Glassb

D1592182

Data Structures on the IBM PC

Acquisitions Editor: Chris Williams
Production Editor/Text Design: Deborah L. Corson
Art Director: Don Sellers
Cover Design: Robert Blair
Assistant Art Director: Bernard Vervin
Manufacturing Director: John Komsa

Typesetter: Ampersand Publisher Services, Inc., Rutland, Vermont
Typefaces: Eras (display), Aster (text), and American Typewriter (pro-grams)

Data Structures
on the IBM PC

Steve Roski

Brady Communications Company, Inc.
A Simon&Schuster Publishing Company
New York, NY 10020

Data Structures on the IBM PC

Library of Congress Cataloging in Publication Data

Roski, Steve, 1935–
    Data structures on the IBM PC.

    Includes index.
    1. IBM Personal Computer—Programming. 2. Data structures (Computer science) I. Title.
QA76.8.I2594R665   1985   001.64′2   85–9639

    ISBN 0-89303-481-9

Printed in the United States of America

85 86 87 88 89 90 91 92 93 94 95   1 2 3 4 5 6 7 8 9 10

To Sally Anthony

a good student
a good teacher

Limits of Liability and Disclaimer of Warranty

Note to Authors

Have you written a book related to personal computers? Do you have an idea for developing such a project? If so, we would like to hear from you. Brady produces a complete range of books for the personal computer market. We invite you to write to Chris Williams, Senior Editor, Simon&Schuster, General Reference Group, 1230 Avenue of the Americas, New York, NY 10020.

Registered Trademarks

Contents

13 Our Library 265

Contents

A long time ago, as a young engineering student, I was lifting yet another heavy concrete block onto the bed of a test machine, when a friend mentioned a course in computers that could be substituted for Concrete Testing 101. I took that course and never did return to mechanical engineering.

This book is for application programmers, for those who aspire to that occult occupation, and for those who just want a career without heavy lifting. The theme of the book is that programmers must be in charge of their software and in control of their computer. While everyone else can talk about the insolence of computers, the programmer has to do something about it. Fortunately, programmers can reprogram their software environment to suit their needs. The reward is artistic freedom and the opportunity to be imaginative and creative.

The book begins where most introductions stop. It assumes the reader already knows something about programming and has written an original program or two in some higher level procedural language. The first chapter is a hasty introduction to BASIC. The second chapter develops PREBASIC, a preprocessor program that gets rid of the line numbers, adds symbolic labels, and introduces the subroutine stack that later supports our library subroutines. Chapters 3-9 look at some elementary space and data structures. The last three chapters lay the foundation for a permanent personal subroutine library for the career programmer.

There is enough material for a solid second semester or—if teamed with any good introductory text—for a comprehensive two-semester introduction to programming. I reluctantly omit much that "absolutely" should be covered. How can one introduce data structures without a chapter on algorithms? How can one write about pipelining without exploring multitasking? And what about the file, the directory, the tree, or the heap, or about sorting, indexing, hashing, parsing, pattern matching, and artificial intelligence?

You may wonder about my choice of BASIC as a presentation language. You, too, may remember "naked" BASIC from the sixties, without integers, without strings, without files, and with those useless matrix algebra statements. All I can say is: Take a good look at modern BASIC. It has grown up in 20 years, and today it has features matched by no other microcomputer language:

- immediate, interpretive, or compiled execution
- true strings and n-dimensional string arrays
- double-precision floating arithmetic
- random files, buffer mapping, symbolic devices
- easy access to batch, DOS, and memory levels
- keyboard and error trapping and resolution
- syntax for joystick, lightpen, cursor, and modem
- bit-mapped screen and printer graphics and color
- overlays, virtual disks, tree directories
- stable, compatible, ANSI standard, international
- large base of tutorials, textbooks, and software
- available without royalties, license, copyright

S. Roski
San Diego
August 1985

About the Author

STEVE ROSKI started his computer career in the sixties as a member of the trajectory programming team for the first lunar landing missions. He has worked with software since then, as an engineer, programmer-analyst, and teacher. He holds degrees in engineering, computers, and law and lives in San Diego.

Acknowledgments

I thank the editors and reviewers for helping with the immediate production of the book. More generally, I thank the thousands of programmers who invented and developed the techniques over the last 20 years.

BASIC Review

1.1 Welcome to Programming

This book is about advanced programming: about being in control of your machine and your software, about selecting the right techniques and building your own data structures, and—by no means least—about the joy of programming. In short, this book is for programmers.

I chose BASIC on the IBM PC as a presentation language because it is the best vehicle for the job. It offers the novice, as well as the advanced programmer, a surprising range of sophisticated features such as variable-length character strings, error trapping, keyboard interrupt handling, built-in file and graphics commands, data communications, program overlays, direct interfacing to the machine language level, and direct input/output of data at the port level.

BASIC is available on most microcomputers, is reasonably uniform from machine to machine, and transposes readily into other procedural languages. Most of the techniques in this book can be used with, say, FORTRAN. Literally hundreds of introductory BASIC textbooks are available, so I can skip the introduction and focus quickly on "second semester" material.

Programming a computer is an exciting intellectual trip. Being able to design your own universe, with its own players and its own rules, can be fascinating: to create a mechanism and then watch it work; to make the rules and then to break them; to change the rules and, when you tire of that, to let the program change them randomly.

Bon Voyage!

1.2 Welcome to BASIC

This chapter summarizes the elements of the BASIC language as found on the IBM PC and covers a few special topics not often found in introductory texts. It is intended for programmers familiar with one or more other programming languages, for those who know BASIC on some other computer, and for those old-timers who learned and forgot BASIC years ago on some "mainframe" computer. (Old-timers are in for a surprise!)

Whatever your background, this chapter can also serve as a filter test. If anything is unfamiliar in this chapter, you may want to catch up on it so we can start into the book with a common background. If the material is completely over your head, you might want to put the book aside for a month and learn a procedural programming language such as BASIC, C, FORTRAN, PASCAL, PL/1 from a competent source.

The chapter compresses one semester of BASIC into a few pages; it is a concentrated review, *not* a tutorial. That is not to say that a motivated reader cannot learn the language anyway. BASIC was designed for beginners and its rudiments can still be learned in a weekend.

If you insist on teaching yourself, use the book index to find more detailed introductions scattered throughout the book. Your IBM PC BASIC language reference manual will supply some of the details. And most importantly, use the computer itself to answer your questions. One of the great features of BASIC is that it can act as a teacher. Using the interpretive mode, you can answer many "what if" questions by typing a short program and running it immediately.

Most of all, relax and enjoy yourself! It is all right to experiment, to make mistakes, to write infinite loops, and to (gasp!) play games on the computer. Provided you back up your disks before you start, you cannot damage the system. At worst, you lock up the system so thoroughly that you have to restart the computer from scratch.

Have Fun!

1.3 Overview

BASIC is a procedure-oriented language. It is used to write an explicit sequence of steps to be followed by the machine. A source program consists of one or more lines. A line contains a line number followed by one or more statements, separated by colons. A statement consists of a verb followed by some parameters. Any text following the REM verb or following an apostrophe is treated as a comment. For example:

```
10 '   Your Name In Lights
20 INPUT "What is your name "; USER$
30 L = LEN(USER$)
40 FOR I = 1 TO L : PRINT LEFT$(USER$,I) : NEXT I
50 GOTO 40
```

BASIC is not a structured language. A program is a single physical entity. It is not organized into hierarchies, levels, procedures, blocks, modules, sections, and so on. Every variable name is known everywhere in the program; there are no scope rules, private or public data, imported or exported arguments, call by name or call by value, and no information hiding.

BASIC has no restrictions on transfer of control. Program execution proceeds in line number sequence until directed elsewhere by a statement. Subroutines are handled with the GOSUB-RETURN construct. Loops take the FOR-NEXT and WHILE-WEND forms. The GOTO and ON-GOTO statements are used to branch to explicit or computed line numbers. For example, here is the above program rewritten with subroutines and a WHILE-WEND loop. Now it only runs until the user enters a null string:

```
1       '   Your Name In Lights
2       INPUT "What is your name "; USER$
3       WHILE USER$<>""
4           GOSUB 10
5           WEND
6       END
7       '
8       '       subroutine
9       '
10      FOR I = 1 TO LEN(USER$)
11          PRINT LEFT$(USER$,I)
12          NEXT I
13      RETURN
```

BASIC was designed as an interpretive language. A BASIC program can be executed in source form by an interpreter that dynamically translates each source statement into machine language and executes it. That means your program remains in source form, so you can change it and rerun it at once, without going through a compile step. That is not to say that BASIC cannot be compiled into machine language. Several compilers are available that convert interpretive BASIC into machine code and thus obtain the same speed advantages of other compiled languages.

BASIC is an elementary language. It provides the fundamental data and control mechanisms, but it does not have the built-in features of other languages. It does not legislate "good" programming: as implied in its name, you get the "basic" programming tools and you are let loose on the machine.

1.4 Programming in BASIC

Writing a program in BASIC typically consists of designing the data and control structures on paper, as always. (Designing and composing at the keyboard is invariably a waste of time in any language.) For smallish programs, the source code is entered from the keyboard. Larger programs are better entered with a text editor and stored as source files. These files can then be merged with library routines and supplied with test data files. This technique is used throughout this book.

You load the source program and run it. To test it, you might interrupt the program in the middle of a run to study the dynamic contents of variables and to execute loops and subroutines that will diagnose problems and isolate errors. You can continue the program where interrupted with the CONT command or you can enter a command that continues execution at a suitable point. When the program runs correctly in interpretive mode, it can be compiled into machine language.

1.5 Variables

Variables are named with symbols consisting of letters and digits. As in most languages, the name must start with a letter to distinguish names from numbers. The name can be any length; however, only the first 40 characters are used internally. Lowercase letters in names are converted to uppercase.

There is a list of reserved words that cannot be used as variable names. However, they may be used freely as part of another name: PRINT is an invalid variable name, but PRINTT is not.

The data type of a variable is specified by appending a type symbol to the variable name. Thus, TAX% is an integer, TAX$ is a byte string, TAX! is a single-precision floating point number, and TAX# is a double-precision floating point number. These are four distinct scalar variables in BASIC. Array names are formed in the same way, except that a subscript is appended to the name, for example TAX!(25) and TAX#(I,J).

If no type symbol is appended, a single-precision floating-point number is assumed. This default type can be changed by using the DEFINT, DEFSNG, and DEFDBL statements. Thus, DEFINT I-N changes the default type to integer for variable names beginning with I through N.

1.6 Numbers

BASIC handles numbers in three forms:

1. **Integer.** Whole numbers from −32768 to +32767. These are stored as two bytes, using 2s complement notation for negative numbers. The integer is also used as a 16-bit word with Boolean operators for bitwise logical operations. Integer constants are written as signed or unsigned literals such as 81% or −349%.
2. **Single-precision floating point.** Floating-point numbers with seven digits of precision, used for fractional numbers. These are stored as a string of four bytes with special coding. Constants are written as 12.34567! or .1234567E2!.
3. **Double-precision floating point.** Floating-point numbers with 14 digits of precision, used for applications requiring special precision. These are stored as a string of eight specially coded bytes. Constants are written as 12.345678901234# or .12345678901234D2#.

1.7 Strings

A string is a variable-length stream of bytes, containing codes in the exact form and sequence as stored in memory. In fact, a string *is* a snapshot of recorded data: it represents the bridge between the logical level where programs are written and the physical level where they are executed.

On the IBM PC, the BASIC interpreter limits the string length to 255 bytes; most BASIC compilers have a limit of 32767 or more. However, there is no theoretical limit to the length of a string, other than the maximum memory of the computer.

Whereas the numeric data types have many restrictions on data sizes and allowable formats, there are no restrictions as to the physical codes or combinations of codes that can be stored in a true string. At the same time, BASIC strings are not logically interpreted as to content. They are treated strictly as streams of codes. For example, a string containing one blank is not "equal to" a string containing two blanks. In fact, the very use of the word "blank" in the preceding sentence is anathema to the true string aficionado, because "blank" is already an interpretation of the code 32 as ASCII code. Many other perfectly valid interpretations are possible for the number 32, such as a CPU operation code, as 2 raised to the power 5, or as a subscript pointer to the 32nd element of some array.

BASIC is one of the very few programming languages that support the true string data type. This simple fact helps to account for the continuing popularity of BASIC, because it is easy to become addicted to the ease of programming with strings. Other languages use the word "string" for watered-down concepts, such as for fixed-length character arrays with restricted byte codes and with arbitrarily appended delimiter codes. These languages will do such astonishing things as arbitrarily deleting bytes containing pure 0 or dropping trailing blanks from a string. It took mankind thousands of years to invent the zero digit, but it is still not allowed as a valid code in some languages!

Because of its variable length and its completely flexible symbolic content, the string is the most powerful data type found in BASIC. It can represent numbers, lists of numbers, symbols, variable names, and even machine language subroutines written for any 8-bit computer in the world. It is not specially formatted in any way, so that it is independent of the recording device and medium. It can be written on a disk file, received from a distant computer via satellite, sent to a voice output device via radio waves, or read from an optical disk with a laser.

Strings are typically used for user messages, instructions, screen displays, printer report lines, and other textual data. But the string has many other uses in advanced programming, such as symbol manipulation, parameter passing, and even subprogram execution. (*See* Chapter 4.)

1.8 Operators

BASIC provides the standard operators found in most languages. (The original matrix algebra operators are rapidly vanishing from modern BASIC. And not too soon, I might add.) There are four classes of operators:

1. **Arithmetic**   + − * / ∧ \ MOD

The \ operator computes the integer quotient. The MOD operator finds the integer remainder. Thus, the expression 29\4 has the value 7 and 29 MOD 4 is 1.

2. **Relational**   < <= = >= > <>

These operators compare two values for equality. The result is expressed as an integer with the value −1 (true) or 0 (false). Comparison expressions can be used as conditions as in the following fragment

```
IF 5<9 THEN PRINT "5 is less than 9"
WHILE DAY$<>"TUESDAY" AND COUNTRY$<>"BELGIUM"
```

They can also be used as normal integers 0 or −1 in computations. For example, the following function will return the larger of the given values X or Y:

```
DEF FNMAX(X,Y) = -X * (X>=Y)  -Y * (Y>X)
```

Here, if X is greater than Y, then X>=Y has the value −1 and Y>X has the value 0, so it computes −X*(−1)−1*(0), which is X. If Y>X, it returns Y in a similar manner.

Strings are compared left to right, strictly on the binary values of the byte codes. Thus, the expression "A" < "a" has the value −1 (true) because the ASCII code for "A" is 65 and "a" has the ASCII code 97.

3. **Boolean**   NOT AND OR XOR IMP EQV

Boolean operations are done on integer values. BASIC treats the integer as a string of 16 bits and operates on each bit independently. For example (numbering the bit positions from right to left as ...6543210):

```
G% = G% OR       16%   ' set bit 4 to 1
G% = G% AND NOT 16%    ' set bit 4 to 0
G% = G% XOR      16%   ' reverse bit 4
```

Because relational operators return integer values, relational expressions can be combined by using Boolean operators. Thus, IF 5<7 AND 7<9 THEN PRINT "EUREKA" will print EUREKA every time. And IF A$=B$ OR A$<>B$ THEN PRINT "AHA" will always print AHA because one of the two possibilities is always true in the condition.

4. **String** +

Only one string operation is implemented as an operator; the other operations are done as function calls. The lonely operator is concatenation, expressed with a + sign between two strings. The concatenation operation joins the strings to form a new string, so that "HELLO" + "THERE" becomes "HELLOTHERE". The following fragment concatenates several strings and prints

   TO BE OR NOT TO BE, THAT IS THE QUESTION

on the screen.

```
+----------------------------------------------------------------------+
:      T$  =  "TO BE"                                                   :
:      Q$  =  "THAT IS THE QUESTION"                                    :
:      PRINT  T$  +  " OR NOT "   +    T$  + ", " + Q$                  :
+----------------------------------------------------------------------+
```

Note how the blanks are carefully manipulated in the concatenations; blanks inside quotes are characters with equal rights. Outside the quotes, that is, between the words of a statement, blanks have no special significance.

1.9 Expressions

An expression is an alternating sequence of values and operators, suitably parenthesized, in the form

   value operator value operator ... operator value

For example,

.17 * (INCOME − DEDUCTIONS) − EXEMPTIONS

The values in an expression can be constants, variable names, or function calls. Strings and numbers can be freely mixed, as long as they are appropriately converted; BASIC does not have automatic type conversion. The programmer must write expressions so that the type matches the operators. Several conversion functions are provided to assist in this.

Function references can be nested. Thus the expression ASC(MID$(G$,2,1)) finds the ASCII code of the second byte of string G$.

Operator precedence in evaluating an expression is typical. First parenthetical subexpressions are evaluated. Then comes exponentiation, multiplication and division, addition and subtraction, relational operators, and finally Boolean operators.

1.10 Arrays

The array is implemented in classic FORTRAN fashion. Array names are simply variable names, including type symbols, followed by a subscript in parentheses. Before you use an array of more than 10 elements, you must declare it with the DIM statement. Multidimensional arrays are supported up to 255 dimensions. Then you can use individual elements as individual variables in expressions:

```
DIM TAXRATES (2000)
DIM CHECKERBOARD (8,8)
TAXRATES (1329) = .17
CHECKERBOARD (3,5) = CHECKERBOARD (2,4)
```

There are no array-level operators. To process an array, you must use a loop that processes each element in turn.

Both strings and numbers can be stored in arrays by using the appropriate type suffix, such as TAX#( ) for floating point numbers and TAX$( ) for strings. String arrays are arrays of variable-length string elements. Thus, string arrays become an effective structuring tool at the byte level. (*See* Chapter 4.)

An array element can be used anywhere a single variable is used, except as a FOR-NEXT loop control variable. The subscript origin is 0 by default, but it can be changed with the OPTION BASE statement. The variable TAX is distinct from the variable TAX(0).

1.11 Functions

BASIC functions come in two flavors: built-in and user-defined. Built-in functions handle a number of standard operations:

```
+---------------------------------------------------------------+
:  SYSTEM        DATE$  ERL    ERR    FRE    TIME$              :
:                                                              :
:  CONVERSION    ASC    CHR$   CVD    CVI    CVS    HEX$        :
:                MKD$   MKI$   MKS$   STR$   VAL                :
:                                                              :
:  MATHEMATICS   ABS    ATN    COS    EXP    FIX    INT         :
:                LOG    RND    SGN    SIN    SQR    TAN         :
:                                                              :
:  INPUT-OUTPUT  EOF    INKEY$  LOF   SPC    TAB                :
:                                                              :
:  STRING        INSTR  LEFT$  LEN    MID$                      :
:                RIGHT$ SPACE$ STRING$                          :
+---------------------------------------------------------------+
```

The built-in string functions may not be familiar to you. First, the LEN function returns the length of a string. Then, there are three functions that copy a substring out of a given string: LEFT$, MID$, and RIGHT$ return a substring from the left end, from somewhere in the middle, or from the right end of a given string, respectively.

The INSTR function reports the location of a specified substring in a given string. This function is useful to analyze strings for content. For example, we may want to know if a file name entered by the user contains a dot:

DOT = INSTR(INFILE$,".")

If INFILE$ contains no period, variable DOT will be set to zero; otherwise DOT will be set to the position where the first period occurs.

In addition to these built-in functions, you can define your own functions. You use the DEF statement to specify the parameters and the functional relationship. IBM PC BASIC limits function definitions to a single statement; in effect, you can only define functional expressions. Single-statement function definitions are generally useless except for very specific mathematical function applications. As a result, I lean heavily on the subroutine for developing programs. In this book, we will develop a powerful subroutine mechanism that supports local variables, nested subroutine calls, and recursive subroutines. We will scarcely miss the function.

1.12 Control Flow

A BASIC program is a sequential file of numbered lines. A line contains one or more statements separated by colons. The default program control flow is from beginning to end, from line to line, and from statement to statement within each line. Certain definitional statements in the control path are ignored, such as DEF, DEFINT, DIM, and DATA.

There are no special procedure blocks. If program control reaches what the programmer considers to be a subroutine, the subroutine code is entered as normal mainline code. Any RETURN statement then returns control in normal fashion to the last executed GOSUB.

Default program control can be altered in various ways. Aside from the classic statements that explicitly control what is to be done next, a BASIC program can manage both voluntary and involuntary interrupts. Voluntary interrupts are those the program expects and prepares for, such as the user pressing function keys or joystick buttons. Involuntary interrupts are those unexpected or unpredictable conditions that are commonly called "errors" such as END-OF-FILE or OUT-OF-MEMORY or DISK-DOOR-OPEN. The statements involved in these forms of control handling are:

1. **Explicit control**

CALL CHAIN END ERROR FOR GOSUB GOTO IF NEXT ON-GOSUB ON-GOTO RETURN STOP SYSTEM WEND WHILE

2. **Voluntary interrupts**

KEY-OFF	KEY-ON	KEY-STOP	ON-KEY-GOSUB
PEN-OFF	PEN-ON	PEN-STOP	ON-PEN-GOSUB
STRIG-OFF	STRIG-ON	STRIG-STOP	ON-STRIG-GOSUB

3. **Involuntary interrupts**

ON-ERROR-GOTO RESUME

1.13 Loops

BASIC provides three forms of loop control: FOR-NEXT, WHILE-WEND, and (what I call) the GOTO loop. The GOTO loop is simply the do-it-yourself loop widely used by assembly language programmers. The FOR-NEXT form is the classic iteration-counting loop. The WHILE-WEND form is the condition-testing loop introduced as one of the structured programming techniques.

BASIC offers the program flow-control statements without any restrictions on their use or abuse. You may design all of your loops yourself, thus paying a price in design and debugging time but writing tighter and faster code. Or you may choose one of the built-in loop mechanisms, thus saving yourself much labor but paying a price in flexibility, execution time, and storage space. For most applications, this price is very small compared to the savings in labor; so the FOR-NEXT and WHILE-WEND loops are usually a better choice. (You can, of course, mix these methods in the same program; for an example, see the HORSE RACE program later in this chapter.)

NOTE:

One important aid to writing and reading looped code is to indent the statements inside the loop under the main loop entry statement. I follow this practice throughout the book; but I deviate from industry practice in one small detail. I consider the loop-terminating statements such as NEXT and WEND to be part of the code inside the loop, and so I indent them, also. One can go both ways on this. My way serves to isolate the loop code completely from the code outside it. I use the same convention on subroutines, by indenting all the subroutine code (including all the RETURN statements) under the subroutine label line.

The FOR-NEXT loop simply counts iterations, by using a loop-control variable (lcv):

```
FOR   lcv  =   v1   TO   v2   STEP   v3
      loop body statement(s)
      NEXT lcv
```

The FOR statement sets up a loop-control mechanism behind the scenes. It saves the values of v1, v2, and v3 so that the loop limits will remain the same even if these variables change during the loop. The first value of lcv will be v1. If the STEP clause is omitted, v3 is 1.

The NEXT statement increments the lcv by v3 and tests the incremented value to see if it has passed the limit v2. If not, it branches to the statement following the FOR. Otherwise it tears down the loop mechanism and goes to the statement following the NEXT.

Inside the loop body, the lcv can be accessed and manipulated like a regular variable. This feature is very useful to vary program behavior on the basis of the current iteration count; the loop is then simply a number of similar statements "rolled up" into a concise package. For example, to display the square and the square root of numbers from 1 to 20:

```
+----------------------------------------------------------------+
:              FOR I = 1 TO 20                                   :
:                  PRINT I, I*I, SQR(I)                          :
:                  NEXT I                                        :
+----------------------------------------------------------------+
```

The lcv can also be changed to vary the loop limits dynamically. You can change the value of lcv inside the loop and "fool" the loop mechanism. You can loop forever:

```
+----------------------------------------------------------------+
:              FOR I=1 TO 2 : I=1 : NEXT I                       :
+----------------------------------------------------------------+
```

BASIC places no restrictions on branching into or out of the body of a FOR-NEXT loop with a GOTO statement, but it is not a good idea. Branching into a loop won't work because the mechanism won't be set up by the FOR statement. Branching out of the loop body will leave the loop mechanism behind like a skeleton bleaching in the desert. One or two of these do no harm, but if this is nested inside some larger loop, all these old bones fill up memory and cause mysterious "Out Of Memory" errors.

To leave a loop prematurely, make the loop mechanism think it has just done the last iteration: Set the lcv to the value v2 or beyond and branch to the NEXT statement. The following loop will only print one HELLO, in spite of what the FOR statement specifies:

FOR P= 1 TO 5000 : PRINT "HELLO" : P=5000 : NEXT P

It is perfectly proper and useful to call subroutines inside a loop. When they RETURN, things continue as before inside the loop, assuming the subroutine did not change any variables that affect the loop.

1.14 WHILE-WEND Loops

The WHILE-WEND loop mechanism is designed for loops that should iterate as long as some specified condition is true (non-zero) at the beginning of each iteration.

```
+------------------------------------------------------+
:             WHILE cond                               :
:                 loop body                            :
:                 loop body                            :
:                 loop body                            :
:             WEND                                     :
+------------------------------------------------------+
```

The WHILE-WEND loop is controlled by the expression cond, which evaluates to a number. As long as this number is not zero, the loop will continue. When this number is 0, control jumps around the loop statements and continues after the WEND statement. Any kind of expression can be used as a WHILE condition, as long as it evaluates to a number:

```
+------------------------------------------------------+
:   WHILE 0           ' doesn't loop at all            :
:   WHILE X           ' loops as long as X is not 0    :
:   WHILE X < 0       ' loops as long as X is negative :
:   WHILE NOT EOF(#1) ' loops until end-of-file on #1  :
:   WHILE LEN(A$)>0   ' loops as long as A$ is not empty :
:   WHILE LEN(A$)     ' loops as long as A$ is not empty :
:   WHILE A$<>""      ' loops as long as A$ is not empty :
:   WHILE 1           ' loops forever                  :
+------------------------------------------------------+
```

The WEND statement is a GOTO statement in disguise. It simply passes control back to evaluate the condition for the next iteration. It also marks the physical end of the WHILE-WEND loop, so that the WHILE statement knows where to GOTO when the condition is 0.

Here is a good example for the WHILE-WEND loop form. You want to copy FILE1 to FILE2; but you have no idea how many lines there are in FILE1, so you cannot easily write a FOR-NEXT loop. You want to write "keep looping until you reach the end of file 1." WHILE-WEND is ideal for that. Open both files and then copy from FILE 1 as long as function EOF(#1) is false:

```
+------------------------------------------------------+
:   OPEN "I",#1,"FILE1"                                :
:   OPEN "O",#2,"FILE2"                                :
:   WHILE NOT EOF(#1)                                  :
:           LINE INPUT #1, A$                          :
:           PRINT #2, A$                               :
:           WEND                                       :
:   CLOSE                                              :
+------------------------------------------------------+
```

1.15 GOTO Loops

In some situations, neither the FOR-NEXT nor the WHILE-WEND form is satisfactory. When loop limits change dynamically, when loop conditions cannot be written as a nice expression, when errors or other interrupts can change the loop statement processing sequence, or when you cannot afford even the small amount of overhead time used by the built-in mechanisms, then you have to construct your own loop mechanism out of IF and GOTO statements.

Sometimes you want to execute a loop just one more or one less time than the built-in mechanism allows. Sometimes you want to test for a condition halfway through the loop body and abort the loop or short-circuit an interation. Sometimes you want to restart a loop from scratch in the middle, because you have discovered after a few iterations that the initial limits are all wrong for the data at hand.

To debug a loop, you need to know the components of a loop. Here is a checklist:

1. Pre-Loop
2.   Loop Body
3.   Change
4.   Test and Branch
5. Post-Loop

Most loops contain all of these steps, although perhaps in a different sequence. In some cases, one or the other step may be absent. If there is no step 2, then the loop does nothing—it may be a pure time delay loop. If you omit step 3, nothing changes inside the loop, so it will run forever. Step 4 tests something to see if another iteration is wanted. This step can also appear before step 2, as it does in the WHILE-WEND form.

GOTO loops have a poor reputation because it is easy to do too much or too little. For example, beginning programmers typically forget step 1, so that they execute the loop without preparing for it. Once they learn to include step 1, they typically branch to it from step 4, which forever restarts the loop! Once they master the 5 steps shown above, they can write GOTO loops with flair.

Here is the WHILE-WEND example shown above, rewritten as a GOTO loop:

```
+-------------------------------------------------------------------+
:         1 OPEN "I",#1,"FILE1" : OPEN "O",#2,"FILE2"               :
:         2 IF EOF(1) THEN GOTO 5                                   :
:         3 LINE INPUT #1, A$ : PRINT #2, A$;                       :
:         4 GOTO 2                                                  :
:         5 CLOSE                                                   :
+-------------------------------------------------------------------+
```

To write nested loops, using any loop form, is easier if you write the innermost loop first and then write the embedding loops around it in succession. Incidentally, the NEXT statement can be written without the lcv. This fact can be useful to emphasize that the NEXT is simply a part of the matching FOR statement. Pithy comments also help to identify the various loop shells:

```
+-------------------------------------------------------------------+
:     ' how to drink 100 bottles of beer in 5 gulps each           :
:                                                                   :
:     FOR B = 1 TO 100          ' 100 bottles of beer              :
:         FOR G = 1 TO 5        ' 5 gulps                          :
:             gulp                                                  :
:             NEXT              ' next gulp                        :
:         NEXT                  ' next bottle                      :
+-------------------------------------------------------------------+
```

1.16 Subroutines

BASIC supports the concept of a subroutine in the form of program code that receives control from some caller via the GOSUB statement, performs some set of operations, and returns to the caller via the RETURN statement. The subroutine code does not have to be declared or identified in any way. Any body of code can serve as a subroutine by terminating with a RETURN statement.

No arguments or parameters can be passed to the subroutine. Subroutines operate on globally known variables as does all BASIC code. This feature is a handicap; but it can be overcome with some effort by using a subroutine stack mechanism. All of this is explained fully in Chapters 11 and 12.

1.17 Error Handling

To program a computer means to be in control and to retain control of the computer, especially under adverse circumstances. One attribute that marks a useful programming language is its ability to retain control when errors or exception conditions occur. BASIC shines in this respect.

BASIC uses two cooperating mechanisms to handle errors: an error trap and an error handler. To set the trap, you specify the line number of the error-handling code:

ON ERROR GOTO 32000

If an error does now arise, BASIC interrupts the program wherever it is and transfers control to the error handler, here line 32000. It reports the error number and the line number where it occurred in two special system variables ERR and ERL. (Had you set no error trap, BASIC would have printed an error message on the screen and stopped, which is what many other languages do.)

Inside the error handler, you continue to be in control. You can use any and all BASIC statements to analyze the program status and to take appropriate action. You can ignore the error signal, you can resolve the problem and continue, you can inform the user and wait for directions from the keyboard, or you can print an illuminating message and stop.

To return to the statement that triggered the error in the first place, you use the RESUME statement. This acts much like a RETURN from a subroutine, except that it returns control to the point where the most recent error occurred. In other words, the error handler is a subroutine that is invoked for you by BASIC in the form of an involuntary interrupt. You service the interrupt and then RESUME normal program operation.

The following fragment shows one simple way to trap and process errors in BASIC with a global error handler. This is only an illustration. For a better routine, *see* Chapter13.

```
+------------------------------------------------------------------+
:      ON ERROR GOTO ^GLOBAL ERROR HANDLER^    ' set trap           :
:      . . . .                                                      :
:      your main program                                           :
:      . . . .                                                      :
:                                                                   :
: ^GLOBAL ERROR HANDLER^    ' the error handler                     :
:      E=1                                                          :
:      IF ERR = 27 THEN E=0 : PRINT "Printer Is Off"                :
:      IF ERR = 53 THEN E=0 : PRINT "File Missing"                  :
:      IF ERR = 61 THEN E=0 : PRINT "Disk Is Full"                  :
:      . . . .                                                      :
:      IF E=0 THEN RESUME    ' back to main program                 :
:      PRINT "Error Number"; ERR; "At Line"; ERL                    :
:      STOP                                                         :
+------------------------------------------------------------------+
```

1.18 The Keyboard

The keyboard can be handled in three ways: at the variable level, the line level, or the character level. The plain INPUT statement accepts one or more values separated by commas and stores them into named variables. The fancier LINE INPUT statement works at the line level. It accepts an entire line terminated by the ENTER key and stores it—commas and all—in a single string variable. It can handle lines up to 255 characters long.

At the character level, keyboard input is handled by the INKEY$ function. This function returns the next character, if any, from the keyboard buffer. Its major advantage is that the program can continue execution while it monitors to see if anything has been typed at the keyboard. Its drawback is that INKEY$ does not echo nor does it support keyboard editing keys. You have to do all the work.

Here is a program template for doing some chores while keeping an eye on the keyboard. If A, B, or C is typed at the keyboard, the program responds some way. All other keys are ignored:

```
     WHILE 1
       I$=INKEY$
       WHILE I$=""          ' while no key is pressed
         ...                ' do some other things
         I$=INKEY$          ' time to check the keyboard
       WEND

       ' user has pressed a key !!!
       IF I$="A" THEN PRINT "Alhambra"    'response for A
       IF I$="B" THEN PRINT "Benzene"     'response for B
       IF I$="C" THEN PRINT "Cathedral"   'response for C
     WEND                   ' go back to do other things
```

1.19 The Screen

The PRINT statement formats and outputs one or more data items to the screen. Simple formatting is provided by control items that are interspersed with the data items to be printed: A comma specifies a cursor move to the nearest tab position; a semicolon inhibits cursor motion after the item is printed. Fancier formatting is available with the PRINT USING statement.

Many statements and functions are provided to manipulate screen data. The CLS statement clears the screen. The LOCATE statement moves the cursor to a specified spot on the screen and lets you alter the shape of the cursor. The POS and CSRLIN functions report the current position of the cursor on the screen. The SCREEN statement sets up screen attributes such as blinking and underlining.

Here is a quickie horse race program, where the horses run the wrong way, just to prove a point:

```
+--------------------------------------------------------------------+
:   ' HORSE RACE                First horse in column 1 wins  :
:   1 CLS:DEFINT A-Z:DIM COL(24)                              :
:   2 FOR C=1 TO 24:COL(C)=80:NEXT    ' horses into the gate  :
:   3 ROW=1+INT(24*RND):COL(ROW)=COL(ROW)-1  ' pick a horse   :
:   4 LOCATE ROW,COL(ROW):PRINT CHR$(ROW+64);      ' move it  :
:   5 WHILE COL(ROW)=1:WEND        ' stop if we have a winner  :
:   6 GOTO 3                        ' move another horse       :
+--------------------------------------------------------------------+
```

But there is more to the screen than character or graphics output. Did you know, for example, that the screen is also an input device? Using the SCREEN function, a program can capture information currently displayed back into a variable. Did you know that, internally, the screen is really a memory space that can be mapped as an ordinary string? If you ever run short of memory, you can use the screen as temporary memory.

In the graphics mode, the SCREEN statement can also select one of seven different internal screen areas. This ability allows interesting techniques with multiscreen output, windows, and motion of graphic shapes on the screen, entirely from the BASIC program level; you need not go to the machine level at all.

CAUTION:

The memory used for the screen starts at different addresses depending on whether you are running on a monochrome or color adapter. See routine VIDEO.LIB (Chapter 13) for a way to let the program determine which adapter you are using.

1.20 Files

BASIC supports three types of files:

1. DATA files
2. Sequential access files
3. Random access files

BASIC uses the DATA statement to define a data file embedded into the program itself. This data file is always open after the program is loaded. It is read-only and is accessed with the READ statement. The RESTORE statement positions the file pointer to any desired line number. In this way, the DATA file can be accessed either sequentially or randomly. Here is a program that uses a data file to display program instructions. The first data statement specifies how many DATA statements are to follow:

```
READ N          ' how many data lines to read
FOR I=1 TO N : READ A$ : PRINT A$ : NEXT I
DATA 4
DATA "Welcome to the tax program.  To compute"
DATA "your federal tax, you must provide the tax"
DATA "journal name.  For state tax, use the same"
DATA "figures, but indicate STATE to the program."
```

BASIC implements the sequential file in the standard open, read or write, close fashion. Here is a program that creates a file from keyboard input:

```
OPEN "O",#1,"BOZO"  ' create and open file BOZO
INPUT A,B,C         ' read 3 numbers from keyboard
PRINT #1,A,B,C      ' write them to file BOZO
CLOSE #1            ' secure from writing
```

A random access file is implemented like a fixed-length string array written to bulk storage. Any record in the file can be read or written directly, by giving the record number. The file buffer is mapped into string variables with the FIELD statement. (*See* Chapter 4 for details.) The following simple example reads and displays records 27-46 of a random file of 80-byte records:

```
OPEN "R",1,"RANDFILE",80
FIELD #1, 80 AS B$
FOR I=27 TO 46 : GET 1, I : PRINT B$ : NEXT I
CLOSE #1
```

Don't overlook the special implementation of files in random access memory (RAM), known variously as the RAM disk, the electronic disk, or the virtual disk. Essentially, when you configure your operating system (long before you get into BASIC itself), you can declare an area of memory to behave like a disk drive. You can use this "soft" drive exactly like a real one; the program does not know the difference. The advantage is that input and output with a RAM disk is marvelously fast, since it is done entirely in memory. The drawback is that you need to increase the memory size of your machine and that the data written on the RAM disk are as evanescent as the rest of RAM. If the RAM disk data are to be saved, you need to COPY them to a real drive before you power down.

1.21 The BASIC Environment

Since its beginning in 1981, the IBM PC has seen BASIC versions 1.0, 2.0, and, most recently, 3.0. These versions essentially match their corresponding DOS versions, and the major differences among these versions relate to DOS features such as tree directories and environment specification. The fundamental BASIC language features have not changed significantly, although here and there some improvements have been made. For the purposes of this book, any version of IBM PC BASIC is sufficient.

To get into the BASIC interpreter, get into DOS and load BASIC by typing BASIC or BASICA. You can provide switches here. For example, if you want to open more than three files at a time (say 7) you must type BASIC/F:7. If you want to open random files with record size greater than 128 (say 512) you must load it via BASIC/ S:512.

After BASIC loads, you get a display of the function key settings on line 25. Type KEY OFF to erase this. Now you are in the interpreter, which always prompts with "Ok" . You can enter and run source programs from the keyboard or from files. In addition, you can enter BASIC statements without line numbers, to be executed immediately, appropriately called "immediate" or "direct" mode.

Programs can be entered in two ways. You can enter them from the keyboard or load them from disk or cassette. (You can, of course, do both. Sometimes I load from disk a skeleton program that I modify at the keyboard and then run.) Type the numbered lines in any order; the interpreter sorts them by line number. To delete a line, just give the line number. To overwrite a line, just enter the new line. **Caution**: It is easy to silently wipe out a line; no warning is given.

To list the current program on the screen, type LIST. LLIST lists the program on the printer. Type RUN to run the program. Type Ctrl+Break to stop a running program and CONT to continue running.

As your programs become larger, you will not want to enter or modify them at the keyboard. You will probably use a text editor to generate the programs as regular text files and then load them to run them. This procedure is assumed in most of this book.

Compiling a BASIC program is the ultimate step in creating a production version of a BASIC program. If a program's work is done mostly in memory and does little disk I/O, you will see as much as a five- to sevenfold reduction in execution time. But one caution applies: While all commercial compilers handle the standard BASIC statements with competence, significant differences exist when it comes to special features such as dynamic array allocation, graphics, direct access to memory, data communications, or interfacing to machine language programs. If you use these features, you should check your favorite compiler before you purchase it.

1.22 Summary

There used to be a programming exercise that required one to write a source program that prints itself. Contests were held and prizes awarded for the shortest program. Even the best programs contained dozens of lines. Since you can execute any interpreter or DOS command from inside a BASIC program (see the SHELL statement of BASIC version 3.0), this exercise can now be done in one statement:

```
1 LIST
```

That summarizes BASIC as well as anything. BASIC has grown tremendously in its 20 years. It is still the original friendly language, easy to learn and easy to remember. It can still be used to learn programming from the ground up without having to commit to a particular machine.

BASIC has been enhanced with many features that make it a language used in production around the world today. Some of its warts have disappeared; some are still with us. In the rest of this book, we will see what can be done with it.

PREBASIC

Now that we have refreshed our recollection of BASIC, let's explore its capabilities. Let's begin by doctoring it up a little to make it more our own language and to improve a few of its features. Being programmers, we may be too embarrassed (or too poor) to go to the software store and shell out $500 for someone else's BASIC that still doesn't exactly fit our needs. We would rather do it ourselves.

Some years ago I got tired of keeping track of BASIC line numbers. I decided to write a simple utility program that would accept numberless BASIC and add the line numbers for me. It would call the first line of the text line 10, the second line 20, and so on. To identify a line of code in such statements as GOTO, GOSUB, and RESUME, I simply inserted a label line into my text by using a couple of framing "hat" characters to flag it as a label line. The program was smart enough to detect the ∧label∧ and to substitute its line number wherever I referenced it. The result looked something like this fragment:

```
+----------------------------------------------------------------+
:                                                                :
:      input               output                               :
:                                                                :
:      ^MORE^                                                    :
:      INPUT A,B           10 INPUT A,B                          :
:      PRINT A+B           20 PRINT A+B                          :
:      GOTO ^MORE^         30 GOTO 10                            :
+----------------------------------------------------------------+
```

Over the years, this utility program grew as I added features such as Continued Lines, Library Files, and Comment Suppression. I used it on several computers, and it became one of my most useful tools. This chapter presents it as PREBASIC, a language preprocessor written in and for IBM PC BASIC. It is used as a presentation language throughout this book.

2.1 About Language Translators

Programming languages are basically computer programs that translate code from one format to another. The input is in some human-oriented format using familiar words and expressions such as PRINT, A+B, IF-THEN, TAX$, and so on. The output is in pure machine language, consisting of a stream of binary operation and operand codes that can be executed by the central processing unit (CPU) (Figure 2-1).

"Compilers" translate the entire program without ever executing it. "Interpreters" actually execute the program by translating each statement just before it is executed. Some languages translate in several stages by using intermediate code forms such as tables, tokens, or pseudocode. Some languages first translate the program into another human-oriented language such as assembly language. (An "assembler" is not a different type of translator; it is simply a compiler for assembly language.)

Contrary to popular usage, a language by itself is not an "interpreted" or "compiled" language. It is really inaccurate to say things like "since BASIC is an interpreted language, it is..." Although some languages are easier to interpret than others because they were designed for interpretation, any language can be compiled as well as interpreted. The question is simply which design is used for a given translator program.

Each translation method has its advantages and its drawbacks. Compiled programs run faster. Interpreted programs can be changed as they run. During program development, when changes and testing require many stops and starts, an interpreter is appreciably faster. For production use, when no changes are made for long intervals, a compiled program is better because it runs much faster.

BASIC offers the best of both of these methods, since both interpreters and compilers are available for it. If you do much work in BASIC, you should acquire a BASIC compiler, if only to save a good part of your life spent waiting for some utility to run interpretively. Be advised that not all compilers are alike. Compilers for the same language differ significantly in the language syntax they support and in the time and space requirements of the compiled programs. (*See* Section 1.21).

So much for interpreters and compilers. There are still other types of language translators. Since a source program is really nothing but a sequential text file, it can be physically manipulated as text by utility programs that reshape, convert, indent, expand,

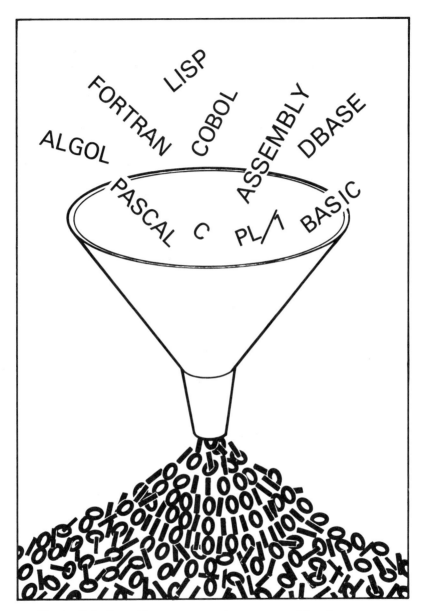

Figure 2-1. Every language ends up as machine language.

compress, and even generate new source text in some way. In this chapter, I develop a "preprocessor", that is, a utility program that must be run before the program text can be handed to a commercial BASIC compiler or interpreter (Figure 2-2).

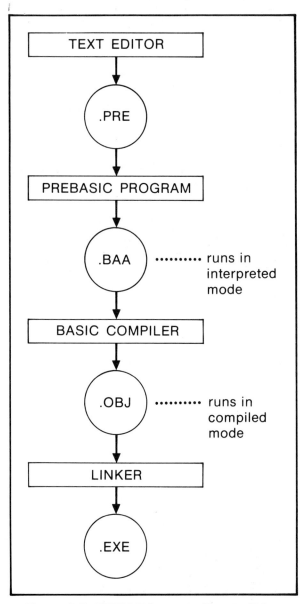

Figure 2-2. PREBASIC runs before BASIC.

In the remainder of this chapter, a preprocessor program for BASIC is developed, called PREBASIC, that converts our own brand of BASIC into legal BASIC. Once we have written PRE-BASIC, we will use it to process all of the programs given in this book.

This preprocessor will be a very useful tool for us because it will let us modify and enhance official BASIC with minimal effort. At the input end, we will be able to invent our own, personalized language syntax to fit our special application needs. At the output end, we will still generate standard BASIC, so we can use any compiler or interpreter.

2.2 The PREBASIC Language

Like all programming languages, BASIC is not perfect; but we can overcome some of its shortcomings with a preprocessor. In the bargain, we get a working language of our very own. Technically, of course, PREBASIC is not a language until we write a compiler or interpreter for it. Nevertheless we will call PRE-BASIC a language because it is simply easier to talk about "writing in PREBASIC" than to talk about "writing text in a code form to be converted by the PREBASIC utility program into BASIC."

The PREBASIC program is nothing more than a rather simple program that converts PREBASIC syntax into BASIC syntax. For all its simplicity, it has significant benefits:

- PREBASIC is a mechanism by which we can implement language features that we want to add to BASIC. We can teach PREBASIC a number of tricks to make our life easier, such as label names and library routines. We can add special syntax and personalized abbreviations.
- PREBASIC supports detailed program documentation that can be stripped off before execution. One of the big short-comings of most programming languages, including BASIC, is their lack of documentation facilities. Programmers have always been berated for not documenting their programs, yet all we get from language designers is the lowly comment. Have you ever tried to document a lunar trajectory program or a heart surgery monitor with REM statements?
- PREBASIC is under your control. You can modify it to suit our needs. It decouples us from the "official" language and lets us maintain and extend the major tool of our trade. If we like, we can write several PREBASIC language processors, one for each computer we are interested in.
- PREBASIC preserves that most useful feature of BASIC: the ability to run in either compiled or interpreted mode. Coupled

with the immediate availability of the personal computer, this advantage is enormous for the **BASIC** programmer.

- **PREBASIC** does not impose any restrictions on us. Every program in this book can be converted manually to standard **BASIC** by simply pencilling in the requisite line numbers. Nothing is introduced by **PREBASIC** that binds us to it.
- The philosophy behind **PREBASIC** recognizes one of the facts of life of advanced programming: the programmer is responsible for developing the tools of programming. Beginners can complain about a language not doing this and not doing that; professionals are expected to write software to solve problems. If a programming language, a utility, or an operating system does not suit you, modify it or write your own. The software buck stops here.

PREBASIC serves four purposes in this book: First, it eliminates some of BASIC's drawbacks. We get rid of the annoying line numbers. We solve the lack of local variable names like every other language solves it—with the use of a stack. We overcome the poor documentation tools by allowing unlimited white space and providing a feature to strip comments out of the generated BASIC program.

Second, it is itself a good tool to increase programmer productivity. **PREBASIC** is *not* a theoretical concept that you discard after the final exam. It is a working tool that I have used for years for my own use as well as my professional work. It encourages the use of a text editor to write programs, and the development of a library of useful routines.

Third, writing a book on BASIC with line numbers is difficult and discouraging for both the author and the reader. With PREBASIC, I can develop a subroutine completely independent of other subroutines. I can refer you to library routines and don't have to repeat them in every program. Best of all, you can fit the pieces together to suit your own needs.

And, lastly, PREBASIC may help plant an important seed in the mind of programmers at the beginning of their careers: Be in control of your language and your software, and you will be in control of your computer. If you develop your own tools, you will be controlled less by other programmers.

Beginning programmers write small programs. They design and code, debug, and execute directly at the keyboard. Sometimes this is done in one session; sometimes the program is saved on disk and loaded back in at a later session. BASIC was designed for this programming, and for this use it serves well. Its utility is attested to since it is the most popular microcomputer language in the world.

Advanced program development is quite different. By definition, advanced programs are larger, more complex, and take longer to develop. They usually require dozens of interrelated programs, reference tables, data files, batch procedures, utility processing, and so on. Their logic is often "fuzzy," poorly defined, and not well understood. The final software is often pieced together from existing code, from subroutine libraries, and from fresh or freshly modified code. All this work must be supported with mountains of documentation.

Advanced programs are not so much written from scratch as they are evolved from earlier programs. They are too large to be typed in and tested at the keyboard, and they are too complex to be tested in one session. They are more commonly written in word processing style with text editors and then stored as text files. They look much like the text of this book: program descriptions and documentation interspersed with programs, fragments, subroutines, figures, alternatives, and such.

Programming by evolution is an excellent tool for the advanced programmer with many benefits:

- You always have a running program. When the boss drops around and asks how you are doing, you run the latest version and show it off.
- You seldom have massive debugging bouts because you debug in small steps as the program evolves.
- You can alter course quickly when program requirements change. And Murphy's Law guarantees that they will change.
- You can stop when the program works well enough. Quite often, programs are acceptable with less than perfection.
- Documentation is easier, because it, too, evolves in small steps. The prospect of having to document two years of development can weaken the knees of the most dedicated professional.

PREBASIC is a tool that supports readability and productivity. You can hardly hope for more from a program as simple as you are about to see.

In the following sections, we look at the major features of PREBASIC.

2.3 No Line Numbers

To look at the features of PREBASIC, let's start with one of the best. You can omit the line numbers from your programs; PREBASIC will supply the necessary line numbers for each line. Here is a program written in PREBASIC:

```
+-------------------------------------------------------------------+
:               INPUT "Enter 2 numbers "; A,B                       :
:               PRINT "Average is "; (A+B)/2                        :
:               END                                                 :
:                                                                   :
:   and here is the program generated by PREBASIC:                  :
:                                                                   :
:               110 INPUT "Enter 2 numbers "; A,B                   :
:               120 PRINT "Average is "; (A+B)/2                    :
:               130 END                                             :
+-------------------------------------------------------------------+
```

Other than the line numbering, the above program is standard BASIC. By eliminating the need to physically number lines, we take a giant step forward in simplifying programming. We can now use a text editor to freely move and copy sections of code to suit ourselves. We can store favorite code sections in a library and copy them in, wherever we like, without having to renumber them.

2.4 Label Names

Not having to code line numbers is a wonderful relief; but how will we reference lines for GOTO, GOSUB, ON, RESUME, and other such statements? Not to worry, PREBASIC is smart enough to handle label names.

A label name consists of any word or phrase between two "hats" such as ^START^ or ^SORT THE FILE^. The hat character is the Shift-6. It is not used much in normal programming, and it has an elevated air that calls attention to itself as befits a label. To change the hat character to another character, change the PREBASIC program variable HAT$.

PREBASIC deletes blanks and converts lowercase to uppercase letters. Other than that, there are no special restrictions on label names; you can specify any string. This feature lets you use the label as an identifier as well as a comment, a very convenient feature. Here is the program just shown, slightly modified to exhibit a label name:

```
+----------------------------------------------------------------+
:        ^START^                                                 :
:            INPUT "Enter 2 numbers "; A,B                       :
:            PRINT "Average is "; (A+B)/2                        :
:            GOTO ^START^                                        :
+----------------------------------------------------------------+
```

To assign line numbers, PREBASIC simply numbers every line it encounters. When it finds a ^label^, it remembers the associated line number. At the end, it substitutes the line numbers for the labels in the output text. The generated BASIC program looks like this:

```
+----------------------------------------------------------------+
:        110 INPUT "Enter 2 numbers "; A,B                       :
:        120 PRINT "Average is "; (A+B)/2                        :
:        130 GOTO 110                                            :
+----------------------------------------------------------------+
```

The starting line number and the interval between lines are here set to 110 and 10, respectively. This can, of course, be changed in the PREBASIC program.

The use of symbolic labels has a number of useful side effects:

- You have the option to retain the label names as comment statements in the BASIC program. This option is convenient for finding your way around in the BASIC program for debugging. Using this option, the output would be slightly different:

```
+----------------------------------------------------------------+
:        110 REM    ----   START   ----                          :
:        120 INPUT "Enter 2 numbers "; A,B                       :
:        130 PRINT "Average is "; (A+B)/2                        :
:        140 GOTO 110                                            :
+----------------------------------------------------------------+
```

- You can now give meaningful names and phrases to your subroutines, loops, and special areas of the program. A descriptive label can serve as a comment and as a guide to the human reader.
- If you exdent labels as I do throughout this book, label names serve as an obvious flag for all points in the program where control can enter from some distant point. This is an excellent aid for reading, debugging, and maintaining the program.
- You can arrange subroutines in alphabetical order. No more

searching high and low for that important input subroutine. You find it immediately by scanning down the listing margin.

- Program fragments are easier to move around and to copy. Subroutines, tables, and commonly used code, such as Copyright Notices, can be stored on a disk and loaded by name.

2.5 Relative Labels

A relative label is written as a signed integer such as $^\wedge+2^\wedge$ or $^\wedge-3^\wedge$. It is not really a label but rather a count or an offset of lines relative to the line in which it occurs. As discussed below, it should be used only as a very local line reference, best limited to no more than plus or minus 5 lines. Moreover, the line count should not include any pure comment lines since these can optionally be suppressed.

One good use for relative labels is to avoid the proliferation of minor local labels that can quickly clutter the program landscape. They are also nice to use in source code to be copied into different locations or even different programs since you don't have to worry about generating duplicate labels. One example of this is inside library routines, where symbolic label names must be invented carefully lest they interfere with programs using the library.

CAUTION

Relative labels require care to avoid subtle errors. One common mistake is to code a relative label, say $^\wedge+4^\wedge$, and later to insert or delete a line so that the count is no longer valid. The cure for this is just good programming practice: whenever you plan to change a program, consider the local code environment for side effects of your changes. This rule applies not just to labels but also to the use of constants, the contents of variable names, and the status of file pointers—in short, the entire machine state at the point of change. Only raw beginners shove new code into a program without ensuring that it fits into the physical and logical program context.

This error of miscounting lines is somewhat aggravated by the fact that various PREBASIC options can change the lines generated for the final program. For example, continuation lines appear in PREBASIC as several lines but they are catenated into one line before labels are resolved; hence, a continued line should be counted as one line. Again, if the range of lines included in the relative count contains comment lines, then the count will be off if comment lines are suppressed by the PREBASIC comment option.

There are two solutions. For one, you can avoid the whole problem by only using relative labels that don't straddle comment or continued lines. In practice, I have found this to be sufficient: I simply treat the relative label with the utmost respect and only use it sparingly for very short ranges of solid BASIC code.

For another solution, you can modify the PREBASIC program so that it adjusts relative label counts when intervening comment lines are optionally deleted. This solution gets you into a more difficult level of intelligent translation, which can be fun if you enjoy that sort of thing.

Whether or not you do it, the important point here is that you are entirely in control of which features of PREBASIC you want to change. This is one of the joys of developing your own language.

Here is the previous program written with a relative label:

```
          INPUT "Enter 2 numbers "; A,B
          PRINT "Average is "; (A+B)/2
          GOTO ^-2^

     It generates the identical output,
     without using a label name:

     110 INPUT "Enter 2 numbers "; A,B
     120 PRINT "Average is "; (A+B)/2
     130 GOTO 110
```

2.6 Library Search

When you run PREBASIC, it asks you to specify a disk drive for the library. This is a disk that contains commonly used subroutines, each as a separate file. Whenever PREBASIC cannot find a label, it automatically searches the library disk for a file with the label name. If it finds such a file, it reads its contents and appends them to the program being processed, as if it had been there from the start. If the library file itself references missing label names, the search and append steps are repeated to load more files from the library disk. If PREBASIC does not find a file for a missing label, it creates stub code, as explained in the next section.

The library feature is very handy. It lets you build a library of subroutines that you can invoke without having to include them explicitly in every program you write. You end up focusing on the new code while existing subroutines take care of themselves. This concept is so powerful that the last three chapters of this book are devoted to it.

For structured programming, this feature can be used effectively to build an entire program with a very brief main routine that calls the routines one level below it. These routines call (and thus load) others, and so on down to the library routines at the lowest level. For example, in the PREBASIC program later in this chapter, the major routines are HANDLE A FILE, RESOLVE LABELS, and WRITE OUTPUT. These routines don't have to be part of the PREBASIC program file; they could just as well be stored on the library disk for PREBASIC, to be loaded when the program is preprocessed.

You can also use automatic file loading to append different routines to customize programs. For example, a payroll program might be written to load the routine that computes the state tax from a library. To generate a program for, say, a Vermont customer, you simply supply the Vermont State library disk to PREBASIC. On this disk, it finds the routine that knows all about the tax laws of Vermont.

2.7 Automatic Stubs

In handling labels, the question arises: What happens if a referenced label cannot be found in the given program or on the library disk? Most compilers treat a missing label as a fatal error. PREBASIC is smart enough to generate a label and stub code for you. A "stub" is a sort of stump for a missing limb of a program. If control is ever transferred to the missing label, the stub code will print a message to that effect and let you take some action at that point.

This feature is very convenient because programs can be run for testing long before they are finished. We often have to work with skeletal programs on which we have only completed one or two portions. When we test these, we know full well that we will not pass control to one of the unfinished limbs of the program. And if we do, we may want to simply ignore the reference and continue, or we may want to supply some dummy data to represent the output from the missing limb.

2.8 Comments

The first step to good documentation is to realize that there is no such thing! Documentation is "good" when it answers a reader's questions; but there is a vast audience of readers for any given program. The president of an aerospace firm expects something else from documentation than does the data processing manager, the computer operator, or the maintenance programmer. We can seldom satisfy one of them, let alone all of them.

Programmers are admonished to write documentation, but programmers are programmers—not tech writers. Moreover, most programming languages not only make documentation difficult, but they often cause the program to be less efficient if it is well documented! When forced to choose between good programming and good documentation, the professional programmer will always choose good programming, and that is as it should be. (*See also* Section 11.3)

In IBM PC BASIC, there are two comment verbs: the REM and the apostrophe. Since we have two forms, we can make them do different duty. PREBASIC treats the REM statement as a fixed comment that is never deleted and the apostrophe as a comment that can be (optionally) deleted. This means you can freely comment your PREBASIC program and still have a small and fast BASIC program. You can comment as much or as little as you deem appropriate. If you like, you can write programs embedded inside massive documentation, so that the program becomes the small raisin in the document cake.

2.9 Continuation Lines

For those pesky long lines that don't fit into your nice margins, PREBASIC has the hyphenation feature. You can break any line into two (or more) pieces and write each piece on a separate line. To let **PREBASIC** know that a line is a continuation line, you prefix a hyphen to it. Hyphenation is very useful when—as for this book—you need to force source code into specific margins, yet have it run as written. It can also make compound statements easier to read.

```
                 PRINT "Report generated and";
                 -NRECORDS; "records printed"

 will generate the output line

   100 PRINT "Report generated and"; NRECORDS; "printed"
```

CAUTION

PREBASIC blindly appends the hyphenated line to its predecessor, with one blank between them. It does not treat the continuation lines as different statements. You must supply the required statement separators, as is done in the following example with colons. For the same reason, relative label references should count continued lines as one line. Example:

```
   IF AGE<0 THEN ^+1^ ELSE
      - PRINT "Negative Age" :
      - INPUT "Do You Wish To Proceed (Y)   "; U$ :
      - IF U$<>"Y" THEN GOTO ^ABORT^
```

2.10 Documentation

PREBASIC supports good documentation practices in a number of ways. In the last section, we saw how comments can be freely used in the program and how they can be optionally suppressed in the generated program. In addition, **PREBASIC** simply ignores blank lines; you can make your programs more readable by including ample white space between program elements.

PREBASIC requires no special indentation and produces none. You have complete freedom to arrange your source text. Here are a few possible versions; each has merits and drawbacks; the whole thing is purely a matter of personal preference:

```
+-----------------------------------------------------------------+
:                        ^START^                                  :
:           INPUT "Enter 2 numbers "; A,B                         :
:           PRINT "Average is "; (A+B)/2                          :
:           GOTO ^START^                                          :
:                                                                 :
:                                                                 :
:     ^START^  INPUT "Enter 2 numbers "; A,B                      :
:              PRINT "Average is "; (A+B)/2                       :
:              GOTO ^START^                                       :
:                                                                 :
:                                                                 :
:    ^START^   ' this program computes the average of            :
:              ' two numbers entered from the keyboard           :
:              ' and prints it on the screen.                    :
:                 INPUT "Enter 2 numbers "; A,B                   :
:                 PRINT "Average is "; (A+B)/2                    :
:                 GOTO ^START^                                    :
+-----------------------------------------------------------------+
```

PREBASIC does not examine your syntax beyond the labels, so you can write any code you want. If you code multiple statements per line, PREBASIC will copy them into the output program:

A=1 : B=1 : C=3

produces the program line

110 A=1 : B=1 : C=3

2.11 The PREBASIC Source Program

This section examines the design of the PREBASIC program and its source code. The program is itself written in PREBASIC and, thus, serves to illustrate some of its own features. The program was deliberately written with simple algorithms to highlight the features and to make the code easily extensible. I know very well, for example, that the search of the label table would be faster with hashing techniques or that the preprocessing could be done in one pass instead of two. These techniques are simply not worth plowing through for this simple application. My personal (compiled) version of PREBASIC, which is encrusted with many special additions and variations, uses nothing fancier than this, yet processes a 1000-statement program in under two minutes, and that is fast enough for many uses.

The physical structure of PREBASIC is straightforward: the main logic is at the beginning and is followed by a few subroutines and terminated by the global error handler. As written, it can handle up to 1000 lines of code and 100 labels.

The main function of the PREBASIC program is, of course, to convert an input text file written in PREBASIC into an output text file in standard BASIC with numbered lines. To do this, PRE-BASIC reads the entire input file into array I$( ), processes lines from I$( ) into O$( ), and finally writes O$( ) to the output file.

The lines from O$( ) are written to the output file with line numbers prefixed starting at 110 for O$(1), 120 for O$(2), and so on to O$(MAXO). The LAB$( ) array is parallel to O$( ). It contains the labels, if any, that have been given to the matching line in O$(). Thus, if line 7 were the assignment statement A=5 and had been labelled ^START^, LAB$(7) would contain the label "START" and O$(7) would contain "A=5" as the source code.

PREBASIC uses the array LAB$( ) to track labels for a given line in case the user wants the option to identify the label names with REM statements in the output program (Option 2). If the user does not want option 2, PREBASIC generates code lines only, with line numbers running 110, 120, 130, and so on. Lines start at 110 to leave some room for manual additions in the front of the program at execution time.

If the user selects option 2, PREBASIC generates a REM line just before each labelled line, using a "halfstep" line number ending in 5. The net effect is that REM --- LABEL --- lines are transparent to the program. It makes no logical difference if they are included or omitted:

```
+---------------------------------------------------------------+
:                                                               :
:          160 COUNT=0                                          :
:          165 REM    --- START ---                             :
:          170 A=5                                              :
:          180 B=3                                              :
+---------------------------------------------------------------+
```

The parallel arrays S( ) and S$( ) serve as the stack for passing parameters to and from subroutines. Their general uses are discussed in the later chapters on the Stack, the Library, and the Subroutine.

The parallel arrays L$( ) and L( ) serve as the label table (Figure 2-3). L$( ) contains the label names, and L( ) contains the pointer to the element of O$( ) where the corresponding output line is stored. For example, in the example above, if START had been the fifth label encountered in the program, L$(5) would contain "START" and L(5) would contain 7 to indicate that START is the label for line 7.

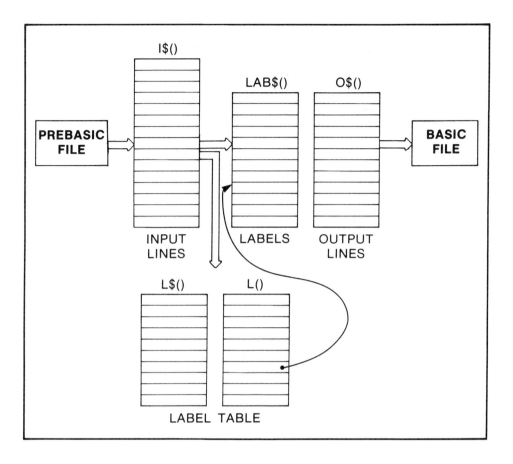

Figure 2-3. Arrays used by PREBASIC.

The routine HANDLE A FILE expects an open input file on channel 1 and reads it into I$( ). Then it processes each line. It strips off any label names and stores them in the label table, taking care to check for duplicate labels first. It handles comments as requested and concatenates continuation lines. Finally, it stores the line into the O$( ) array. (Note that the routine is used again later to load and process any library files).

The RESOLVE LABELS routine is responsible for translating all embedded label references into line numbers. It examines each line in O$( ) to see if it contains a label reference. This process is fairly simple because all it has to look for is the "hat" characters that enclose all label names. Once it finds a label, it has to convert it into a line number. First it checks for relative labels of the type

$\wedge+3\wedge$. These labels are easily converted into absolute line numbers by adding the increment to the current line number CL. If the label is not relative, the routine uses the subroutine SEARCH TABLE to see if the label name was present in the input file. This is the normal processing sequence.

If the label is not found in the table, then it is first assumed to be the name of a library file. If the file exists, routine HANDLE A FILE is pressed into service once again to read and append it to the existing program in O$( ). If the file does not exist, **RESOLVE LABELS** generates a stub, which is a line of code that will print a message about the missing label and stop if it is ever executed.

The PREBASIC program calls several library subroutines, characterized by the file extension .LIB. These routines are not contained in the PREBASIC listing because they are loaded by PREBASIC when it processes the code. (*See* Section 2.6.)

The GLOBAL ERROR HANDLER traps all errors and issues appropriate messages.

Here, then, is the listing of the PREBASIC preprocessor, written in PREBASIC code. In some areas, the code was adjusted to fit between the book margins. The processed version, with line numbers as you will have to install it on your system, is given in Chapter 13.

```
+--------------------------------------------------------------------+
:  ^PREBASIC^     ' Program to translate PREBASIC to BASIC           :
:                                                                    :
:         '              TABLE OF VARIABLES                          :
:     ' APOST$     the ' character used as trailing comment          :
:     ' CL         current O$() line being processed                :
:     ' HAT$       the hat character used as label delimiter         :
:     ' HAT1       label hat 1 -- first hat found in line            :
:     ' HAT2       label hat 2 -- second hat found in line           :
:     ' I$()       the program as read from the input file           :
:     ' IFILE$     name of input file                                :
:     ' L()        label table - pointers to O$()                    :
:     ' L$()       label table - labels                              :
:     ' LAB$       label currently being processed                   :
:     ' LAB$()     label defined for parallel element in O$()        :
:     ' LIBDRIVE$  disk drive of library disk                        :
:     ' MAXI       number of program lines stored in I$()            :
:     ' MAXL       number of labels stored in L$()                   :
:     ' MAXO       number of program lines stored in O$()            :
:     ' NEXTO      next available O$() element                       :
:     ' O$()       the BASIC program as processed so far             :
:     ' OFILE$     name of output file                               :
:     ' OPT1$      option 1: if Y then leave all comments in         :
:     ' OPT2$      option 2: if Y then show label names              :
:     ' QUOTE$     quote character                                   :
```

```
:      ' S() and S$(S)    subroutine stack;  S is pointer       :
:      ' S1,S2.. temp variables used locally in subroutines     :
:      ' TL       current I$() line being translated            :
:      ' WL       current O$() line being written out           :
:                                                                :
:      DEFINT A-Z                                                :
:      DIM I$(1000)       ' input PREBASIC text                  :
:      DIM O$(1000)       ' output BASIC text                    :
:      DIM LAB$(1000)     ' labels for O$() lines                :
:      DIM L(100),L$(100) ' label table                         :
:      DIM S$(10),S(10)   ' subroutine stack                     :
:      QUOTE$=CHR$(34) : HAT$="^" : APOST$="'"                    :
:      MAXL=0 : MAXO=0 : NEXTO=1 : S=1                           :
:      CLS : ON ERROR GOTO ^GLOBAL ERROR HANDLER^                :
:                                                                :
:      PRINT "   Welcome To PREBASIC    Version 2-13-85"         :
:      PRINT                                                     :
:      INPUT "Input  File Name       "; IFILE$                   :
:      OPEN "I",#1,IFILE$                                        :
:      INPUT "Output File Name       "; OFILE$                   :
:      OPEN "O",#2,OFILE$                                        :
:      INPUT "Library Drive (as X:) "; LIBDRIVE$                 :
:      S$(S)= "Leave Comments": GOSUB ^YESNO.LIB^                :
:      OPT1$=S$(S)                                               :
:      S$(S)= "REM --- Label ": GOSUB ^YESNO.LIB^               :
:      OPT2$=S$(S)                                               :
:                                                                :
:      PRINT "Reading Input   ..." : GOSUB ^HANDLE A FILE^       :
:      PRINT "Re-labelling    ..." : GOSUB ^RESOLVE LABELS^      :
:      PRINT "Writing Output  ..." : GOSUB ^WRITE OUTPUT^        :
:      PRINT MAXO; " Lines Written To File "; OFILE$             :
:      PRINT "Normal End Of Program"                             :
:      END                                                       :
:                                                                :
:                                                                :
: ^HANDLE A FILE^  ' Sub to process a PREBASIC file              :
:     ' enter with file open on channel #1                       :
:                                                                :
:     S=S+1    ' must preserve stack because sub is              :
:              ' also called to process library files            :
:                                                                :
:     ' read the file into I$()                                  :
:     MAXI=0                                                     :
:     WHILE NOT EOF(1)                                           :
:        LINE INPUT #1, I$(MAXI+1):MAXI=MAXI+1:WEND              :
:                                                                :
:     ' translate I$() into O$()                                 :
:     FOR TL=1 TO MAXI                                           :
:        S$(S)=I$(TL)   ' line being translated                  :
:        WHILE 1        ' process one or more labels             :
:           GOSUB ^LJUST.LIB^                                    :
:           IF LEFT$(S$(S),1)<>HAT$                              :
```

```
                     - THEN ^HANDLE COMMENTS^
              S1=INSTR(2,S$(S)+HAT$,HAT$)
              LAB$=MID$(S$(S),2,S1-2) ' strip a label
              S$(S)=MID$(S$(S),S1+1)  ' from the line
              S=S+1:S$(S)=LAB$        ' deblank and capitalize
              GOSUB ^NOBLANKS.LIB^
              GOSUB ^UPPERC.LIB^ : LAB$=S$(S)
              ' check if a duplicate
              GOSUB ^SEARCH TABLE^ : IF S(S)=0 THEN ^+4^
              PRINT "Duplicate Label ";HAT$;S$(S);HAT$;
              PRINT " Ignored."
              BEEP : GOTO ^NEXT LABEL^
              MAXL=MAXL+1                 ' record it
              L$(MAXL)=S$(S)             '     in table
              L(MAXL)=NEXTO
              IF LAB$(NEXTO)<>"" THEN ^+2^
              LAB$(NEXTO)=S$(S):GOTO ^+2^
              LAB$(NEXTO)=LAB$(NEXTO)+", "+S$(S)
          ^NEXT LABEL^
              S=S-1                       ' pop the label
              WEND

      ^HANDLE COMMENTS^ ' handle comments

          IF OPT1$="Y" THEN ^HANDLE HYPHENS^
          GOSUB ^LJUST.LIB^
          IF LEFT$(S$(S),3)="REM" THEN ^STORE LINE^
          GOSUB ^DROP COMMENTS^

      ^HANDLE HYPHENS^  ' handle continued lines
          GOSUB ^LJUST.LIB^ ' does line start with hyphen?
          IF LEFT$(S$(S),1)<>"-" THEN ^STORE LINE^  ' no
          ' drop the hyphen and leading blanks
          S$(S)=MID$(S$(S),2) : GOSUB ^LJUST.LIB^
          ' be sure prior line has no trailing comments
          S=S+1:S$(S)=O$(NEXTO-1):GOSUB ^DROP COMMENTS^
          GOSUB ^RJUST.LIB^ : O$(NEXTO-1)=S$(S) : S=S-1
          ' join line to prior line, if not too long
      ^TRY JOINING^      ' used by error handler
          O$(NEXTO-1)=S$(S+1)+" "+S$(S):GOTO ^NEXT INLINE^
      ^TOO LONG^
          PRINT "Continued Line NOT Joined (too long): ";
          PRINT S$(S)
      ^STORE LINE^ ' generate a BASIC line
          IF S$(S)="" THEN ^NEXT INLINE^     ' skip if empty
          O$(NEXTO)=S$(S) : MAXO=NEXTO : NEXTO=NEXTO+1
      ^NEXT INLINE^
          NEXT TL                ' next input line

  CLOSE #1 : S=S-1  ' no more lines in I$()
  RETURN
```

```
^RESOLVE LABELS^     ' Sub to convert labels to numbers
    CL=1
    WHILE CL<MAXO
        HAT1=INSTR(O$(CL),HAT$)    ' do we have a label?
        HAT2=INSTR(HAT1+1,O$(CL),HAT$)
        IF HAT1=0 OR HAT2=0 THEN ^NEXT LINE^       ' no

        ' extract and clean up the label
        S=S+1:S$(S)=MID$(O$(CL),HAT1+1,HAT2-HAT1-1)
        GOSUB ^UPPERC.LIB^:GOSUB ^NOBLANKS.LIB^
        LAB$=S$(S)

        ' is it a relative label?
        IF INSTR("+-",LEFT$(LAB$,1))=0 THEN ^+2^
        S(S)=CL + VAL(LAB$):GOTO ^REPLACE LABEL^      ' yes

        ' is it in the label table?
        GOSUB ^SEARCH TABLE^
        IF S(S) THEN ^REPLACE LABEL^   ' yes

        ' is it on the library disk?

        S$(S)=LAB$
        ' error handler tests this label
        ^TRY LIB FILE^   OPEN "I",1,LIBDRIVE$+S$(S)

        ' library file exists and is open; append it
        GOSUB ^HANDLE A FILE^
        ' if label is in table now, we are happy
        GOSUB ^SEARCH TABLE^:IF S(S) THEN ^REPLACE LABEL^

    ^MISSING LABEL^    ' label is not in table or disk
        PRINT:PRINT "Missing Label ";HAT$;LAB$;HAT$;
        PRINT "   Stubbed In New Line "; 100+10*CL

        ' generate output code to stub the line:
        O$(NEXTO)="PRINT " + QUOTE$ + "Stub For Label "
        O$(NEXTO)=O$(NEXTO)+ LAB$ + QUOTE$ + " : STOP"
        MAXO=NEXTO : NEXTO=NEXTO+1
        ' enter label into table
        MAXL=MAXL+1:L$(MAXL)=LAB$:L(MAXL)=NEXTO
        ' set S(S) as expected
        S(S)=MAXO

    ^REPLACE LABEL^   ' convert label ref to line number
        ' enter with S(S) the output line number
        S1$=LEFT$(O$(CL),HAT1-1):S3$=MID$(O$(CL),HAT2+1)
        O$(CL) = S1$ + MID$(STR$(100+10*S(S)),2) + S3$
        S=S-1      ' top is now the BASIC line again
        GOTO ^SAME LINE^    ' check for more labels
```

```
:         ^NEXT LINE^   CL=CL+1                                      :
:         ^SAME LINE^   WEND                                         :
:         RETURN                                                     :
:                                                                    :
:                                                                    :
: ^WRITE OUTPUT^                                                     :
:     FOR WL=1 TO MAXO                                               :
:         IF LAB$(WL)="" OR OPT2$="N" THEN ^+3^                      :
:         PRINT #2, USING "#### &"; 95+10*WL;                        :
:         PRINT #2, "REM        --- " + LAB$(WL) + " ---"            :
:         PRINT #2, USING "#### &"; 100+10*WL, O$(WL)                :
:         NEXT WL                                                    :
:     RETURN                                                         :
:                                                                    :
:                                                                    :
: ^SEARCH TABLE^   ' Sub to seek label S$(S)                         :
:     S1=MAXL                                                        :
:     WHILE L$(S1)<>S$(S) AND S1>0 : S1=S1-1 : WEND                  :
:     S(S)=L(S1)                                                     :
:     RETURN                                                         :
:                                                                    :
:                                                                    :
: ^DROP COMMENTS^    ' Sub to delete ' xxxxx                         :
:     S1=INSTR(S$(S),APOST$) : IF S1=0 THEN RETURN                   :
:     ' verify that ' is not part of a quote or label               :
:     IF INSTR(S1,S$(S),QUOTE$) THEN RETURN                          :
:     IF INSTR(S1,S$(S),HAT$  ) THEN RETURN                          :
:     ' drop the comment and blanks                                 :
:     S$(S)=LEFT$(S$(S),S1-1) : GOSUB ^RJUST.LIB^                    :
:     RETURN                                                         :
:                                                                    :
:                                                                    :
: ^GLOBAL ERROR HANDLER^                                             :
:     IF ERL=^TRY LIB FILE^ THEN RESUME ^MISSING LABEL^             :
:     IF ERL=^TRY JOINING^ THEN RESUME ^TOO LONG^                    :
:     RESUME ^+1^     ' we have a general error                      :
:     BEEP : PRINT : PRINT "Error"; ERR;                             :
:     PRINT "At Line"; ERL; "In PREBASIC Program"                    :
:     END                                                            :
+--------------------------------------------------------------------+
```

2.12 Installing PREBASIC

Technically, you don't really need to install **PREBASIC** at all. Short programs written in **PREBASIC** can easily be processed by hand. Simply write line numbers alongside the program and then substitute the appropriate line number for each label where it is referenced. Although hand-compiling is not much fun, the point is that PREBASIC does very little that you cannot do yourself. It is simply faster and more accurate!

To install PREBASIC, you have to type in its numbered version (given in Chapter 13) with some text editor or directly from the keyboard and store it as a standard text file. If you can compile it, all the better, since it will run faster that way.

If the thought of entering this long program depresses you, take heart: this is the last time you will ever have to type a numbered BASIC program of great length. From here on, you can develop small routines and store them in the library. Sooner or later, you will think a program is massive if it exceeds two pages.

Existing BASIC programs can be easily converted to PRE-BASIC by stripping off their line numbers and replacing line numbers references with labels. For simplicity, use the original line numbers enclosed between hats as labels. This is exactly what the BASPRE utility program does for you. (*See* Chapter 13 for details.)

2.13 Using PREBASIC

First a word about file names. I use the extension .PRE for all PREBASIC programs and .LIB for library routines. After they are run through PREBASIC, I call them .BAA, for "BASIC As ASCII." This is the file type obtained when you SAVE "filename",A. It is also the file type required by the BASIC compiler. I almost never use the file type .BAS because it cannot be manipulated by text editors, by compilers, or by PREBASIC. This means that I have to specify the extension .BAA whenever I LOAD or RUN the source file, but that price is little enough to pay in exchange for never getting the wrong file type.

PREBASIC can be treated as if it were a compiler. While it adds a step to the program development procedure, it also simplifies program development; in my experience, its advantages far outweigh the added step. Keep in mind that you are *not* removing yourself from the BASIC environment at all. You can work with both the PREBASIC and the BASIC version of a program, thus using each to its advantage.

Developing a new program with PREBASIC is no different than in any other language. However, for those readers who have only written BASIC directly by entering numbered statements at the keyboard, I want to recommend a better way: use a text editor to write the program. Treat the program as a data file while you sketch it out in pseudocode, move functional blocks around, and start to rough in the code.

Many parts of a program such as the welcome message, the main command menu, and the error-trapping mechanism occur in every program and are easily copied from a library of standard program pieces. At least 25% of a new program can usually be whipped up from a template program by reading a few standard files. Chapter 13 includes a skeleton program for this purpose.

Which brings us to an important point. It does not matter what word processor you use, but be sure it is not one of those that robs you of control, that thinks all users ever want to do is write business letters or memos. You need one that lets you quickly move blocks of text around, as well as copy code lines, one that lets you list occurrences of a given word in the text, and one that does not get in your way with automatic word wrapping or justification.

Be sure the editor generates standard sequential text files without hidden text-formatting characters. If you want fancy program listings, build a listing option into PREBASIC—that's where it belongs. Most of all, you need an editor that lets you insert a file from disk anywhere in your text and lets you write any set of lines to the disk as a named file. This should be one simple command.

Run PREBASIC to generate the BASIC version of the program, which is of course the standard numbered BASIC file I call .BAA. Debug the .BAA program in interpretive mode until it performs well enough to compile. Don't bother to recompile the program for every adjustment. Instead, change the loaded program and make a note in red pencil on a hardcopy of the PREBASIC version. After one or two hours of testing, you can then make all changes at once in the PREBASIC version.

For many programs, this work is sufficient and no further work is necessary. But to make the program run five to seven times faster, compile it into a .OBJ program and link-edit it into a .EXE form. This step converts the program to machine language.

2.14 Extending PREBASIC

The PREBASIC presented in Section 2.11 was deliberately limited to those features you need to install the PREBASIC program as well as the programs concepts in this book. You can add many features to evolve it into a formidable programming tool of your own. A few suggestions follow:

- You might want to add an option to generate a program listing with numbered pages, an index to labels, and other goodies.
- To analyze the performance of your programs, you could add an option that automatically generates a call to a monitor subroutine between every two lines of the program. When the program runs, the monitor subroutine gains control between every two statements. This way you can observe where your program spends most of its time, which, in turn, is useful information for speeding up the program. You could also use the monitor to give you control at the keyboard between lines, so you could step through the program one line at a time.
- As written, PREBASIC reads the entire input file into memory and then processes it. To accommodate larger programs, you could modify PREBASIC to write an intermediate file out to (RAM) disk instead of the O$( ) array.
- You could enhance PREBASIC to let you specify several files to be processed and merged into a single output file. You could then develop large programs out of separate files.
- You might want to improve the way PREBASIC handles missing labels to let you supply a library file name from the keyboard. This feature would give you a chance to mount the correct library diskette when PREBASIC cannot find a library file.
- You might add macros to PREBASIC, commands to modify its functions as it runs. For example, you could have a .DO and a .NODO command that would suppress preprocessing for large segments of the input programs. This would let you have large text blocks inside your program without having to cast them into the form of comments. Or, you might want to save some comments and delete others with a .COMM and a .NOCOMM macro.
- You might design your own language commands, which PREBASIC recognizes and converts to standard BASIC syntax. For example, you could generalize the concepts presented in the chapter on Dynamic Storage Management so that you can issue a single command to reserve or release dynamic storage. Or you could add new syntax to, say, PUSH and POP values to and from the subroutine stack S$( ).
- One very useful feature would be to expand the label comment option so that PREBASIC includes the line numbers that reference the label. This feature would be a terrific

debugging aid. The generated BASIC program would look something like this:

1230 REM --- LOAD --- referenced in 970, 1010

- It would show at a glance where the label is used. You would be the envy of all the kids on your block, whose expensive languages do not provide this feature. (If you look closely, you will note that the BASPRE utility already has this feature. It lists all references to a given line, as a comment. You might want to copy this feature and install it into PREBASIC.)
- You could extend the preprocessing function to include a check for syntax errors. Then you might as well add a compiler for PREBASIC. Suddenly, you are a language designer!

Whatever features you select, PREBASIC can grow with you over the years. It can become your personal tool, tuned to your way of programming and thoroughly familiar with your idiosyncrasies. In conjunction with a good subroutine library, you can write programs faster and faster, without sacrificing quality. As new languages emerge, you can copy their features into PRE-BASIC. If you decide to abandon BASIC for another language, you can adapt PREBASIC to generate the new code, or you can at least take the preprocessing concept with you. You will save money and effort, but most importantly: you will end up saving a good portion of the most precious computing resource of all: your own life. That seems to be a worthwhile goal.

Data Objects

3

How does a program process data? Physically, it sends electrical impulses through various hardware circuits that remember, move and compute and display data, and so on. But how does a program process data logically? How does a program "see" the data it processes well enough to control traffic, to map the human brain, to simulate an ecosystem, or to guide a spacecraft? What does the world look like from inside a program?

The subject of this chapter is variously called "data structures" and "data types" and "data objects" and "data management." I much prefer "data objects" because it encourages us to visualize internal data constructs like objects of the real world. But I will also use the more common word "structure," especially where the shape or format of a data object is of interest.

Programmers see data as objects in the sense that astronomers see the universe as objects. A data object comes in all shapes and sizes. It is simply any collection of data of any type, with any structure, that is convenient for the problem at hand. An object may be as light as a gas or massive as a star. It may be a single object, or a group, or a group of groups, just as stars form galaxies and galaxies form clusters. It may be physically connected like the Red Spot of Jupiter or functionally connected like the Moon is captured by the gravity of Earth. It may be a real object (planet), a mathematical formula (orbit), a theory (black hole), a pictorial aid (constellation), or a totally abstract invention (parallel universe).

A data "structure," however, is a more ambiguous concept: it can mean the parts of something, the elementary components (chemical structure); the way these elements are put together, their method of connection (sentence structure); their existence as a specific object (as in "the Great Wall of China is the only man-made structure that can be seen from outer space"); as a generic object as a class of all objects composed in some way (array, tree, RAM disk); or some combination of these meanings.

To make matters worse, "structure" has in recent years acquired a special meaning of "technical quality," as if all structured things are automatically good and all bad things are unstructured. Structured analysis means (good) thinking about a problem before developing a (good) design. Structured design means modularizing the problem (well) and then designing each module (well). Structured programming means writing (good) code in a (good) readable style, with (good) defined names and (good) independent blocks of (good) code. Structured testing means (correctly) verifying the (correct) operation of a program in a (correct) sequence. Structured documentation means a (good) set of manuals and (good) program comments.

Add to this the fact that some languages use the word "structure" as a verb to define a record, and it is no wonder that beginning programmers have trouble understanding what they hear as "structured structure structuring of structured structures." And yet, the concept is absolutely essential to good programming. As programmers, we must know as much about designing data objects as about writing programs. We must define data spaces and format data values so they fit into these spaces. We must define logical data objects so that we can manipulate them directly in their logical setting. We must evolve from the elementary data types that represent the computer hardware, such as numbers and arrays, to logical data objects that more closely resemble the real world.

In this chapter, I present this idea in some depth. In other chapters I focus on the fundamental data structures such as the array, the queue, the pipeline, and the stack. Advanced structures such as the tree and the net will have to wait for a future volume.

3.1 Data Objects: Definition

Computer programs work with data in various forms and sizes at various levels, as tiny bits and as giant data bases. And don't just think of the application program's data; they are not the only data floating around the computer. The programs themselves, the operating system, the compilers and utilities, the directories and batch files—all are at one time data that must be correctly manipulated for the whole thing to work.

Data must be shaped and formatted and connected, physically

and logically, temporarily and permanently, in ways that allow the various programs to access and to manipulate them. A machine with 64K bytes of memory contains 500,000 bits, and a typical diskette holds almost 3,000,000 bits; you really don't want to manipulate data at the bit level. You have to lump data into larger groups that you can manage as a whole with standard procedures and canned subroutines.

To do this, you create certain favorite data objects, like numbers and arrays and files and strings. A data object is simply anything that a program manipulates internally. Bits, bytes, characters, numbers, strings, arrays, files, and so on are data objects. Keys, drives, disks, screens, printers, and circuit boards are not.

This book is not the place for a formal definition of the concept. We will learn it by example, and content ourselves for now with this deliciously tautological definition: a data object is anything that a program manipulates, and a program is anything that manipulates data objects. Here are some of the essential properties of a data object:

- It is stored in a data space. A data object resides somewhere, be it magnetic tape, disk, memory, or some chip register.
- It has an address. The space location where the object is stored is its address, by which it can be uniquely identified and accessed.
- It has some value. The value may be as simple as one bit or as complex as the contents of several data bases stored around the planet in an international research network.
- It consists of pure data. Even though a data object can be manipulated to cause external manifestations such as characters on the screen or beeps on the speaker, it is essentially an internal object known only to programs.
- It has a format and a structure. A data object might be structured as a simple bit stream, as a contiguous array, or as a network of related values scattered throughout the data space.
- It may be a group of data objects. A data object can be constructed from other data objects to any desired level. The object as a whole always has some properties not found in any of its separate components (else there would be no need to build the object).
- It can have many logical interpretations. The numeric data object .145 can be a poor batting average, a good interest rate, or the alcohol reading of a drunk driver.

3.2 Seeing with Data Objects

In theory, programming is a snap: take some real world system, model it as a collection of data objects, and write a program. What could be simpler?

The problem is that model making is not so simple. The real world does not come precisely packaged and arranged for data processing. It is variable, complex, intertwined, n-dimensional, nonlinear, elusive, ambiguous, obscure, and unknowable. It contains paradoxes, duplications, errors, irrelevances, contradictions, deceptions, metaphors, inferences, implications, interpretations, and assumptions.

The real world contains many unrelated actors and processes that simultaneously make independent decisions, sometimes cooperating and sometimes not, involving conditions, options, choices, random chance, accidents, omissions, errors, lies, misunderstandings, minor rule violations and major crimes. There are inconsistent policies, conflicting laws, nonstandard formats, mixed media, and obsolete devices.

All of this has to be coded, formatted, and forced into a shape that can be stored in the data space. The intertwined aspects of the real world must ultimately be formed into a single bit string of ones and zeros, without losing track of the properties to be studied. Somehow we have to chop the world into bits without chopping it to pieces.

Data objects are the computer models of the real world. They reduce its richness and variety without destroying its essential properties. They encode data into forms that the program can access. In this way, they let the program (and through it, the programmer) actually "see" the data. Of all the properties of data objects, this one—giving the program access to the data—is perhaps the most important one from the programmer's standpoint.

There is a fable of several blind men examining an elephant to describe it. Each man examines a different part and reports that the animal is a tree (leg), a snake (trunk), a rock (tusk), a rope (tail), and so on. The point is that an object cannot be described merely by examining its parts. One may dissect and reshape an object for internal storage, but one must preserve its essence, its relevant properties as a whole.

Programmers recognize this fable as describing exactly how computer programs work. Programs are like moles, blindly burrowing through the tunnels of memory, examining a bit stored here, a byte stored there, having to recognize a data item by its shape, or being guided to it by another data item. A program does not "know" what a keyboard looks like, what a diskette is, or how the screen output looks to a human. It sees nothing but an unending stream of bits that appear in input buffers, are operated on, temporarily stored, and then mysteriously disappear from the output buffers.

Isn't it terrifying to realize that essentially blind programs control traffic, fly airplanes, and guide missiles? It is amazing that they can do it at all; it 'is astounding that they do it millions of times a day around the globe. Whenever I read how stupid computers are, I wonder just how smart I would be without my eyes.To illustrate the difficulties involved, imagine that you are a program that plays a simple game of tic-tac-toe. Figure 3-1 shows what you, the program, "see" in memory.

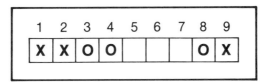

Figure 3-1. Tic-tac-toe as seen by a program. The game board is stored in row order, one byte for each cell.

How quickly can you tell the winning move in this game position? It is difficult without (at least mentally) drawing a board on scratch paper (Figure 3-2). But programs *must* analyze the position in this form, by feeling their way along the string: If there is an x in cell 1 and an x in cell 2 and no marker in cell 3, then the winning move is an x in cell 3. If there is no marker in cell 1, but there is an x in cell 2, and there is an x in cell 3, then the winning move is an x in cell 1. If there is . . .

That was an extremely simple example. What about something a little more useful: Imagine that you are a program that controls a traffic light at a street intersection. You allow automobile and pedestrian traffic to cross safely during rush hour. You cannot "see" the traffic or the intersection; you must rely entirely on position and speed data fed to you as a data stream from various sensors embedded in the street surface.

If you try to do this with data objects stored in the usual row-column array format, you will encounter great difficulties because cars and people arrive and leave in random fashion and interfere with each other in complex ways that are hard to handle at high speed with simple arrays. If instead you use more

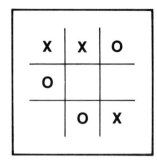

Figure 3-2. Tic-tac-toe as seen by a human. The same position modelled as a board. It is easier to see the winning move if you can "see"!

advanced data objects, you can build a model of the intersection to suit your processing needs. You can keep track of those cars waiting for a left turn, cars approaching a red light, cars that have stalled in the intersection, pedestrians still on the street even though the light has changed, emergency vehicles with priority, and so on. You can use this information to decide what action to take next to help the traffic flow.

3.3 Contiguous Data Objects

We have seen that a data object can play many roles. It can be an empty space where data will be stored, a special method by which data are connected or related, an internal model of the real world, or just the scratch paper of a blind program.

Not all data objects need to be actually stored in some space. Later in this chapter, we will see that a data object can be computed as you go. But for those objects that are in fact stored, a useful distinction is between those that are stored in a single place and those that are scattered all over. I call them "contiguous" and "linked" data objects, respectively. First, let's look at the contiguous object (Figure 3-3).

Contiguous data objects are stored as one single chunk. Their elements are stored adjacent to each other like cigars in a box. The usual example is the array, whose elements are stored next to each other in one long byte stream. Other examples are the integer (a stream of 16 contiguous bits), the character string (a stream of contiguous bytes), and the random access file (a stream

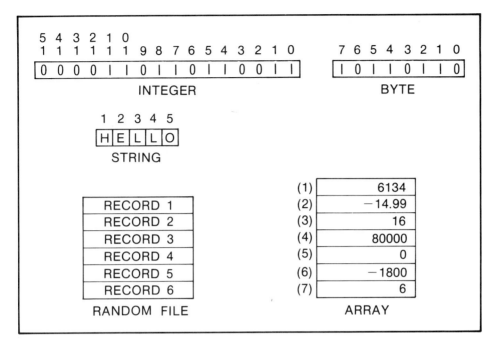

Figure 3-3. Contiguous data objects consist of data elements packed next to each other.

of fixed-size records). Computer memory itself can be thought of as a contiguous data object partitioned into a stream of 8-bit bytes; each byte is numbered with a unique address.

The main advantage of contiguous data objects is that it is easy to process them at the element level. Sequential access is straightforward: once you know the address A of an element, the next element is at address A+1. In a similar manner, it is easy to compute the 50th element, the 5000th, and so on. This, in turn, leads to what is known as "direct access"—the ability to determine the address of any element by a fast simple computation.

Their major disadvantages are their need for a single chunk of connected and addressable space and their relative inflexibility. To insert a new element into the middle of a contiguous object you have to shift aside all elements on one side or the other.

3.4 Linked Data Objects

Linked data objects (Figure 3-4) look like stick figures made of data nodes and links between nodes. The nodes are stored all over

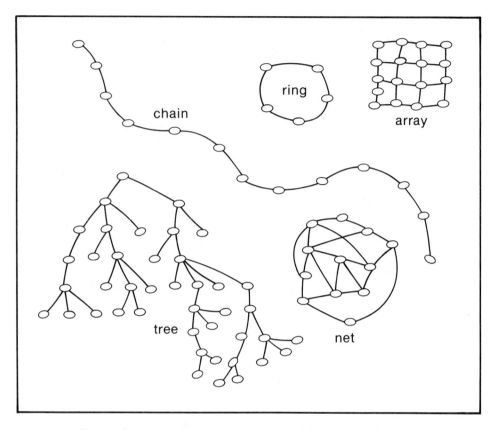

Figure 3-4. Linked data objects consist of data elements, stored in various parts of memory, that are linked by pointers from one element to the next.

the place; the links connect the nodes into a single object. Linked objects store data wherever space is available and use address pointers to link the scattered data into a coherent object. They focus on the data and use space as if it were a disposable resource to be allocated and discarded as needed.

Data nodes contain the values that describe a real-world object. In fact, the only things a program knows about a real-world object are those attributes encoded into the data object as values. The real-world object "exists" in the computer entirely in terms of its attributes!

(This view did not start with computing. A venerable philosophical view holds quite convincingly that there are no real objects, only attributes: If you stub your toe on a stone, there is no toe and no stone, only the attribute "hard and sharp" whose nature it is to combine with the attribute "soft and unprotected" to produce the attribute "black and blue." Quantum physics extends this view to say that even these attributes are only probabilities. Not every encounter of stone and toe produces a bruise.)

The nodes of an object might represent people, cars, nations, concepts, planes, or cucumbers. For example, on a transportation map, the cities might be the nodes, and the highways might be the links. In a family, the people (Jane, Tom, Bill) are usually the nodes, and the links represent their relationships to each other (mother-of, father-of, son-of). If we are modelling an office elevator system, our objects would be people, elevators, and floors. If we manage an airline, our objects would be passengers, planes, airports, crews, tickets, money, baggage, fuel, meals, lost children, and so on.

Of course, data objects are not always tangible things of the real world. They can be more abstract notions such as a performance, a dialogue, a party, a conspiracy, a trial, a love affair, a hypothesis, a fantasy, or a joke. In our airline example, a "flight" is an abstract object. When you think about it, there is no such "thing" as a flight. It really does not exist per se, yet everyone recognizes it and talks about it. A flight is an event, a happening that combines other objects (a plane, a destination, passengers, baggage, meals, fuels, a crew, and so on) for some time and then exists no more. The next day after a flight, its components have scattered, some belonging to other flights now, others belonging to new abstract objects such as families, governments, or criminal conspiracies.

The links between nodes represent the relationships among objects (Figure 3-5). (They are also called "relations," "implications," or "interfaces.") They may represent true physical connections, such as a rope between climbers or a highway between cities. They may represent invisible bonds such as magnetism or greed, groupings such as a choir, or classifications such as all cars. They may be arbitrary connections such as the constellations of the zodiac (most stars of any given constellation are nowhere near each other in space, they are just convenient groupings as seen from earth). Another connection might be in terms of cause and effect, such as the impact of British cotton prices on India's struggle for independence.

The fundamental idea of linked data objects, then, is to represent the real world inside the computer by collecting attributes into records and connecting the records to each other to represent their connections. If we repeat this for every record, we create an integrated whole, a stick figure of nodes and links between nodes.

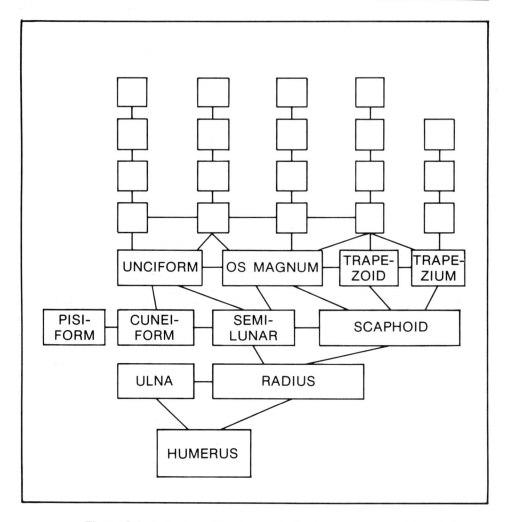

Figure 3-5. A model of the bones in the human arm and hand. Nodes represent bones and links represent bones that are directly connected as a mechanical linkage.

Note carefully that the structure of a linked data object is itself stored as part of the object; thus, the way an object is constructed can be created and changed by the program as it runs. This is powerful medicine, equivalent in the real world to being able to change a car into a truck by changing license plates.

The idea can be applied to files, to data bases, and to systems that are only partly automated. For example, the maintenance log of an airplane is typically so massive that it is not in machine-readable form. In that case, the log field in the plane's data base record would contain some identifying number for the hardcopy log; simply another form of pointer.

Files are a mix of contiguous and linked data organizations designed to handle the special problems associated with input from and output to peripheral media. The random access file is nothing but an array stored on disk, and the sequential file can be seen as a disk queue of variable-length character strings. All of the contiguous and linked data objects presented in this book can be used directly or in adapted form for bulk storage. For example, the random file can be used effectively to allocate disk space among competing processes, and the sequential file makes an excellent queue for pipelining bulk data.

Typically, data records are collected into files and stored on bulk media such as disk and tape. It is conceivably possible to describe any complex subject with a linked data object by using suitable pointers to identify those portions of the model stored as files, on other computers, on other media, or as manual records. Using the Dewey Decimal system, any book in the Library of Congress can be logically included in a data object.

This flexibility is what makes the linked data concept so powerful. It lets us include as much or as little detail as we need. Various portions of our model can be on different media, it can be encoded, classified, abstracted, indexed, and cross-referenced to suit the application. Ultimately, a pointer can point to a program which, when activated, will compute the desired data. This lets us include data in our model that are computed as needed, data that don't even exist when we design the model.

Linked data objects offer an enormous step forward toward intelligent programs, and they are not that difficult to construct. In fact, one reason I chose BASIC as the vehicle for this book is to show just how simple these objects are. If we can set them up in a few lines of code in BASIC, then we can surely implement them in the high-octane languages.

3.5 Computed Data Objects

Beginning programmers learn to distinguish programs and data. They write a program, read data into the program, massage the data a little, and write the data out. There is a clear distinction between the active program (process, operation, verb) and the passive data (parameter, operand, noun).

But programs and data are not always clearly separable concepts. The first hint comes when you learn about functions. Just what kind of animal is a function? It looks like a little program, because you define a function in terms of what is to be done, such as DEF FNSUM(X,Y) = X+Y. Clearly, you have here a tiny subprogram that computes the sum of x and y. But when you use it, you don't use it as a program, you don't give it control as a sequence of executable operations, you don't call it as a subroutine. You use it like a data item, as in PRINT FNSUM(1234,5678). What is going on? It seems a function changes coats from program to data.

Advanced programmers know that programs and data cannot always bc distinguished. True, at a given instant in time, there is always a processor and a processee, an operation and an operand. But over time, the roles may reverse. For example, programs are data when they are being written with some text editor, when they are stored as files, and when they are being compiled. On the other hand, data can become programs, as when a function is referenced, or a program file is loaded and run, or a string is executed (*see* Sections 4.17 and 4.18).

A "computed data object" is an object that is not stored anywhere but is computed at the instant that it is required. It is a phantom data object that only exists when a program creates it. As an example, a patient's medical record may only contain the birthdate; yet the program can compute and display the age of the patient as a data item. The user at the keyboard cannot tell whether the age was stored or computed. We have already touched on another example: the function. When you execute

PRINT LEFT$("FREE",1)+RIGHT$("FREE",2)

you print the word "FEE" on the screen. This is a data object, but it is not stored as such anywhere in the memory; it is a computed data object. It is temporary, in the Latin sense of having a short existence in time.

A third example of the computed data object is the electronic spreadsheet, in which each cell of a two-dimensional array contains a "formula." The formula is a tiny subprogram that computes the value of that data cell. No data value exists until you "run" the sheet.

Experienced programmers see programs and data merely as two ends of a continuum. At one end is pure "space" containing pure data, such as a floppy diskette or a RAM chip. At the other end is pure "time" containing pure processes such as "clear screen" and "beep the speaker." Somewhere in between can be placed all programs and all data.

PURE TIME				PURE SPACE
pure actions	computed objects	linked objects	contiguous objects	pure data

Very few programs or data objects exist in pure time or pure space. It is an important insight to realize that most everything that programs do trades off space for time in some way. For example, the code

```
                       A(0) = 0
                       A(1) = 0
                       A(2) = 0
                       A(3) = 0
                       A(4) = 0
                       A(5) = 0
                       A(6) = 0
                       A(7) = 0
                       A(8) = 0
                       A(9) = 0
```

can be replaced by

```
           FOR I=0 TO 9 : A(I) = 0 : NEXT
```

The first version is larger but runs faster since it does not have to test 10 times for the end of the loop. It saves time at the expense of space. In this way, programs swap time for space in their designs and in their coding. Programmers distort real objects not just in space form but also in time form to achieve some purpose. They simulate, round up and down, restructure, condense, approximate, and shape both data and program objects. It makes no difference how much the time-space frame is distorted, as long as we can retrieve the desired information when it is needed, in the required form and precision.

Because the computer is extremely fast, we can sometimes achieve some surprising effects by exchanging time and space. The classic example of this is the timesharing system, where 50 users may be using a computer built for 5. Each of the 50 users thinks he or she is alone on the computer. Actually, the operating system swaps their programs in and out of memory, perhaps 10 times a second. Notice the word "swaps" in the last sentence. What is being swapped here? Programs are moved from memory out to disk. The net effect is that we are swapping disk space for execution time, since we are squeezing 50 users into a time slot where only 5 users should go.

3.6 Abstract Data Objects

For the final topic of this chapter, let's look at the ultimate idea in this area: the abstract data object. It has a forbidding name that has sent shivers down the spines of many programming students who were forced to wade through domains, sets, algebras, functions, mappings, and recursive definitions of recursion.

An abstract data object is nothing but a fancy computed data object, a package of subroutines that, taken as a whole, represents some data object. It is a relatively uncomplicated idea, easily implemented and quite useful in advanced programming.

First a quick review. A data "type" is a class of data objects on which the same or similar operations can be performed. In BASIC, we are familiar with such types as numbers, strings, and files. Thus, all data objects that can be stored on a medium, and opened, accessed, closed, and listed in directories are of the type "file." All objects you can add, subtract, multiply, and divide are of the type "number."

Types have a hierarchy. At the top, there are numbers, strings, labels, files, and more. Each type has subtypes; thus, the number type contains the integer, floating, Boolean, complex, and string number types. The floating type in turn contains the single-precision, double-precision, and extended-precision types.

Fortunately we do not have to worry about the taxonomy of data types in this section. We are not interested here in what a given type includes and excludes or what types others have invented and classified before us. Instead, we want to generalize the type idea, so that we can invent new types beyond those that BASIC gives us. That is how we arrive at the concept of the abstract data type: it is the type for all seasons, the essence, the template for making types.

All data types have two properties in common: they are data objects, and they can be manipulated with operations. The data object can be any one of our old friends such as numbers or strings or arrays or files. Operations are simply a set of sub-routines that perform certain desired services on or with the data object. For example, in BASIC we have the data type "random access file" and the corresponding operations OPEN, FIELD, GET, PUT, CLOSE, KILL, and RENAME. Or we have the data type "program file" and its operations LOAD, LIST, RUN, SAVE, and so on.

If a data type is part of the programming language, both the object and the operations are supplied as "built-in." If we want to create our own data type, we are on our own; we have to create both the object and its operations. To do this, we can only use the tools BASIC gives us. For objects, we can use numbers and strings and arrays and files. For the operations, we can write subroutines. The result will be a data object surrounded by subroutines that perform the required operations on the object (Figure 3-6). That is exactly what an abstract data object is.

That is all there is. The abstract data type is nothing but a program! After all, every program manipulates some internal data object to perform desired services (that is, operations) for the

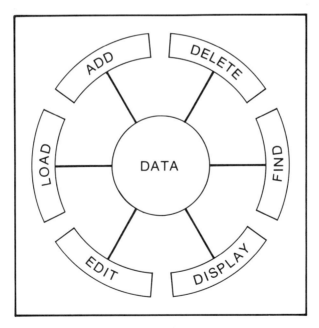

Figure 3-6. An abstract data type is a data object enclosed inside a ring of service routines that perform operations on the object.

outside world. A data base management system manages a data base, an operating system operates a hardware system, and a spreadsheet program manipulates a two-dimensional array. The main difference is that the abstract data type is an object internal to a program, a tool we use to create more flexible models of the real world.

Beginners sometimes have difficulty with the abstraction involved here, with the concept that a set of subroutines can represent an object. After all, a subroutine is a time concept whereas an object is a space concept. Perhaps it helps to point out that most of the things you think of as "objects" inside a program are really temporal illusions, created by the action of some executing process. As we just saw, even a loop—usually considered to be a process—can be interpreted as a form of condensed space. Remember the Wizard of Oz and his admonition to "pay no attention to the man behind the curtain."

For example, you may think a string array is a contiguous data object, since it behaves that way. Actually, behind the scenes, it is a linked data structure. It consists of an integer array that points (that is, links) to the data strings, which are scattered all over the memory. The assignment statement A$(7) = "HELLO" appears to just shove the value "HELLO" into its proper pigeonhole. Actually, the assignment is performed as a sequence of operations on several objects by subroutines that scurry about to find string space, store the value "HELLO" into it, and set the proper pointer for the subscript 7.

The RAM disk is another fine example of an abstract data object. Here we have a piece of memory used as if it were a floppy diskette. It is accessed exactly like a diskette by using the same I/O statements we always use. As far as the program is concerned, it is a diskette because it exhibits all of the functions of a diskette.

Much of programming involves this notion of simulated reality, and it can be addictive. You start to define subroutines for all kinds of objects. You realize that you can invent any kind of operation that you want—nonlinear, unusual, abnormal, and downright unreal. Thus, you can create random objects with unpredictable properties, to simulate some real system. You might create "living" objects that grow and change and replicate. You might even create objects that write programs—then relax and let them earn a living for you!

You can even simulate the computer itself. You can design your own favorite chip and simulate it entirely with subroutines that handle the primitive arithmetic and logical operations. Then you write a BASIC interpreter for this simulated chip. Now you would be completely independent of the underlying hardware. Your entire system—both hardware and software—would be one huge abstract data object. You could move this object to any other real computer, provided you rewrite the primitive operations. Some programming languages have been designed around this very concept of structuring the language into independent layers.

The key concept regarding the abstract data type is that those who use this object only "see" the access routines that surround it. They do not (or choose not to) see the internal details, so that the implementation of the object is hidden behind the curtain. As a result, the object can be modified behind the scenes without affecting the users. In fact, the object may not even exist: it may be completely simulated by using nothing but computed data objects.

3.7 Implementing an Abstract Data Object

An abstract data object consists of a data object and a set of operations, implemented as subroutines that access the object. The object is the typical stored or computed type, or some mix of these, such as found throughout this book.

The subroutines that access the object represent the operations on that object. They are as simple or as complex as the object itself. The minimum set typically contains routines to set up the object, to add to it, delete from it, and report its status. An extended set may include statistical operations such as summing, averaging, and trending, or it may include logical operations such as searching, sorting, replicating, and pattern matching.

Here, then, is a sample application. Let's say we plan to write several card-playing programs and want to use an abstract data object we'll call a "deck." A deck has 52 cards, and each card has the two attributes rank and suit. As users of the deck, we don't want to know anything about how the deck is implemented, stored, shuffled, and dealt. The only operations we need for this demonstration are

SET UP   = set up a new deck.
SHUFFLE = randomize the deck.
DEAL 1   = give me a card.

Each card will be represented by two integer variables named RANK and SUIT. RANK will run from 1 (ace) through 13 (king).

SUIT will be 1-4 for spades, hearts, diamonds, and clubs. SUIT=0 will signal that there are no more cards in the deck.

Four suits times 13 ranks gives us 52 different cards, so we implement the deck as two parallel integer arrays, RANK(52) and SUIT(52). Each pair of elements such as RANK(7) and SUIT(7) represents a different card in the deck. We will use the internal variable CARD to track the subscript of the last card dealt out. When CARD=52 then we are out of cards.

Here are the routines for the operations. They assume that RANK() and SUIT() are externally dimensioned.

```
+-------------------------------------------------------------------------+
:  ^SET UP^   ' New deck: spades,hearts,diamonds,clubs      :
:     FOR I=1 TO 52                                          :
:          RANK(I) = 1 + (I-1) MOD 13                        :
:          SUIT(I) = 1 + (I-1) \ 13                          :
:          NEXT I                                            :
:     CARD = 0                                               :
:     RETURN                                                 :
:                                                            :
:  ^SHUFFLE^    ' Shuffle the deck                           :
:     FOR I=1 TO 100                                         :
:          X = 1 + INT(52*RND)                               :
:          Y = 1 + INT(52*RND)                               :
:          SWAP SUIT(X),SUIT(Y)                              :
:          SWAP RANK(X),RANK(Y)                              :
:          NEXT I                                            :
:     RETURN                                                 :
:                                                            :
:  ^DEAL 1^    ' Return one card as SUIT and RANK            :
:     IF CARD=52 THEN SUIT=0 : RETURN                        :
:     CARD = CARD + 1                                        :
:     SUIT = SUIT(CARD)                                      :
:     RANK = RANK(CARD)                                      :
:     RETURN                                                 :
+-------------------------------------------------------------------------+
```

Taken as a group, these three routines are now the abstract data object "deck." We can use this object to support any number of playing programs, be they games, simulations, statistical studies, or parapsychology tests. Here is a skeleton poker-playing program. All it does so far is present two hands on the screen for your inspection. You must evaluate the hands yourself (or write additional operations such as VALUE and COMPARE):

```
+------------------------------------------------------------+
:  ^POKER.PRE^    ' Program to deal two hands of 5 cards     :
:     DIM SUIT(52), RANK(52)                                 :
:     GOSUB ^SET UP^ : GOSUB ^SHUFFLE^                        :
:     CLS : PRINT "My Hand      Your Hand" : PRINT           :
:     FOR I=1 TO 5          ' 5 cards                        :
:        FOR J=1 TO 2       ' 2 players                      :
:              GOSUB ^DEAL 1^                                :
:              PRINT MID$("A23456789TJQK",RANK,1); " of ";   :
:              PRINT MID$("SHCD",SUIT,1);; "        ";       :
:              NEXT J                                        :
:        PRINT                                               :
:        NEXT I                                              :
:     PRINT                                                  :
:     END                                                    :
+------------------------------------------------------------+
```

Just to show how easy it is, let's also write a quickie program to deal four hands of Bridge.

```
+------------------------------------------------------------+
:  ^BRIDGE.PRE^    ' Program to deal four hands of 13 cards  :
:     DIM SUIT(52), RANK(52)                                 :
:     GOSUB ^SET UP^ : GOSUB ^SHUFFLE^                        :
:     CLS                                                    :
:     PRINT "WEST        NORTH        EAST        SOUTH"     :
:     PRINT                                                  :
:     FOR I=1 TO 13         ' 13 cards                       :
:        FOR J=1 TO 4       ' 4 players                      :
:              GOSUB ^DEAL 1^                                :
:              PRINT MID$("A23456789TJQK",RANK,1); " of ";   :
:              PRINT MID$("SHCD",SUIT,1);; "        ";       :
:              NEXT J                                        :
:        PRINT                                               :
:        NEXT I                                              :
:     PRINT                                                  :
:     END                                                    :
+------------------------------------------------------------+
```

The key advantage of implementing the deck as an abstract data type lies in its isolation from the program that uses it. If you look closely at the Bridge program, you will see that to "write" this program I only used my text editor COPY command to clone the Poker program and then modified the driving variables. This is one of the nice side effects of using abstract data objects: once you have them, you can use them to support other programs, which then become easier to write.

So far, we only have a skeleton program, so the simple object we built here is sufficient. But as the program evolves into a more realistic game, perhaps even a commercial product, the object "deck" will require more and more sophisticated operations. There are many other possible representations for the deck:

- A string of 52 bytes, each encoded with suit and color bits. Several decks could then be simply a string array.
- An integer array dimensioned 52, with attributes encoded as bits.
- A linked list or chain through a set of parallel arrays, to simplify returning discards to the deck as well as tracking hands of various players.
- A random file with 52 records, fielded to carry suit and color information. This would allow permanent storage of special hands.
- A deck of 52 punched cards (the real kind you can fold, spindle, and mutilate), read into memory by a card reader.
- A hardware chip built to represent a card. 52 chips on a board would then sell as a deck.

Obviously, you have a range of choices, some farther out than others. (The last example is not at all unreasonable. In the last years, some ambitious chess programmers have actually built hardware that is dedicated to playing chess.)

3.8 Summary

Programmers use data objects of various types to model the real world inside the computer. A few elementary types are built into the programming languages; the rest must be constructed by the programmer.

Data objects are stored in data space in two general forms: as contiguous objects whose values are stored together or as linked objects whose values are scattered but logically connected with pointer values. A third type of object is not stored at all but is computed on request from stored types.

The most general object is the abstract data type, which is an object surrounded by a ring of routines representing operations on the object. The object is accessed and manipulated entirely via these operations routines.

Data objects are very important components of the total program environment. They support effective modelling and simulation at all levels of detail. They can be used to isolate portions of the programs from each other and thus to promote modularity. Their net effect is to build more and more intelligent application programs.

The String

The string is a data object that contains a variable number of bytes treated as a unit. There is no theoretical limit to the length of a string; the physical limit is the maximum addressable computer memory.

The most common example of a string is the ASCII display string, used to form screen displays, printed reports, and file records. But, as we will see, there are many other uses for the string in advanced programming. Whereas the numeric data types have many restrictions on data sizes and allowable formats, there are no restrictions as to the codes or combinations of codes that can be stored in a string. We will take full advantage of this feature.

4.1 The Conversion Functions

To exploit the power of the string, it is essential to understand its nature as a data object, especially in relation to the number. The conversion functions illuminate this aspect of strings. Because they are not always covered fully or explained correctly in introductory texts, I will begin by examining this aspect. We will look at five pairs of functions:

VAL   STR$
ASC   CHR$
CVI   MKI$
CVS   MKS$
CVD   MKD$

They are paired; that is, one converts from numeric to string, and its partner converts from string to numeric. You can always tell which way you are converting by noting that the function name itself follows the rules of naming variables. Those string functions ending in a dollar sign return a string value; the others return a numeric value.

VAL and STR$

Numeric data can be stored as numbers or as strings. If you write PI! = 3.14159, you create PI! as a "single-precision floating point numeric data type," which is also called a floating point (FP) number. Behind the scenes, FP numbers are specially encoded and stored as four bytes for single precision and 8 bytes for double precision.

If you write PI$ = "3.14159" you create PI$ as a "string data type" or string for short. Strings are not encoded behind the scenes (a very important quality). PI$ will be stored exactly as written, requiring (count them) 7 bytes.

Now, suppose you have the number in the string form PI$ and you want to do some arithmetic involving PI. Arithmetic computations can only be done with numbers, so you have to convert PI$ to a numeric data type first. The VAL function handles this. If you want to print the area of a circle with radius 2, you PRINT 4*VAL(PI$).

The STR$ function performs the reverse conversion. STR$(number) returns the number encoded as a string constant. For example, to create a string such as "MELT 2 OZ BUTTER" when the amount is given as a numeric variable AMOUNT, use the following expression. Note the way blanks are handled: the STR$ function appends a blank on each side of the converted number, so we don't provide any blanks:

"MELT" + STR$(AMOUNT) + "OZ BUTTER"

ASC and CHR$

Now we address a completely different problem. We want to play with the actual code of a single byte, exactly as it is stored in memory. We want to convert a small number between 0 and 255 into a single byte or, the inverse, we want to see what the contents of a single byte are.

The VAL and STR$ functions are useless here. For example, the internal ASCII code for the digit "0" is 49. But VAL("0") returns 0. This is useful in other contexts, but not when we want to see what the actual code is.

The expression ASC(X$) returns the internal code of the character X$. (If X$ is longer than 1 character, the ASC function only looks at the first character.) For example, PRINT ASC("0") will print 49.

The expression CHR$(code) returns a 1-character string whose byte contains the given code. The function gives an error if it gets a number outside the range 0-255. PRINT CHR$(65) will print the letter A, because 65 is the ASCII code for an "A".

CVI and MKI$

Now we are ready to tackle two useful functions that are indispensable when needed. They are kissing cousins of the ASC and CHR$ functions: where ASC and CHR$ play around with one byte, CVI and MKI$ play around with two. MKI$ "packs" an integer number up to 32767 into a 1-byte string, and CVI converts it back into an integer.

Consider the integer 12345. If we convert it to a string via STR$(12345), we get the 5-byte string "12345". If we use CHR$(12345) we get a nasty error message because 12345 is larger than 255. How can we convert 12345 into internal format? With the MKI$ function. As the name suggests, MKI$ "makes an integer into a string". The expression MKI$(12345) returns a 2-byte string that has the binary value 0011000000111001, which is 12345 in decimal.

CVS and MKS$

CVD and MKD$

Now we get the drift of these conversion functions. The MKS$ function converts an FP number to internal 4-byte format; CVS converts it back. The MKD$ function converts a double-precision FP number to internal 8-byte format; CVD converts it back.

The major advantage of these functions is that they pack bulky numbers into very tight form. For example, the number "3.1415926535898" requires 15 bytes as an ASCII string but only 8 bytes as a double-precision FP number. The functions are most often used to encode numbers into record fields, for storage on disk.

4.2 Advanced Strings

Now we are ready to explore some of the ways the string can be used in advanced programming. Each of the following sections highlights some particular technique, some special way of solving a problem with strings. The examples given are only sketches of what can be done; they are not fully developed and polished programs.

Because it is the least regulated and the most flexible data type of BASIC, the string plays an important role in advanced programming. It gives you much freedom to build and shape data objects dynamically. And, since it is an exact representation of what is stored in the physical memory, you can manipulate the machine by manipulating strings. As an example of how far you can take this, in one of the last sections of this chapter, we will store a short machine language program into a string and then transfer control to it as a subroutine!

It is a common misconception that numbers—the objects of mathematics—are somehow "clean" and "precise," while strings are somehow less "scientific" because their content and format is unstructured. How often have you heard that "computers reduce everything to numbers"? The fact is that computers manipulate all data in the form of strings. Keyboard, screen, printer, data communications, disk I/O, and even graphics are all handled as strings.

Aha, you say, isn't at least arithmetic done with numbers inside the computer? Not at all. Nowhere inside the hardware are numbers recognized as such! They are strung like beads on an abacus, and only processes (program or human) assign numeric meanings to them such as counts or amounts or subscripts or addresses or pointers. Integer arithmetic is done by logically ANDing and ORing bit strings together, one bit at a time. Floating point numbers are manipulated in the form of arbitrarily encoded strings of 4 and 8 bytes.

These are the properties of the string that we will exploit here and in later chapters:

- **Variable Length**. A string only takes up as much memory as it needs. There is no need to reserve the maximum and no need to worry about wasting space.
- **Symbolic Content**. A string can contain its own name and names of other variables, files, and programs.
- **Arbitrary Content**. A string can contain any sequence of

codes. Interpretation is strictly up to the program. There are no special byte positions and no reserved codes.

- **Recursive Type**. A string breaks down into smaller strings and combines with others to form larger strings.
- **Direct Access**. Even though a string can be treated as a unit, its byte elements can be directly accessed and individually processed.
- **String Arrays**. Strings can be grouped into arrays, taking advantage of the best of both worlds.
- **Fielded Strings**. Strings can be used to map buffer spaces, with such effects as overlaying strings on each other and defining substrings and even subarrays inside strings.

Because this chapter is a compendium of "things to do with strings," it makes dull reading at one sitting. You might wish to skim the sections lightly, to get an idea of what is possible and to pick out what you like.

We start with two sections that make these very important points:

1. A string is not (just) an array.
2. A string is not (just) an ASCII string.

4.3 A String is Not an Array

Many students confuse the string with the array, and for good reason. Some textbooks define strings as if they were tiny little character arrays. Some languages implement the string only in the form of a character array and sap it of all its strength. Some languages were invented for number crunching and have only recently been upgraded to include the string data type—in the less useful form of an array of "small" integers.

The BASIC language itself is, perhaps, the best illustration. The original BASIC only included the string as a data type for printing (as in PRINT "HELLO"). Later BASIC designs allowed exactly two string variables; they had to be called A$ and B$, if you can believe it! Even the BASIC interpreter supplied by IBM is not without fault here: The string length limit of 255 bytes is a crippling blow to the string's power, especially since it was unnecessary.

So that we might be righteous and never fall into that ancient trap, let's assert the truth loud and clear, especially for those who have learned bad habits. All together now, class, three times:

+--+
| |
| A STRING IS NOT AN ARRAY |
| A STRING IS NOT AN ARRAY |
| A STRING IS NOT AN ARRAY |
| |
+--+

Strings have more flexibility than arrays. Strings are variable-length, dynamic data objects; arrays have fixed length and are predimensioned. You can dynamically create a string of any length, even one extracted from another string. In most BASIC languages, you cannot dynamically create arrays.

You can add data to the head or the tail of a string. Bytes "float" inside a string: you can delete one byte from the middle of a string and close the string around it, or you can insinuate a new byte into the middle of a string. All without the laborious shifting of data values from element to element required for arrays.

Since strings are not arrays, we may occasionally need to convert one type to the other. In older BASIC languages, there was a CHANGE verb that performed this function. This verb was very useful to teachers because it drove home the point that strings are NOT arrays. Today, the CHANGE verb is extinct, so this pedagogic tool is no longer available. Here is the code to convert a string S$ to an array A() and back:

```
+----------------------------------------------------------------+
:    ' string to array                                           :
:    FOR I=1 TO LEN(S$)  :  A(I)=ASC(MID$(S$,I,1))  :  NEXT I     :
:                                                                :
:    ' array to string; array count is in A(0)                   :
:    S$=""                                                       :
:    FOR I=1 TO A(0)  :  S$=S$+CHR$(A(I))  :  NEXT I             :
+----------------------------------------------------------------+
```

4.4 Strings Are Not ASCII Strings

There are two misconceptions about strings: that a string is a text string and that ASCII is a display code. These mistaken notions survive by feeding on each other. At the beginning level, they make little difference because strings are typically used only to store text messages and alphanumeric business records. But to make advanced use of strings, we need to get rid of these misconceptions.

The myth that ASCII is a display code evolved because beginning programmers are usually exposed only to text strings (that is, strings used to store or display alphanumeric text). In the IBM PC, such text strings are, in fact, encoded in ASCII code. This leads the student (and some textbooks) to talk of the string as if it is always and only ASCII. Some texts talk interchangeably about strings and text strings as if there is nothing else in the universe.

But, saying that a string is an ASCII string is like saying that a basket is a breadbasket, or a bucket is a waterbucket: it is correct but does not go far enough. Here are the facts: A string consists of bytes. Each byte consists of 8 bits (Figure 4-1), which is not a law of nature but rather an industry standard in microcomputing today.

Given 8 bits, each with value 0 or 1, Arithmetic tells us that we can store any binary number from 00000000 to 11111111, which is 0 through 255 in decimal. Since only the whole numbers 1, 2, and so on can be represented this way, we can define a string as a stream of integers with any value from 0 to 255.

Now we are on our own! There are no further rules regarding strings that we absolutely *must* obey. Given some binary number in a byte like 01100111, our programs are free to interpret this value in any way we please. We may treat it as Morse code, as Braille, as a count, as a person's age, as the day of a month, or as the open–shut state of eight flow valves along an oil line. The key here is some agreement, if only with ourselves, how each byte is to

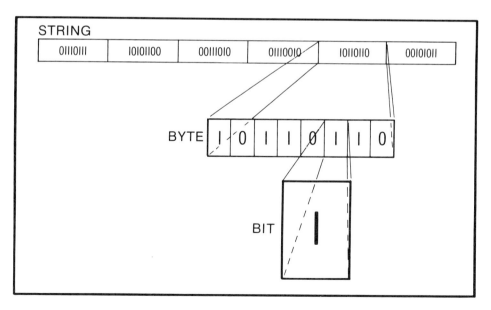

Figure 4-1. Relationship of string to bytes to bits.

be interpreted. Thus, if we want oil to flow along our line, we must see that all 8 bits are 00000000 or 11111111, depending on which value we chose to mean "open."

So far, so good. We can certainly agree with ourselves. But now arises a problem: How will we communicate with each other? If we want to transmit a data stream to a friend across town, we need to agree on a code with our friend. We must specify all the codes for two kinds of data to be transmitted: true data such as ages, dates, amounts, punctuation, numbers, symbols, and valve settings; and control data that tell the recipient where the true data start and stop, where the end of each line is, who sent the message, and how many bytes were sent.

The American Standard Code for Information Interchange (ASCII) was designed for this purpose. It is a code for data communications, not for display. Obviously, a part of the code includes the codes to transmit letters, numerals, and punctuation marks that we do commonly display. But there is a lot more. Some codes specify physical actions, such as "ring the bell at the receiving terminal" (code 7) or the famous "carriage return" (code 13) and its twin "line feed" (code 10).

Some codes work in combinations; thus "end of line" is commonly transmitted as the two-code sequence 13 10, because the code 13 will move the carriage back to the right (or the cursor or the printhead back to the left) and code 10 will move the cursor down 1 line or the paper up one line. Together, 13 10 performs the function "newline." The "backspace," code 8, is another combination code; it begs the receiver to "ignore the character I just sent to you."

Example: The "underline" code has given many a student a headache. Why is an underlined A three characters in my string when it only takes up one position on the screen? Because underlining involves three operations behind the scenes: printing the A, and backspacing, and overprinting the underline character. Each of these three operations requires one character to specify. Therefore, an underlined A requires a three-string ASCII sequence.

Some codes control the transmission itself, such as "abort transmission" (code 3). There is even a code to override the ASCII scheme itself: the "escape code" (27) means literally "what follows is a special sequence; do not necessarily interpret it as ASCII." It is used to escape from the ASCII code into any other code, such as some special printer control code or a code to drive some special device attached to the computer.

Note how the distinction between data and process is somewhat blurred, even at this simple byte level. Some bytes are data, some bytes are commands, some bytes are status messages, some are just spacers waiting for time to pass. Data and processes are thinly disguised versions or variations of the same thing. They are the yin and yang of programming, and we will see more of them throughout the book.

Why, then, do we learn incorrectly to think of display strings as ASCII? Because most microcomputers use ASCII to communicate internally among their various devices, such as keyboard, screen, memory, disk, speaker, modem, joystick, and so on. You can observe this as follows:

```
A$ =    "word1" + CHR$(7) + "word2"
PRINT LEN(A$)
PRINT A$
```

The speaker will beep, the screen will show "11" and the ten characters "word1word2". Internally, the string A$ contains 11 characters, but only 10 are printed. The software treats CHR$(7) as a command to activate the speaker, not to light up the screen.

Only a part of ASCII is a display code; the rest of the codes are control codes, graphic symbols, or simply undefined, depending on what system you are talking about. Specifically, the first 26 codes are the "Control Codes." They are reserved for transmission control. This becomes important when, for example, you try to transmit binary data or object files to other computers by using an ASCII transmission system. In an ASCII transmission, when you send a code 7 (defined in ASCII as "RING THE BELL"), the receiving terminal dutifully sounds the speaker and swallows the 7. It does not know and does not care that, to you, the 7 represents data, perhaps the age of a child patient or an interest percentage.

As if that were not enough, not only was ASCII not designed as a pure data code, but since it is the only common code around, it has been mucked about with so much that it is now often unrecognizable. You simply have to ask yourself at all times to whom you are sending a message, and in what context. For example, PRINT CHR$(3) displays a heart on the IBM PC screen. On other machines, this statement will produce any number of reactions such as an error message, no action at all, some arbitrary graphic symbol, or—most devastating of all—a complete system lockup that forces you to reboot. If you transmit CHR$(3)

to a remote receiver, many will abort transmission and return to the operating system because in true ASCII, code 3 is the infamous "Control-C" command, also known as BREAK.

To summarize, the string is a powerful data structure or data object for carrying data encoded in various forms, either public, such as ASCII; special, such as roman numeral; or private, such as a string of oil-valve settings or a scrambled satellite signal. The point, as always, is to distinguish between the physical code and its logical interpretation by someone.

4.5 Working with Strings

Strings are a useful bridge between the human and the computer. Humans represent information as strings and communicate it as strings. So do computers. Humans use strings to compute answers to problems. So do computers. Humans store bulk information in the form of strings. So do computers. Humans write source programs in the form of strings. Computers execute machine language programs in the form of strings.

Strings are highly flexible data objects that can be used effectively to model real-world data as well as format and process data inside the hardware. One testimony for the power of the string is that string processing languages are widely used in artificial intelligence, where sophisticated data processing tools are required.

It is all the more surprising that language designers as a whole have generally ignored the string or treated it like an orphan. For example, in BASIC there are about 14 operators for integers, but only 1 for strings. And yet, BASIC programmers are indeed fortunate to even have the string. Many other languages don't even offer it, or they offer it in some awkward form as a fixed-length integer array, or they prohibit certain characters because they are used as delimiters.

You will find working with strings to be very easy and very natural—you have done it since grammar school! And you will find hundreds of uses for the string. In fact, there are so many that all I can do in the rest of this chapter is summarize some of the more typical uses and illustrate a few of them. First, we will look at the ways strings can be packed and translated. Then we will look at a few applications and work out a few to illustrate how strings can be used.

4.6 Verifying String Contents _____

Let's start with a very simple string operation that is not offered as a BASIC string function. Given some data string, we often need to verify that all of its codes are valid, meaning that all of its codes come from a set of valid codes called an "alphabet." For example, we may need to verify that a social security number contains only decimal digits. To do that, we would verify it against an alphabet of "0123456789" to detect alien characters. We would use "0123456789ABCDEF" to verify a hexadecimal number.

IBM PC BASIC provides the string function INSTR to find the first occurrence of a key string in some given string. We want to write a function that will return the location of the first character that does *not* belong into some given string. If the function returns 0 we are happy, because it means that the given string is clean, it contains no alien characters.

Here is a subroutine to verify the contents of a string INFO$ against an alphabet ALPHA$. The routine tests one data byte at a time against the alphabet string. If the byte is *not* in the authorized alphabet, the routine returns its location in the string. Otherwise, it loops through INFO$ and returns ALIEN = 0 to signal a valid string:

```
: ^ALIEN^
:    ' enter with  INFO$ = the string to be checked
:    '              ALPHA$ = the authorized characters
:    ' Return with ALIEN = location of first alien (or 0)
:
:    ALIEN=0    ' location of alien character in INFO$
:    WHILE ALIEN<LEN(INFO$)
:       ALIEN=ALIEN+1
:       BYTE$=MID$(INFO$,ALIEN,1)
:       IF INSTR(ALPHA$,BYTE$)=0 THEN RETURN
:       WEND
:    ALIEN=0
:    RETURN
```

The routine ALIEN merely reports the location of the unauthorized or unwanted character. The next step is to write a routine CULL that removes the alien bytes and returns a nice clean data string containing only good characters. The routine uses ALIEN to find the alien bytes and then mercilessly deletes them from the INFO string:

```
+---------------------------------------------------------------+
:   ^CULL^                                                      :
:      ' Enter with  INFO$ = data string to be culled          :
:      '              ALPHA$ = good characters                  :
:      ' Return with INFO$ = the cleaned data string            :
:                                                               :
:      WHILE 1                                                  :
:         GOSUB ^ALIEN^                                         :
:         IF ALIEN=0 THEN RETURN                                :
:         INFO$=LEFT$(INFO$,ALIEN-1)+MID$(INFO$,ALIEN+1)        :
:         WEND                                                  :
:      RETURN                                                   :
+---------------------------------------------------------------+
```

One quick example for using the CULL routine is in editing raw data input. Suppose you ask the user at the keyboard for a telephone number. You might get it in the form 5551234 or 555-1234 or (619)555-1234 or even 1-619/555-1234. You want to cull the input string for the good digits and to ignore the punctuation noise:

```
+---------------------------------------------------------------+
:   ...                                                         :
:   INPUT INFO$             ' get the raw data                  :
:   ALPHA$="0123456789"     ' good characters                   :
:   GOSUB ^CULL^            ' delete bad characters             :
:   ' INFO$ only contains digits now                            :
:   ...                                                         :
+---------------------------------------------------------------+
```

4.7 Packing Data into Strings

Unlike a number, to which only a single data value can be assigned, there are many ways to structure and arrange data into a string. A string can contain any combination of letters, digits, blanks, commas, words, phrases, pointers, labels, variable names, file names, and so on. An entire word processing document can be stored as a single string.

No matter how intricately the physical data are packed, they have to be unpacked and processed as logically separate units. Programmers use the word "field" to distinguish the logical data from each other inside a string. Fields can have fixed or variable length and can be formatted in a number of useful and interesting ways:

Fixed Field

The string is partitioned into fields whose lengths remain fixed for the duration. This concept is simple and easily implemented. It has the advantage that a given field can be located easily with the MID$ function. Its major drawback is that fixed fields have to be defined large enough to accommodate the largest possible data value to be stored. This means that space is always wasted unless the data themselves have fixed length.

```
+--------------------------------------------------------------------+
:     '        Last Name           First    Middle      Age  Sex     :
:                                                                    :
:     DATA   Gray                  Richard  Frederick    3   M       :
:     DATA   Green                 John     A.          36   M       :
:     DATA   Greene                Betty    Jane        24   F       :
:     DATA   Greensleeves          Al                   62   M       :
+--------------------------------------------------------------------+
```

Note: Be sure to distinguish this method of packing data as fixed fields into a string from the technique of fielding a file buffer with the FIELD statement, discussed below. Any string can be packed with fixed fields; but only file buffers can be FIELDed. But as we will see, we can use the FIELD statement to help us manipulate fixed-field strings.

Delimited Fields

Fields with variable length can be strung together into a list as long as they are separated by some special character or characters called a "delimiter" or "terminator."

Here are some simple examples in the form of a program fragment. The first line uses the colon to delimit variable-length source statements. The next two lines use the blank and the comma to separate their data fields. In the fourth line, the first byte of the string specifies the delimiter:

```
+--------------------------------------------------------------------+
:     GOSUB ^A^ : B$="abcdefg" : GOSUB ^B^ : A=3                     :
:     A$ =    "Joe 3 Jane 8 Tom 6 Elizabeth 13"                      :
:     A$ =    "Joe,3,Jane,8,Tom,6,Elizabeth,13"                      :
:     A$ =    "\This\is\delimited\by\left\slash\"                    :
+--------------------------------------------------------------------+
```

The delimiter can be more than one character long. In fact, if you use the 2 bytes CHR$(13)+CHR$(10), which are carriage return + line feed, you can store several print lines into one string. The delimiter not only separates the lines, it causes a new print line to be set up for each field. As a result, you can print an entire document stored in some giant string D$ with a single statement PRINT D$. This trick might be good for a bar bet the next time you are with programmers of less sophistication!

Counted Fields

Sometimes the use of delimiters is not possible. If the data values themselves contain all possible codes, we have no codes we can use as delimiters. One cannot use a period to delimit sentences that contain periods.

In such cases, we count the bytes in each field and store the count itself as part of the string. The count acts as a computed delimiter, and each field is found by carefully counting the bytes of its predecessors. The count is usually stored just in front of the field itself, or all counts are lumped and placed in front of the data:

```
+----------------------------------------------------------------+
:          DATA    3APE8ELEPHANT5SHEEP7GIRAFFE                    :
:          DATA    3857APEELEPHANTSHEEPGIRAFFE                    :
+----------------------------------------------------------------+
```

Note that in the example we stored the counts as ASCII digits of one byte each. If any field lengths exceed 9, additional bytes would be required for the count fields. To avoid wasting many bytes, the counts are often converted to 2-byte binary using the MKI$ function discussed earlier. This conversion makes the string "unprintable" since it contains non-ASCII count bytes; but it lets us handle fields up to 65535 bytes long with fixed-length count fields of 2 bytes each.

Ordered Fields

One major problem of packing many fields into a single string is keeping track of which field is which. So far, the packing examples have been arbitrary lists of data values; what if the order of the fields is important?

One method of identifying specific fields in a string is to simply insist on listing the fields in some fixed order, leaving empty spots where a data value is missing. For example, a typical address string can be designed as a comma-delimited list to contain name, street, city, state, and zip code. The fields must occur in this order or else address labels will not print right. If a field is missing, we must carefully leave a spot in the form of an empty field:

```
+----------------------------------------------------------------+
:   DATA    John Green,923 Main St,San Diego,CA,12345,           :
:   DATA    UCLA,,Los Angeles,,,                                 :
:   DATA    Jane Blue,456 Elm Way,,Oklahoma,,                    :
:   DATA    The White House,,Washington,,,                       :
+----------------------------------------------------------------+
```

(For an application of this method, *see* Chapters 11 and 12, where we will use it to pack parameters into a string that we pass to the subroutine for processing.)

Labelled Fields

Another way to track fields in a string is to label them. Since we are playing with symbolic data, why not use symbols to identify them? In some applications this can save space, especially where there can be many possible fields, but only a few usually appear, such as in business or personnel records:

```
+------------------------------------------------------------------+
:   DATA    NAME=UCLA,CITY=Los Angeles,                            :
:   DATA    STREET=456 Elm Way,NAME=Jane Blue,STATE=Oklahoma       :
:   DATA    NAME=The White House                                   :
+------------------------------------------------------------------+
```

A program that wants to process this type of string has to use the INSTR function first to locate a desired field, such as L=INSTR(INFO$,"NAME="). This function yields the location L where the field name starts. To find the name itself, we find the delimiting comma with C=INSTR(L,INFO$,","). Finally, we extract the name value itself, via N$=MID$(INFO$,L+6,C−L−5). One convenient side effect of labelling the fields is that they need not be in order anymore. To add a new data value to a string, we simply concatenate it, prefixed with a comma and the field label.

Cross-Referenced Fields

A field need not just contain a single data item. You can use a field to correlate two or more data items to each other. Examples are: a book index, a label-line number table for PREBASIC, an abbreviations list, a beginner/expert menu, and a dictionary:

```
+------------------------------------------------------------------+
:   DATA    queue 123, string 56, stack 234                        :
:   DATA    400=^START^ 1200=^VERIFY^  680=^BOOT^                   :
:   DATA    oz=ounce  bbl=barrel  w/o=without  N=North             :
:   DATA    APPEND=APP=7, WRITE=W=3, OPEN=O=4                       :
:   DATA    merci=thank you, rue=street, monde=world               :
+------------------------------------------------------------------+
```

These are a few of the techniques for packing data into strings. Each has its advantages and its drawbacks; the fancier we get with our packing methods, the more complicated the unpacking becomes. As always, several judgments are involved in selecting a method. Theoretically, we want to minimize our labor, the data space, and program execution time. As a practical matter, these three resources must be traded off for each other: tight packing requires more packing time but saves space. Fancy packing may conserve both space and time, but requires much design time. In some cases, such as the graphic representation of data in a string array, the benefit of having an understandable, viewable data object can far outweigh any savings derived from other representations.

4.8 The FIELD Statement

The FIELD statement basically subdivides a file buffer into a set of fixed fields, each with its own string name. It lets you map a buffer to match the record format of the file you are accessing. This simplifies access to random file records, which are typically stored as fixed-field strings.

To FIELD a buffer, you first open some file as a random access file and then execute one or more FIELD statements. A FIELD statement creates a template of string names that is overlaid on the buffer as long as the file remains open. Each FIELD statement is independent of the other, so that you can create different templates for the same buffer.

After you read any record (say 123) of the file, you can refer to the whole record with a single name (for example, RECORD$ in the following example). Or you can reach into the record and refer to any substring by name (for example, INFO$). The following dummy program shows the typical statements used in conjunction with the FIELD statements:

```
+-----------------------------------------------------------------+
:    ' Dummy program to show FIELD syntax and semantics          :
:    OPEN "R",#1,"SOMEFILE",200                     ' open        :
:    FIELD #1, 200 AS RECORD$                       ' map 1       :
:    FIELD #1, 100 AS HALF1$, 100 AS HALF2$         ' map 2       :
:    FIELD #1, 50 AS NAME$, 50 AS INFO$             ' map 3       :
:    GET #1, 123                              ' read record       :
:    A$=NAME$     ' convert buffer string to regular string      :
:    LSET NAME$=B$      ' convert regular to buffer string        :
:    PRINT HALF1$                    ' display name and info      :
:    LSET INFO$ = "New info for record 123"  ' change info        :
:    PUT #1, 123            ' rewrite record 123 with new info    :
:    PUT #1, 456            ' write record 456 with same info     :
:    CLOSE #1                             ' done with file         :
+-----------------------------------------------------------------+
```

So, what is the catch? We programmers know from experience that we never get any software feature without paying some awful price; but, surprisingly, no strings are attached to the FIELD statement. (The only price you have to pay is that recursive pun.)

Although no one will tell you so, the FIELD statement really defines a new string type that we might call a "buffer string." As always, when you have a new data type, you must know and respect its properties to use it correctly. For one thing, a buffer string has a fixed length. Just as you cannot store a number larger than 32767 into a 2-byte integer, you cannot store a string longer than 100 bytes into a buffer string that has been FIELDed to 100 bytes. It will be chopped to exactly 100 bytes.

Since buffer strings are mapped onto open file buffers, they require special internal processing. To do this, BASIC provides two assignment statements: LSET and RSET. An LSET statement stores a regular string into a buffer starting at the left end of the buffer string. If the string is too long for the buffer string, the tail is chopped off. The RSET statement right justifies the string into the field, padding on the left if the string is too short. Both LSET and RSET chop off the string if it is too long for the field.

To unFIELD, that is, to convert a buffer string to a regular string, simply use it in a regular assignment statement such as INFO$="". This statement signals BASIC that you wish to use INFO$ as a regular string again. It is also the most common mistake made with FIELDed strings. If you are debugging a program that seems to write the same field to every record, no matter what you assign to the field, you have probably fallen into this subtle trap.

Buffer strings can be used in various ways to simplify programming. You can pack numbers into a record by using the conversion functions CVI and MKI$ (and their floating-point cousins). You can use several FIELD statements to define several record types within the same file. You can arbitrarily "chunk" a record into more convenient lengths for display or plotting.

You can provide some protection for your data files by embedding nonsense fields into the middle of valid data. A single random nonsense letter embedded into the city field of a customer address list can help to thwart or at least delay snoopers or data thieves. Yet they do not interfere with authorized processing if you simply field the buffer around them.

On the other hand, if you are a snooper, you can use a large buffer to detect how some foreign file was originally fielded, by searching for patterns. Or, if you don't know the record size of a random file, you can step through a FIELD loop until some pattern emerges.

You can construct records out of 1-byte fields and map an entire disk into one giant fixed-field string of individual characters. You might map screen layouts as file records. You can even define arrays of buffer strings by using the FIELD statement in a loop that maps a string array to successive buffer fields. Here is how:

```
'  Program to define a buffer string array B$()
DIM B$(100)
OPEN "R",#1,"SOMEFILE",200
FOR I = 1 TO 100
    FIELD #1, 2*(I-1) AS DUMMY$, 2 AS B$(I)
    NEXT I
```

The array B$( ) starts out as a regular string array. Each iteration of the loop fields a different portion of the buffer. The DUMMY$ string is used to skip over the fields already mapped in previous iterations. After the loop, B$( ) is a buffer string array, each element covering 2 bytes of the buffer. B$(1) is the first 2 bytes of the buffer. B$(2) is the second 2 bytes. B$(100) is byte 199 and 200. You can assign data to the buffer as if it were an array. For example, to set the 17th byte pair to the integer 3456, you would write LSET B$(17) = MKI$(3456). Conversely, to extract the value from a record just read from disk, you might write A = CVI(B$(17)).

Finally, consider the use of a dummy file just to exploit the mapping powers of the buffer string. If you open a dummy file (that is, a file you never read or write), the system sets up a buffer for you. Using multiple FIELD statements, dummy fields, and buffer string arrays, you can then pack data in highly specialized formats to suit your needs.

4.9 Parallel Strings and String Arrays _____

You can increase the power of the string by using several strings in parallel or by dimensioning a string array. When many strings with fixed-field formats are arranged into a table or an array, their fields line up vertically. Once the location of a given field is known in one string, it is known in all other strings. Whether defined as an array or an individual string variables, strings arranged in parallel like this can be used effectively for synonyms, for cross-referencing, for translation, and in general for any tabular use where alternate versions of some string have to be rapidly located.

As one example, you can use parallel strings or string arrays to store entire graphics for display or analysis.

```
+------------------------------------------------------------------+
:       DATA     "  *                 x "                          :
:       DATA     "    *             x   "                          :
:       DATA     "      *         x     "                          :
:       DATA     "        *  x          "                          :
:       DATA     "           x *         "                         :
:       DATA     "         x     *      "                          :
:       DATA     "             x     * "                           :
+------------------------------------------------------------------+
```

As another example, consider the use of parallel strings to store a command menu for some program. You want to provide command words for novices, for beginners, and for experts. In addition, you want to give each command word a number for use by internal subroutines, and you want to tell the program how many parameters are required with each command and whether or not it is privileged. You elect to store your menu as a parallel string table, like this:

```
+------------------------------------------------------------------+
:    NOVICE$ = "ADD DELETE FIND HELP QUIT READ WRITE"              :
:    EXPERT$ = "A    D      F    H    Q    R    W"                  :
:    WORDNO$ = "7    4      2    1    3    6    5"                  :
:    PARAM$  = "2    2      1    0    1    1    3"                  :
:    PRIVIL$ = "Y    N      Y    Y    Y    Y    N"                 :
+------------------------------------------------------------------+
```

As a group, this set of parallel strings supports three different functions: it translates alternate user names to each other, it cross-references user symbols to internal numbers, and it contains information for command execution. NOVICE$ and EXPERT$ are synonym strings; you can enter the table by either command word. WORDNO$ cross-references the symbolic English command words to some command word number used internally by the program. Together with the WORD$ string, PARAM$ and PRIVIL$ strings make up a little look-up table that helps the program look up information required to perform the command.

A major advantage of this technique is that the table can be changed even as the program runs. You can add new menu items as you go, perhaps letting the user define his or her own command names. You can eliminate inappropriate commands, or read a new command set from some prepared file. In short, the program can learn as it runs.

Other uses that come to mind are

- Two parallel strings can hold the before and after codes, as detailed in Section 4.11.
- Building file symbol tables, so that external users are not restricted to the complicated file names used internally. Instead of entering "B:PR850331.DAT" to access a payroll file, the user can enter "MARCH PAY" and let the program translate this with parallel strings.
- In the area of artificial intelligence, parallel strings can be used to teach a program about a data object. The program can piece together partial data as it gains information about an object over time. The parallel strings serve as a Rosetta Stone or as a holograph to correlate different views of the data object to help describe it.
- Use parallel strings to keep track of the current location or status of a number of data objects, for example, to track disk records currently in memory this way. This tracking avoids reading a record that is already in memory or writing a record that has not been changed since it was read into memory.

See also Chapter 5 for similar ideas in the array area. Arrays of strings are the ultimate in convenience for parallel string methods. You have the best of both worlds: the array gives you addressability with subscripts you can compute; the string gives you variable-length symbolic data values. Who could ask for more? If that is not enough, imagine what you could do with parallel arrays of parallel strings, stored on parallel files.

4.10 Translating Strings

Because the string is such a flexible data object, there is no end to the codes and formats and possible uses. In addition to the packing format we saw above, there are many official codes such as ASCII, EBCDIC, Grey, Hexadecimal, CDC Display, and so on. Murphy's Law says that a string will always be in the wrong code or the wrong form, and you will need routines to translate strings.

Often, data streams need to be examined to verify that they

contain only valid codes. Invalid codes must be eliminated, and codes may need to be standardized. For example, you may want to translate all lowercase letters to uppercase, or to edit brackets and braces to parentheses.

For security and privacy reasons, you will want to encode data into your own private code. If you are one of the dreaded teenage "hackers" that are currently terrifying our Defense Department, you will need translation routines to decode national defense secrets. (Hey you guys, don't carry me off . . . just kidding, honestly . . . I never . . .)

In the following sections, some of the translation methods are detailed.

4.11 Parallel Translation

To translate a string, we need to specify what each given code is to be translated to. One method is to have two parallel strings BEFORE$ and AFTER$ that specify the codes to be translated. For example, we may need to standardize all braces, brackets, and angles as parentheses, so that < and [become (, and > and] become) (Figure 4-2).

To translate, all we have to do is find a code in BEFORE$ and pick its matching code out of AFTER$. Here is the routine:

```
+-----------------------------------------------------------------+
:   ^PTRANS^     ' Sub for parallel translation                   :
:      ' Enter with  INFO$   = string to be translated            :
:      '             BEFORE$ = these codes become                 :
:      '             AFTER$  = these codes                         :
:      ' Return with INFO$   = the translated string              :
:      FOR I = 1 TO LEN(INFO$)                                    :
:          B = INSTR(BEFORE$,MID$(INFO$,I,1))                     :
:          IF B THEN MID$(INFO$,I,1) = MID$(AFTER$,B,1)           :
:          NEXT I                                                  :
:      RETURN                                                      :
+-----------------------------------------------------------------+
```

As an example, suppose we wish to reverse the font of some document on file by converting all the uppercase letters to lowercase and vice versa. The BEFORE and AFTER strings simply consist of the letter fonts. Here is the code. using parallel translator strings to translate file BOZO1 to BOZO2. (For presen-

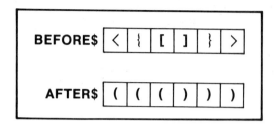

Figure 4-2. Parallel "⟨{[]}⟩" and "(((())))" strings can be used to translate various forms of parentheses.

tation reasons, the BEFORE and AFTER strings are shown with some of the letters suppressed):

```
+-----------------------------------------------------------------+
:   BEFORE$="abcdef...opqrstuvwxyzABCDEF...OPQRSTUVWXYZ"           :
:   AFTER$ ="ABCDEF...OPQRSTUVWXYZabcdef...opqrstuvwxyz"           :
:   OPEN "I",#1,"BOZO1" : OPEN "O",#2,"BOZO2"                      :
:   WHILE NOT EOF(1)                                              :
:      LINE INPUT #1, INFO$                                        :
:      GOSUB ^PTRANS^                                              :
:      PRINT #2, INFO$                                             :
:      WEND                                                        :
:   CLOSE                                                          :
:   END                                                            :
+-----------------------------------------------------------------+
```

4.12 Indexed Translation

The translation codes can also be specified by using only one string AFTER$. We generate AFTER$ so that each byte contains the translated code corresponding to the byte's position in AFTER$. That is, we use the code to be translated as an index into the AFTER$ string (Figure 4-3). The first byte of the translator string tells what to translate code 1 to, byte 2 tells what to translate code 2 to, and so on until it reaches the 255th byte of AFTER$, which specifies what code 255 is to be translated to. (I am ignoring code 0 here to simplify the presentation. It is handled easily by treating it as code 256 and adding it to the end of the AFTER$ string.)

The following translation routine uses an indexed translation string AFTER$ to translate a given string INFO$:

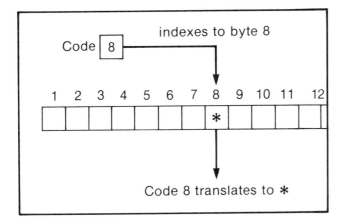

Figure 4-3. An indexed translator string can be used to translate one code into another.

```
+------------------------------------------------------------------+
:   ^IXLATE^   ' Sub to translate using an indexed string          :
:      ' Enter with  INFO$  = the string to be translated          :
:      '             AFTER$ = the translator string                :
:      ' Return with INFO$  = the translated string                :
:      FOR I = 1 TO LEN(INFO$)                                      :
:          S2 = ASCII(MID$(INFO$,I,1,))                             :
:          MID$(INFO$,I,1) = MID$(AFTER$,S2,1)                      :
:          NEXT I                                                   :
:      RETURN                                                       :
+------------------------------------------------------------------+
```

Let's use this idea on the last example of section 4.11. We will reverse the fonts of file BOZO1 to BOZO2 again. We know that the ASCII codes near the letters have this pattern, written horizontally. For example, an ASCII 65 is the capital letter A:

```
+------------------------------------------------------------------+
:  ... 64 65 66 ... 89 90 91 ... 96 97 ... 122 123 ...             :
:        @  A  B     Y  Z  [      '  a       z   {                  :
+------------------------------------------------------------------+
```

To reverse the letters only, the 65th byte should contain the lowercase "a" and the 97th byte should contain the uppercase "A". We need a translator string like this:

```
+------------------------------------------------------------------+
:  ... 64 65 66 ... 89 90 91 ... 96 97 ... 122 123 ...             :
:        @  a  b     y  z  [      '  A       Z   {                  :
+------------------------------------------------------------------+
```

This translator string is formed by this code:

```
+------------------------------------------------------------------+
:   FOR I=  1 TO   64 : AFTER$ = AFTER$ + CHR$(I)  : NEXT I    :
:   AFTER$=AFTER$ + "abcdefghijklmnopqrstuvwxyz"               :
:   FOR I= 91 TO   96 : AFTER$ = AFTER$ + CHR$(I)  : NEXT I    :
:   AFTER$=AFTER$ + "ABCDEFGHIJKLMNOPQRSTUVWXYZ"               :
:   FOR I=123 TO 255 : AFTER$ = AFTER$ + CHR$(I)  : NEXT I    :
+------------------------------------------------------------------+
```

We set up the translator string AFTER$ as above and now we can translate file BOZO1 to BOZO2:

```
+------------------------------------------------------------------+
:   OPEN "I",#1,"BOZO1" : OPEN "O",#2,"BOZO2"                  :
:   WHILE NOT EOF(1)                                          :
:     LINE INPUT #1,INFO$:GOSUB ^IXLATE^:PRINT #2,INFO$;      :
:     WEND                                                    :
:   CLOSE                                                     :
:   END                                                       :
+------------------------------------------------------------------+
```

In general, parallel string translation is simpler to set up and to control. Also, you only need to define those codes to be translated. Indexed translation takes more design and setup effort; but it is far more handy when you need to translate a lot of codes. For example, on its larger commercial computers, IBM uses Extended Binary Coded Decimal Interchange Code (EBCDIC). Converting EBCDIC to ASCII is easy with indexed translation, even though setting up the translator string can be a bit of a headache. (For one neat solution, *see* Section 4.15.)

Also, don't overlook the value of indexed translation in the other direction. If you need to convert some arbitrary list of characters into another sequential number code, use INSTR to give you the code. For example, if C$ is an uppercase vowel, you can convert it to a 1-6 code with the simple expression INSTR("AEIOUY",C$). This idea is applied later in the section on hexadecimal translation.

4.13 Translating to Hexadecimal

As discussed earlier, strings containing pure binary numbers from 0 to 255 cannot be transmitted with ASCII code because the ASCII code defines certain codes as transmission control commands rather than as data. To transmit binary values or graphic character bytes with ASCII transmission software, we must force them into ASCII display codes such as letters, digits, and punctuation which do not control transmission. In other words, we must fool the transmission system by translating our 8-bit data into artificial ASCII. The receiving program then translates the artificial ASCII back to the true binary values and graphic codes.

Since we are free to select any translation rule we please, we select the hexadecimal code. This is a code in which each digit represents 4 bits, so that it has 16 code values from 0 to 15. These code values are traditionally represented as digits 0–9 and A–F. The following table shows the hexadecimal digits and their binary representation:

0	1	2	3	4	5	6	7
0000	0001	0010	0011	0100	0101	0110	0111
8	9	A	B	C	D	E	F
1000	1001	1010	1011	1100	1101	1110	1111

By choosing hexadecimal, we not only solve our transmission problem, but we can also use the routines to examine the internal binary values of the binary code. For example, if we have a bit string 0010111001011010 0101, we segment it into 4-bit chunks: 0010 1110 0101 1010 0101, and translate the chunks into hexadecimal as 2E5A5. This is the technique used by machine language programmers to tame the confusing bit strings they have to work with at that level.

To translate a binary string into hexadecimal ASCII (Hex ASCII), we break each byte into halves, called "nybbles." A nybble has 4 bits, which can have the values 0 to 15. Each nybble is converted to a hexadecimal digit that occupies a full ASCII byte. It sounds confusing, but it is nothing but a doubling of the string length (Figure 4-4).

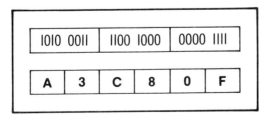

Figure 4-4. In Hex ASCII code, each binary byte expands into two Hex ASCII bytes.

For transmission purposes, the sender and the receiver must each have a routine to encode and decode the binary data stream, respectively. Here are both of them. Because translating to Hex ASCII doubles the length of the data string, you can only translate strings up to 127 bytes long in interpreted BASIC. In compiled BASIC, strings can contain up to 32767 bytes.

```
: ^HXLATE^      ' Sub to convert string to Hex ASCII            :
:    ' Enter with  INFO$ = the string to be converted          :
:    ' Return with INFO$ = the converted string                :
:    FOR I = 1 TO LEN(INFO$)                                    :
:        INFO$=MID$(INFO$,2) + HEX$(ASCII(LEFT$(INFO$,1)))      :
:        NEXT                                                   :
:    RETURN                                                     :
```

```
:^AXLATE^   ' Sub to compress a Hex ASCII string to ASCII      :
:    ' Enter with  INFO$ = Hex ASCII string                     :
:    ' Return with INFO$ = Compressed string                    :
:    BEFORE$="123456789ABCDEF"     ' indexed translator         :
:    FOR I = 1 TO LEN(INFO$)                                    :
:        N1$ = MID$(INFO$,1,1)    '   left nybble               :
:        N2$ = MID$(INFO$,2,1)    '  right nybble               :
:        C = 16*INSTR(BEFORE$,N1$) + INSTR(BEFORE$,N2$)         :
:        INFO$=MID$(INFO$,3) + CHR$(C)                          :
:        NEXT                                                   :
:    RETURN                                                     :
```

AXLATE takes the bytes of the given string two at a time. The bytes are looked up in a (reverse) indexed translator string to convert them to binary values. Then the nybbles are concatenated into one byte and appended to INFO$.

4.14 Applications for Strings

The string finds many uses throughout data processing. To present at least an overview, this and the remaining sections outline the more common uses and detail some of them.

Data Compression

If data storage space is limited or data transmissiion time is expensive, you may want to compress data into a denser code. For example, if the data only contain digits 0 to 9, you can force two digits into each byte by using a nybble for each digit. Or you may want to replace lengthy blank strings with shorter strings that tell how many blanks were at that point.

Data Transmission

As mentioned earlier, transmitting binary data in ASCII code is impossible because certain binary values are misinterpreted as transmission control commands. To send binary data, you have to disguise them as valid ASCII display codes, such as Hex ASCII.

Parsing

Interpreters, compilers, and other programs that process source statements need to break down the source lines (that is, source strings) into syntax elements that can be translated into machine language. Parsing involves sophisticated string manipu-. lation, since source programs are really nothing but symbol strings.

High-Precision Arithmetic

A string can carry numbers to any desired precision. If you want to study prime numbers, you need absolute precision. A string filled with digits can handle numbers to any desired length, in any number system, in any number base. You like roman numerals— you got them. You want to study the Babylonian base 60 system— no problem. (A sample routine is included in Our Library as ASTRADD.LIB).

Screen Display

The IBM PC maps the screen as a 4000-byte string in memory. If you know how to access and code it, you can form fancy text displays directly simply by moving a data string to the correct memory location.

Parameter Strings

A string can be used to pass control information to a process. One example is the ASCII code itself, which transmits data by embedding them in strings between control codes. Another example is in the PRINT USING statement, where a string is used to specify how data are to be printed.

Fielded Strings

The string plays an important role in file access because data are typically stored as strings on external media. Sequential files are written and read in terms of single lines, that is, character strings. Random access file records are mapped as strings via the FIELD statement, which is described in Section 4.8.

Symbol Manipulation

One of the most fascinating ideas of all is to manipulate real-world symbols as such inside the computer. Word processing is one example of this. A more esoteric example is symbolic manipulation such as in the integral calculus and in propositional logic. In symbolic arithmetic, you don't need precision. If you want to store the infinite repeating decimal 0.333333..., you simply assign the entire operation to a string as "1/3" and let the recipient worry about how to evaluate it.

Data Objects

Since strings can contain any mix of programs and data, they can be used to store all kinds of data objects and structures, including abstract data objects. Moreover, the string can contain its own name and can, therefore, reference itself.

Executed Strings

A string can be used to store executable program code. Executable strings can be very small operations or very large programs. (As I said earlier, all programs are nothing but strings to be executed!) One example of a tiny program was just given: the string "1/3" is really a division operation to be carried out later. It is a mini-program, entirely contained in a string variable. All it needs is a routine that can parse it, perform the division, and save the answer. Other example are given in sections 4.18 and 4.19.

4.15 Common String Library

Once you begin to use strings in a variety of ways, a number of string constants will begin to appear over and over in your programs. String constants can be quite complicated and sophisticated and, therefore, more difficult to specify. I don't mean such simple strings as "Hello" and "Enter File Name" but entire report headings, code translating strings, short machine language programs stored as strings, and so on. The idea here is to develop a library of commonly used strings, ready for use by any program. Using a library routine to generate standard string constants is useful for several reasons:

- The exact form or content of a string constant is not always easy to remember or to code. Examples: the value of PI to 50 places, the correct translation string for EBCDIC to ASCII, the escape sequence needed to underline on your printer.
- Duplicating string constants throughout a program wastes memory space. A common string library lets independent programs use the same constant strings, such as disclaimers, directions, and letterheads.
- Using common strings lets you change program logic without modifying programs. For example, when your business changes addresses or phone numbers you need only change one business letterhead string in the library. All reports immediately come out with the new letterhead.

Here is a routine for your subroutine library. It works quite simply: You request a string constant via S(S) and it returns it in

```
+------------------------------------------------------------------+
:  ^STRING.LIB^  ^ Sub to get string constant   11-20-84           :
:     ^ Enter  with S(S)  = the desired number                     :
:     ^ Return with S$(S) = the desired string constant            :
:                                                                  :
:  ON S(S) GOSUB ^+1^,^+2^,^+3^,^+4^,^+5^,^+6^,                     :
:        -  ^+7^,^+8^ : RETURN                                      :
:     ^  1    Capital Letters in ASCII (65 - 90)                   :
:  S$(S)="ABCDEFGHIJKLMNOPQRSTUVWXYZ" : RETURN                      :
:     ^  2    Lowercase Letters in ASCII (97 - 122)                :
:  S$(S)="abcdefghijklmnopqrstuvwxyz" : RETURN                     :
:     ^  3    Base 10 Digits in ASCII (48 - 57)                    :
:  S$(S)="0123456789" : RETURN                                     :
:     ^  4    Base 10 Digits in Binary (0 - 9)                     :
:  FOR S1=0 TO 9:S$(S)=S$(S)+CHR$(S1):                             :
:        - NEXT S1:RETURN                                           :
:     ^  5    Hexadecimal Digits in ASCII                          :
:  S$(S)="01234567890ABCDEF" : RETURN                              :
:     ^  6    String byte index codes  (1 - 255)                   :
:  FOR S1=1 TO 255:S$(S)=S$(S)+CHR$(S1):                           :
:        - NEXT S1:RETURN                                           :
:     ^  7    PI to 50 places                                      :
:  S$(S)="3.14159265358979323846264338327950                      :
:        - 28841971693993751O"  : RETURN                           :
:     ^  8    Date-Time as ASCII  "CCYYMMDDhhmmss"                 :
:  S$=DATE$+TIME$:S$=MID$(S$,7,4)+LEFT$(S$,2)                      :
:        - +MID$(S$,4,2)+MID$(S$,11,2)+MID$(S$,14,2)               :
:        - +MID$(S$,17,2,2):S$(S)=S$:RETURN                        :
+------------------------------------------------------------------+
```

S$ (S). Note that the routine will be included by PREBASIC as a subroutine in your program exactly once. So you save space if you use a lot of the constants; but you waste memory if you only use one. This routine can also serve as a convenient reference source for esoteric string constants. As they say, there is never a table of PI to 50 places around when you need one!

4.16 Common String Files

Another way to implement common strings is to store them as a random access file. This saves memory because it only loads the needed strings, but it costs time to load the strings. It also lets you define strings longer than 255 bytes, and so it can be used for more application-dependent strings such as report headings, help messages, and boilerplate text for contracts.

For example, in one application that analyzes blood samples and prepares diagnostic reports, I used a common string array to store the medical diagnosis sentences. The program computed the chemical blood composition, looked up the numbers in some medical charts and nomographs, and then converted the results into English sentences that it pieced together and printed as the diagnostic report for the physician. Consider how easy it would be to convert this program for export to other countries. Because the calculations are the same in every language, all I would have to do is convert the common string file to the new language.

4.17 Programmer's Holiday

As an illustration of the concept of the executed string, consider the PLAY statement of Advanced BASIC. The complete statement is PLAY S$, where S$ is a string that contains musical instructions: notes to be played, tempo, pauses, and so forth. For example, the following program plays the theme of Beethoven's Ninth Symphony:

```
S$ = "EEFGGFEDCCDEEDD"
PLAY S$
```

The string S$ is really a tiny musical program that is executed by the PLAY statement, which acts as a language interpreter of S$. Several musical "commands" are provided that can be included. For example, "O6" will change all notes following to a high octave. The most interesting command of these is the X command. If you include the command "X Y$;" in the string S$, the PLAY statement will perform the (music) string Y$ at that point. The variable name Y$ is used as a pointer, and the string Y$ is a subroutine of the string S$! For example, to complete the theme, we can repeat it with a slight change at the end each time:

```
THEME$ = "EEFGGFEDCCDE"
S$ = "X THEME$; EDD  X THEME$; DCC"
PLAY S$
```

The embedded music string can itself use the X command to invoke still other music strings, so that you can compose with a whole hierarchy of themes. (As an aside, if the string S$ contains its own name, for example S$= "C E G S$", you have an excellent example of infinite self-reference, or recursion. More about recursion in Chapter 10.)

To tie this all together into an example, here is an amusing little melody generator. As written, it generates what appears to be random bugle calls in the pattern aab. With some modification to seven or eight notes per line, and lines in the form aaba, it could be used to crank out Country and Western song themes. If you are really ambitious, add rhythm and expand it into a Master's Thesis in artificial intelligence:

```
^BUGLER^    ' Bugle call generator
   DEF FNR$=MID$("CEG",1+INT(3*RND),1)
   WHILE 1
      A$=""  :  B$=""
      FOR I=1 TO 5 : A$=A$+FNR$  : NEXT I
      FOR I=1 TO 7 : B$=B$+FNR$  : NEXT I
      PLAY "XA$; P8 XA$; P8 XB$;"
      SOUND 32767, 60
      WEND
```

The BUGLER program defines FNR$, a function that returns one random note from "CEG". Then it builds two theme strings: A$ with five notes and B$ with seven notes. The PLAY statement executes the string "XA$; P8 XA$; P8 XB$", which simply plays the two themes in the order aab, with a pause between each theme.

The final SOUND statement is a longer pause between themes, to give the listener's ear a much needed rest.

4.18 A Program in a String

The last section might not have convinced you completely that a string can really contain a program. After all, that was a music program, not a computer program. Therefore, for our final string example, let's write a very short but very useful IBM PC machine language program and execute it, entirely inside a regular BASIC string.

We need three things for this technique. First, the machine language subroutine you want to execute. You get this from an assembler or from a friend who has assembled the routine. In our case, we want to write the routine to simulate the Shift-PrtSc keys, that is, to copy the screen to the printer. This is quite useful inside a BASIC program. Without going into the details, here is the program in machine language, given in Hex ASCII notation:

CD05CB

It is a short program, indeed, and it consists of three bytes that ask the operating system to print the screen.

Second, you need a string to store this program in. Let's call this P$:

P$ = CHR$(&hCD) + CHR$(&h05) + CHR$(&hCB)

This statement forms a string of three bytes containing the three codes of the machine language program. Finally, you need a way to give control to the string. This is done with the VARPTR function and the CALL statement. The VARPTR function returns the internal address of the string P$, that is, the memory location where the string P$ is actually stored. The CALL statement transfers control to it. The complete subroutine, then, is written as follows:

```
+----------------------------------------------------------------+
:   ^PRINT SCREEN^    ' Sub to print the screen                  :
:      DEF SEG                                                    :
:      P$ = CHR$(&HCD) + CHR$(&H5) + CHR$(&HCB)                   :
:      A! = PEEK(VARPTR(P$)+1) + 256*PEEK(VARPTR(P$)+2)           :
:      CALL A!                                                    :
:      RETURN                                                     :
+----------------------------------------------------------------+
```

Of course, there is more work to it than this. If you want to pass parameters to the machine language routine, you need to set them up and then reference them in the CALL statement. It's all explained briefly in the back of the BASIC Reference Manual; but it will not be very useful to you unless you are acquainted at least a little with assembler or machine language.

One point of this final section was to demonstrate that the string is a powerful enough data object to serve as a real machine-level program. In fact, machine language programs *are* strings! Another aim was to give you a little ammunition for the next time some other-language bully throws sand in your face and tells you BASIC is a beginner's language. Very few languages can dynamically compute a program and then execute it.

The Array

5.1 A Quick Review

In its simplest form, the array is nothing more than a table of data. If you have 52 playing cards and want to store their face values, you define a variable name such as CARD to have 52 elements and then you manipulate each card by referencing the desired element of the array. To set card 23 to 0 you write CARD(23) = 0, and to print the value of the fifth card, you PRINT CARD(5).

An array is a portion of memory that is subdivided into subspaces called "elements" or "cells" or "nodes." Each element has a unique integer number called its "subscript," and it can contain exactly one data item. All elements of an array have the same data type; string and number data cannot be mixed.

An array is a contiguous data object, and its elements can, therefore, be randomly accessed. A value can be stored into or retrieved from a specific element by using the name of the array and the subscript of the element, such as TAX(23) or NAME$(234).

Array names are standard scalar variable names followed by a subscript in parentheses. Both number and string data types can be stored in arrays by using the appropriate variable name suffix such as TAX#(20) for floating data and TAX$(20) for string data. Array elements can be written anywhere a scalar variable can be used, with very few peculiar exceptions (for example, an array element cannot be used as a FOR-NEXT loop control variable.)

Subscripts can be given as numeric expressions, so they can be computed dynamically, as in TAX(I+K−25). These expressions can themselves reference array elements; thus, indirect addressing such as

```
TABLE1(TABLE2(I)*J) or LINK(LINK(X))
```

is possible.

105

An array is defined with a DIM statement, which specifies the array name, the number of dimensions, and the number of elements to be reserved in each dimension. Up to 255 dimensions can be specified in a DIM statement.

```
DIM MYDIARY$(366)
DIM CHECKERBOARD(8,8)
DIM HHMMSS(24,60,60)
```

The last example requires $24 \times 60 \times 60 = 86400 \times 2 = 172,800$ bytes of memory.

The question arises here whether you can use a variable to specify the dimension in a DIM statement, as in

```
INPUT "Enter a dimension"; N
DIM ARRAY(N)
```

Many BASIC translators, especially the compilers, do not allow this. The IBM PC interpreter documentation does not mention it; but it works as an undocumented feature on some versions.

The same goes for the BASIC ERASE statement, which lets you delete arrays while the program is running. This, too, is *not* supported by many compilers; but do not be dismayed. As always, when there is a language problem, there is a solution. Later in the book, we will build our own dynamic storage manager, one that we can trust to work on all BASIC compilers.

The subscripts of an array can start with element 0 or element 1. This element is selected by the OPTION BASE statement. It lets you choose whether the statement DIM X(200) gives you 201 elements labelled 0 to 200 or 200 elements labelled 1 to 200.

The choice depends on the application. For example, we may have an original disk called DISK0, a first backup disk called DISK1, and a second backup called DISK2. Or, you might refer to the days of the week as 0–6 or 1–7. Also, some algebraic expressions are simpler if the first element has subscript 0. On the other hand, if we are simply counting the elements as first, second, and so on, then element 0 is not needed. I personally always use the zero-origin array. It gives me an extra element to use as a header or count or other information about the array. If I don't use it, it goes to waste—a small price to pay for eliminating one more possible source of errors.

There are typically no array-level statements in BASIC. That is, you cannot process all elements of an array at once with some global statement such as A( ) = A( ) + 1. To do that, you must construct a standard FOR-NEXT loop. In IBM BASIC, the array name written without subscripts becomes a totally different (scalar) variable name (in some other BASICs, A(0) and A reference the first element of array A). In fact, throughout this book, we use array S( ) as our subroutine stack and the variable S as the pointer to the top of the stack. This gives rise to such expressions as S(S), which can be confusing until you realize that it is no different than, say, S(23) or S(Q).

5.2 The Array in Advanced Programming__

Since it is the only formal data structure in BASIC, the array plays an important role in advanced programming. But first, just what is advanced programming? Unfortunately, the word "advanced" means very little anymore in the microcomputer industry. Hype is king, and to sell something you have to name it at least "Ultimate Ecstatic Metamorphosis."

Advanced programming means being in control of the software and of the computer. Beginners are guided into programming along lines carefully designed to control them, to keep them out of trouble. They draw flowcharts with only prescribed symbols, and they use languages that require programs to be written in a certain sequence. They learn programming at a level that is shielded from the more powerful and more dangerous techniques.

Advanced programmers typically have unrestricted access to their entire machine, including data and programs, language and operating system, and software and hardware. They freely manipulate data values, subdivide and combine, encode and transform, and point and index to suit their needs. They shift instantly from program to data domain, from logical to physical data level, from external to internal viewpoints, and from software to hardware. They are in control and freely use the advanced techniques such as unconditional branching, direct memory modification, error management, interrupt handling, space allocation, physical file access, generated and self-modifying code, and so on.

By this definition, the modern BASIC language—as it has evolved on the mini- and microcomputer—is surprisingly advanced. As you see throughout this book, all of these techniques are available to the BASIC programmer. And the array, especially the string array, is one of the key tools for writing advanced programs.

In BASIC we can view the array as our memory and the subscript as our address. Just as machine language programs define the memory as a large 1-byte array, we can design our own data objects around the array. We can use the subscript as address, as pin, as pointer, or even as a count. We can embed entire structures into an array, structures that change dynamically under program control. Ultimately, we can define structures that adapt and learn.

Perhaps another distinction between beginning and advanced programming is the difference in emphasis on data values versus data space. Beginning programmers see the array as a data object, as a list of values to be processed. How and where the values are actually stored is unimportant. Advanced programmers see the array as a space object, as a set of slots that have a unique address and can be directly accessed. The current set of values occupying the space is less important.

In advanced programming, the focus shifts toward the use of space as a resource to structure data and process objects. This is where you can find such oddities as arrays that contain other arrays, arrays whose values are subscripts of other arrays, arrays that simply keep track of available free memory, or arrays that reach beyond memory into disk files.

5.3 The String Array

A string array is declared like any other array; by using a string variable name, such as DIM A$(400). Each element of this array is a variable-length string. Each element string can be as long as the particular BASIC implementation allows. In the case of the interpreter, this is 255 bytes; otherwise it is usually 32767 bytes.

As detailed in Chapter 4, the string has properties that give it special value in advanced programming; it far surpasses the power of the common integer or floating-point number. When strings are gathered into an array, we obtain a structure with even greater powers: we obtain an array that can contain a variety of data items—file names and dates and dollar amounts and even machine language subroutines.

The string array is the playground of the advanced BASIC programmer. Here we have no type restrictions, no numeric range limits, no coding rules. We have married all of the advantages of the string data type to the advantages of the array. It is a fertile field for fabulous data objects.

For example, the poor beginner who tries to dimension an

integer array to track 40,000 integers soon finds out this is impossible because the typical subscript limit is 32767. Instead of struggling with some laborious scheme to break the data into two arrays of 20,000 each, the savvy programmer defines a string array and stuffs each element with, say, 125 integers. This yields a maximum integer capacity of about four million integers.

5.4 The Basket Array

One of the simplest uses for the array is for a plain old container for an arbitrary mix of data items, much like a picnic basket. This use would seem to be obvious, but programmers sometimes have the idea, if only unconscious, that all data in an array must be related, must be of the same type, and must have the same units. One just does not mix apples and oranges!

At heart, the array is nothing but a set of empty slots that can be filled with any data items, be they constant, variable, local, global, static, dynamic, apples, or oranges—a veritable data salad. You are limited only by your inventiveness in how to pack data into each element, made all the easier if you use a string array (*see* Chapter 4).

Many programming texts advise the use of mnemonic variable names for data. This is good advice, but it has its limits. Program documentation should be distinguished from program code: Documentation is for humans and code is for computers. Note how much more precision can be conveyed in the following documentation scheme than in all the complex variable names

```
+------------------------------------------------------------+
:    DIM PL$(100)     ' Pilot Log Information                 :
:             '  0    count of PL$() elements in use          :
:             '  1    #1 engine speed at last check, RPM      :
:             '  2    #2 engine speed at last check, RPM      :
:             '  3    pilot's name, address, phone            :
:             '  4    altitude above local ground, feet       :
:             '  5    flap position, left wing                :
:             '  6    flap position, right wing               :
:             '  7    number of passengers on board           :
:             '  8    radio frequency for emergencies, hz      :
:                ...                                          :
:             ' 47    last bearing, corrected for drift        :
:             ' 48    current autopilot bearing               :
:             ' 49    windspeed, knots                        :
:             ' 50    fuel remaining, left forward tank        :
:                ....                                         :
+------------------------------------------------------------+
```

one can devise. Note also that, being comments, the entire description can be stripped out of the program before it executes, so that it will not interfere with program execution.

This approach lets you document the program to any desired depth without interfering with the program's performance. Of course, it is imperative that the basket array contents be detailed as in the above example. If you do not describe variables within your program, the technique is significantly weakened: Cryptic program statements like PRINT PL$(37)+PL$(36) are hard to decipher without a guide. Properly used, the basket array offers a number of advantages:

- As programs grow in size and complexity, they must often manipulate hundreds of variables, constants, flags, options, modes, conditions, errors, and so on. A basket array gives a single name to this herd and assigns a simple unique integer number to each item of the herd. A simple print loop can display the status of every variable.
- A basket array can serve as a convenient checklist to verify that you have updated all relevant machine state values when you add a new feature to existing code. It makes it easy, for example, to spot a count that needs to be updated or a flag that needs to be reset.
- A named variable is an isolated object that can only be tracked by its name. An array element, on the other hand, can be located by its subscript—an enormous advantage for manipulating data items by computing their location, their offset, their nesting level, and so on. For example, in a program to land a plane, it makes more sense to define an array DIM C(100) and to monitor conditions C(1) through C(100) than to track individually named conditions such as SPEED, ANGLE, RPM, FLAPS, WEIGHT, LOAD, HEIGHT, RATE, LENGTH, SHEAR, PITCH, RATE, HEADING, STICK, LIFT, FUEL, OIL, and so on.
- If you use variable names, you can also be struck down by one of the hideous scourges of western civilization: the Reserved Word. In the innocent variable name list just shown, STICK and LOAD are reserved words that will bomb out your program.
- As variable names proliferate, new errors appear in your program. First you try to add more descriptive content to the names, and you end up looking like a COBOL program (LEFT-WING-FLAP-LAST-CHECK) or like a Navy memo

(LEFWINFLALASCHECK) to mean the "left wing flap setting at the last checkpoint." Then you start to misspell the names.....

- Nobody wants to read a plot that involves 87 people. Elaborate mnemonic names are fine for small programs that handle 10 variables. Larger programs are usually better off with a few well-chosen basket arrays to lump program controls, user options, and application-dependent parameters.

- Even though they are stored as a basket, variables can still be identified with mnemonic names. Simply give the subscripts names. After setting RPM1 = 1 and ALT = 3, you can refer to the rpm of engine 1 as PL\$(RPM1) and to the altitude as PL\$(ALT). This gives you the best of both worlds.

- When you use the CHAIN or the MERGE statements to give control to another program, you usually want to pass some variable values to it. This is much easier if all the variables are in one or two arrays.

- A basket array can become an effective data definition table by adding parallel arrays that contain data descriptors, options, initial values, normal ranges, critical values, and so on.

- The basket array helps to solve the eternal problem of naming temporary variables. Say you are in the middle of writing code, and you need three string variables. You can invent three new variable names such as TEMP1, TEMP2, and TEMP3. But to do that safely, you need to check the entire program to see that these names are not used somewhere else. And then you are stuck with three new names to clutter the landscape.

  A better way is to establish two basket arrays TEMP( ) and TEMP\$( ), to be used throughout the program for temporary integers and strings. Now you have a place to document who uses which variable and when. (Note: Even better techniques are presented in the chapters on Dynamic Space Management, Stacks, and the Subroutine).

- Even if you do not use the basket array as such, understanding its concept is helpful in that it leads naturally to viewing an array as a space that is used to contain something, not as the data set that happens to be occupying it at this moment. The ability to separate space and data is helpful in developing data structures.

- Operating system programmers typically create basket arrays called "control blocks" to track system data. For example, PC-

DOS uses a file access table (FAT) to control file processing. The FAT is where the system keeps track of such diverse data as the current file position, the length of the file, and where the file is stored on the diskette. Just imagine tracking this information with symbolic data names!

- The basket array is a great help for developing multiuser programs. If you start with a basket array to group your variables, you can extend to multiple contexts later by simply adding a dimension to specify the user. Thus, PC-DOS can easily track many files simultaneously by setting up many file control blocks. Or, if you control 20 planes, the #2 engine speed of plane 16 is found at PL$(2,16). This idea later leads you into Context Switching, Resource Sharing, and Multi-tasking—all techniques that can be among the most difficult to design unless space and data concepts are properly separated.

- The use of symbolic variable names can do much to simplify programming, but it comes at the cost of name dependence. Few programmers would make the mistake of hardwiring a date such as "1985" into their program. Everybody realizes the program won't run correctly on January 1, 1986. But once a variable name is used in a program, it is "hardwired" just as solidly. The name becomes "reserved," and the value cannot be accessed except through the symbolic name. The basket array avoids name dependence and lets us access data by convenient numeric "names" in the form of subscripts that can be calculated.

5.5 The Parallel Array

A parallel array is a data structure created by (mentally) arranging several arrays side by side, so that elements with the same subscript line up in a row. Instead of declaring the array as a two-dimensional table, we choose to declare it as a group of one-dimensional tables (also called "lists").

Here is an example of a parallel array describing some heads of state in World War II in terms of name, country, and year they assumed power:

```
+-----------------------------------------------------------------------+
:              N$()                   C$()                  Y()          :
:        (1)  ROOSEVELT         (1)  AMERICA        (1)  1936            :
:        (2)  CHURCHILL         (2)  ENGLAND        (2)  1940            :
:        (3)  HITLER            (3)  GERMANY        (3)  1933            :
:        (4)  STALIN            (4)  RUSSIA         (4)  1929            :
+-----------------------------------------------------------------------+
```

The parallel array is a versatile tool for building data structures. The idea of aligning objects to relate them to each other is hardly novel; it appears everywhere—in parallel strings, translation tables, FIELDed random access files, relational data bases, redundant data transmission, and so on. Backup files are really parallel files. Entire computer systems are duplicated as backup on spacecraft missions. Here are a few more advantages:

- The parallel array is one of those programmer-friendly tools that never lets you down. It is easy to understand and to implement. We are raised with tables, and we use them constantly.
- Since parallel arrays can be composed of arrays of different data types such as strings and integers, they are well suited for defining special data objects. A data object is really a collection of data items—often of diverse size, shape, and location—that are somehow associated for the moment.
- The parallel array simplifies modification of an existing data structure. As a structure evolves, new arrays are simply defined and included in the group of parallel arrays. No code needs to be changed to modify existing array references.
- Because the subscript of a parallel array selects the corresponding element in every member array, the subscript becomes a pin, a spear thrust through the elements of several arrays like a shish kebab made with data instead of beef. The subscript then acts as a unique integer number to define the selected data set. We will look at this important idea in detail now.

5.6 The Subscript as Pin

One of the uses of the array is to arrange disorganized data into a list, thus forming a single line that can be processed. When given the proverbial can of worms, programmers stuff each worm into an array cell, and the cell's subscript automatically gives each worm a unique number.

Seen in this light, the array loses its ominous aura of higher mathematics, n-dimensionality, hyperspace manifolds, and matrix algebra that intimidates so many novices. It becomes a framework that holds data in numbered slots. And the subscript becomes a "pin," an identification number that pins down or pinpoints the location of data.

So far, we have only renamed the subscript as pin. Now we

extend the idea to all of our data objects. Any unique number can be a pin: byte positions in a string, line numbers of a sequential file, record numbers of a random file, or disk sector numbers. Let's examine a couple of typical examples to expose the problems encountered and to show the need for the pin.

Assume you have been asked to organize the student records for a small private college. The college has records dating to 1880. Your first problem is to identify each student, that is, to match a given record to the human being it belongs to. Say a woman, Mary Doe, wants you to verify she received a degree in English in 1943. How will you find her record and distinguish it from the 87 other students named Mary Doe?

Consider a second example: You have been hired as Records Manager for a hospital. It is your responsibility to correctly identify and track patients throughout the hospital. I recommend you buy plenty of malpractice insurance, because you face an impossible task. Sure, most patients are admitted in normal fashion during business hours, when their records can be opened, and new identification numbers can be assigned. You can open any Data Processing textbook and it will show you nice schemes for setting up a records system. But those are not your problem patients!

Your problems start in the evening and grow through the night. First, there is the emergency ward, where there is great confusion and little time for identification. There are the amnesiacs, the unconscious, the drugged, the children, the senile, and the insane, the foreigners who don't know the language, the criminals who lie, and the public figures who want to stay incognito. Then there are the patients you thought were properly identified. Some check out, some sneak out, some get lost, some die. Over in the maternity ward, pregnant patients "generate" new little patients in the middle of the night. Babies are a joy to humanity, but to your program they are unidentified and unadmitted intruders.

Considered at the detail level, it is really quite difficult to uniquely pinpoint the identity of any object of the real world inside a computer. Data identification is not only a major problem in programming, it can be downright intractable. Names are a poor choice for identification. They are poorly structured, have duplicates, and change over time. They are at best arbitrary symbols assigned to human beings, totally useless for more than social identification.

You might think the Social Security Number (SSN) is the most useful way to identify a human being. But in practice, the SSN is also limited: there were no SSNs prior to 1934; foreigners have no SSN; babies and youngsters have no SSN; many older records carry no SSN because it once was a federal offense to use the SSN as an identification number; many people deliberately give bogus SSNs to confuse Big Brother; and the SSN is not a continuous integer.

Even formal mathematics can confuse the issue. For example, the union of the sets [23 45] and [45 67] is the set [23 45 67] to a mathematician but [23 45 45 67] to a programmer. Set Theory treats the two 45s as labels for the same object; programmers treat them as two data objects. As a result, pure relational data base theory cannot handle duplicate items; you have to introduce artificial variations into data to store them into a relational data base.

The idea of a pin comes to our rescue to solve all these problems. No matter what the outside world does, inside our program we store our objects into one or more parallel arrays (or parallel random access files or parallel fields in a data base record) and then use its subscript (or record number) to "pin" down the items. Pins can be used to cross-reference items in different arrays, as pointers to link one set of records to another, or to form special data objects out of records. Thus, a patient giving birth to twins need not upset the program; simply generate two new records and set a pointer to them in the mother's record. Whatever form the pin takes, you will find it a useful concept.

5.7 The Pointer Array

In machine language parlance, a "pointer" is a memory address that is itself stored as a data value somewhere else. A pointer is an interpretation of an integer as the address of one memory byte. Elaborate data structures can be built by storing tables of addresses somewhere, then storing the address of the pointer table as a pointer somewhere else, and so on.

At the BASIC language level, the equivalent to memory is the array, and the equivalent to the address is the subscript. Because the array is widely used to hold various data objects, the subscript often serves as pointer to individual elements. It becomes a link between data and can serve as the "glue" that binds data structures. In fact, the pin and the pointer are really the same concept: the pin is a unique number precisely because it POINTS to a unique element of an array. The pointer builds data structures by PINNING their components together.

When we have many data items, we have many pointers, and it

makes sense to store the pointers into arrays. We simply take the subscripts of the true data items and store them as integers into a new array. Pointer arrays have interesting properties (Figure 5-1). No matter how complex and irregular the data may be, a pointer is a nice, uniform, well-behaved integer that takes up little space and can be manipulated with simple arithmetic statements. It can be used to extract, sort, randomize, repeat, index, cross reference, and so on without ever moving its data. When more complex data structures are required, pointer arrays can be created that point to pointer arrays and so on, all without using any language features other than the modest subscript.

In this section, we explore some of the more common uses for the pointer array.

The Sorted Pointer Array

A pointer array is physically separate from its object data, and so the pointers can be arranged in a different sequence than the

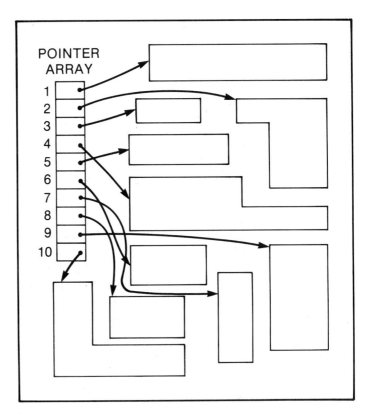

Figure 5-1. A pointer array serves as a collector for dispersed data.

data. This means that a pointer array can be used to specify a second sort order through the data, also known as an "index" to the data. For example, if a data array COMP$( ) lists composers in chronological order of their birthdate, a pointer array BYNAME( ) can be built that lists pointers to the elements of COMP$( ) in alphabetical order:

```
+-------------------------------------------------------------------+
:              BYNAME()              COMP$()                         :
:              (1)   4               (1)    PURCELL                  :
:              (2)   5               (2)    MOZART                   :
:              (3)   2               (3)    PAGANINI                 :
:              (4)   3               (4)    CHOPIN                   :
:              (5)   1               (5)    MAHLER                   :
+-------------------------------------------------------------------+
```

The array BYNAME() might be called an "alpha index." It contains pointers in the order 4 5 2 3 1. If the array COMP$( ) is accessed in that order, it produces the names in alphabetical order: CHOPIN MAHLER MOZART PAGANINI PURCELL. To print the composer names in alphabetical order is trivial:

```
+-------------------------------------------------------------------+
:              FOR I=1 TO 5                                          :
:                  PRINT COMP$(BYNAME(I))                            :
:                  NEXT I                                            :
+-------------------------------------------------------------------+
```

Be sure you understand how indirect addressing works here: The statement PRINT COMP$(I) would print composers in the order stored in COMP$. But PRINT COMP$(BYNAME(I)) prints them in the order that subscripts are stored in the pointer array BYNAME( ). This is called "indirect" addressing because the subscript of COMP$( ) is not specified directly as a number, but is given as the element of another array.

The idea of a sorted pointer array can be extended to more than one index. We simply establish one pointer array for each sort order we want to track:

```
+-------------------------------------------------------------------+
: BYLAST()    BYFIRST()    BYBIRTH()    COMP$()                      :
:    4            4            6        BERNSTEIN, LEONARD           :
:    2            2            4        BARTOK, BELA                 :
:    3            6            2        BEETHOVEN, LUDWIG VAN        :
:    5            3            5        BRITTEN, BENJAMIN            :
:    6            1            3        BRUCKNER, ANTON              :
:    1            4            1        BACH, JOHANN SEBASTIAN       :
+-------------------------------------------------------------------+
```

This method is very useful because the data are stored once and are never moved. Yet, we have all the sequences we might need at our fingertips. We can browse through our by-name index, find a composer of interest, then switch to the by-birth index to find other composers of similar age. This is an effective way of logically grouping data and finding new relations.

The Selective Pointer Array

Pointer arrays are not parallel arrays. They may contain any subset of the pointers to the full data set. If you have a list of 350 composers, you may want to extract the composers of the 19th century as a group, or only the British composers. You can use the pointer array as an "extract array," to list elements of special interest.

One example application might be in text processing. If you have all of the text in an array and want to track the beginning of each paragraph separately, just establish a pointer array that lists the subscripts of the applicable lines in order (Figure 5-2).

The Replicated Pointer

An array containing duplicate pointers is also useful.

A typical use of replicated pointers occurs in cardgames that use several decks. For example, Las Vegas casinos use four to eight decks for Blackjack to discourage savvy players who count cards. To program such games, you can write a library routine that carefully and thoroughly defines a generic deck of 52 cards with suits, values, names, ranks, and colors. Then, when you need a deck of four decks, you simply build a pointer array of 208 elements, store each pointer four times, and shuffle it to make it a random pointer array.

Not only is this exceedingly simple, but the result is a thoroughly shuffled, complete deck that will pass the casino inspector's critical examination.

The Pointer Used as Pin

In Section 5.6, we looked at using the subscript as an external identification number. If we also use it internally as a pointer, this dual use can be very effective. The subscript now becomes a bridge between the real world and its model inside the computer. For example, if you store records into some random access file, you can save the record numbers in an array as pins. Physically, the record numbers are pointers because they point to the record location in the random file. Logically, they are pins because the

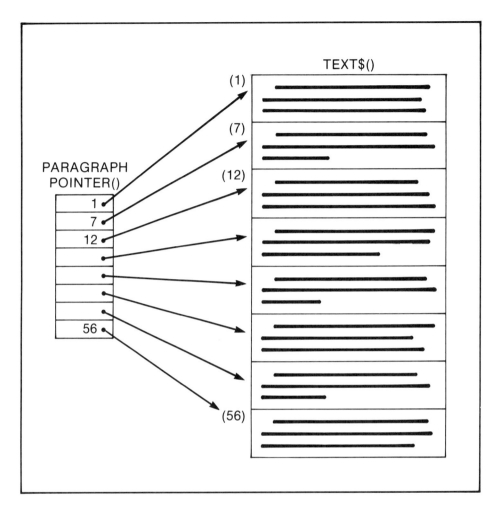

Figure 5-2. A pointer array used to identify variable-length paragraphs in a text array.

user is aware of them and uses them to identify the records later.

The Pointer Used as Decoupler

A pointer isolates and insulates the program from its data. Programs that directly address data are "closely coupled" to them. Any change in one often requires a change in the other. Programs that use pointers address data indirectly; the pointer serves as a "broker" between program and data. The use of a pointer inserts an addressing level between the program and the data. This means the data location can be changed without affecting the program, and vice versa (Figure 5-3).

A simple example occurs when the data array has to be modified for some reason so that each data item now occupies two elements. Perhaps data have grown or the application has expanded to two dimensions, and so on. If you have a pointer array to the data array, you merely adjust the pointers so they point to alternate elements of the data array (Figure 5-4). That is, you change the initialization portion of the program. The rest of the program need never "know" that you changed it. Only those areas need to be changed that are affected by the new data structure.

Someday, when you face a fuzzy design with large arrays whose format may change in later phases of the program, you might want to use a pointer array just to decouple the various parts of the design and not have to commit yourself too early to one design.

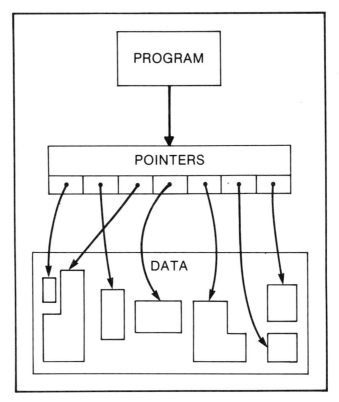

Figure 5-3. Pointers used to decouple program from data.

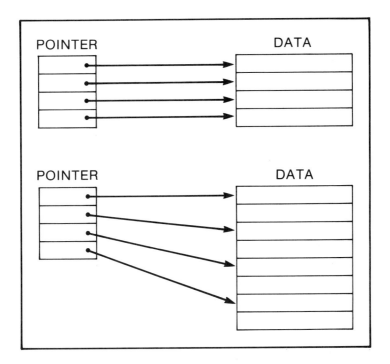

Figure 5-4. Pointers used to select alternate cells of an array.

5.8 The Array as a File

All the data structure concepts discussed in this book apply to file processing—sometimes with major modifications to accommodate the mechanical delays associated with disk access. When the array appears on disk, it is called a random access file. The array elements become "records," and the subscripts turn into "record numbers."

Random access files are not formally dimensioned. You simply open a file and write records to it. It is good practice, however, to "extend" the file, that is, to write some data into the last record. This will ensure that there is enough space on the disk for the full file.

Random file records are stored on disk as fixed-length strings. In memory, records appear in the file buffer, where they can only be accessed by defining names for them with the FIELD statement. (*See* Chapter 4 for details.)

```
+------------------------------------------------------------------+
:       ' Template to read and write array A$()                    :
:       ' assumes no element exceeds 20 bytes                      :
:       DIM A$(1000)                                               :
:       OPEN "R", #1, "SOMEFILE", 20                               :
:       FIELD #1, 20 AS R$                                         :
:       FOR I = 1 TO 1000                                          :
:           GET #1, I : A$(I) = R$          ' to load  A$()        :
:           ...                                                    :
:           LSET R$ = A$(I) : PUT #1, I  ' to store A$()           :
:           NEXT I                                                 :
:       CLOSE #1                                                   :
+------------------------------------------------------------------+
```

If random files are aligned side by side like parallel arrays, they can be used effectively for translation, cross referencing, and other parallel uses. One special use for files is to break up a file too large for one diskette so its parallel halves reside on two diskettes. Another interesting idea is to encode a file with a different code for each record. Then keep the code key as a separate, parallel file on a separate disk. The data file is quite secure without the matching key file to decode the data.

The pointer array technique can also be used with files. For example, to sort a file without moving any data in it, you build a second file (called an index) that only contains pointers into the data file (Figure 5-4). Each pointer is a data record number, and the sequence of pointers in the index file determines the desired sort order for the data file.

Because they only contain pointers, not data, index files are usually smaller than their associated data files. They can often be loaded into memory even if the data file is too large. When several sort orders are required at once, several index files can be set up without duplicating the data file.

A random file can be used as a substitute for (or an extension of) a memory array. Such a use is called a "virtual" array, with the word virtual, as always, meaning "simulated on disk." All you need is a little software mechanism that performs operations to read and write records from and to disk as required. This can often be improved by keeping track of which records are in memory at the moment and which have been changed and, therefore, need to be rewritten. This can speed up processing and avoid rewriting unchanged records. Another approach to virtual arrays is to use a RAM disk.

A final note of caution is in order. There is one crucial difference between memory and disk storage: access time.

Accessing a file record (even after the file is opened) can be up to 100 times slower than accessing an array element. If you design programs with significant disk accesses, you must carefully analyze your detailed use of the disk. A design that works well in memory or for small test files can become unacceptably slow when used with large data files.

5.9 The Random Array

Many applications such as games, simulations, statistics, experiments, and testing require data in random order. Since randomizing is the opposite of sorting, a pointer array can be used to randomize data without disturbing them.

Given an array of data, such as a card deck to be "shuffled" into random order, it is easy to build a parallel pointer array and then to shuffle the pointers. In many cases, this is a better method than shuffling the data array directly. For one thing, the data may already have other arrays pointing to them and cannot be shuffled. For another, the data array may actually be a set of parallel arrays; shuffling these will be confusing and time wasting. Or, the data array may be stored on a file, which turns shuffling into a major exercise.

The code to do this is simple:

```
FOR I=1 TO 100 : PA(I)=I : NEXT I
FOR I=1 TO 100
    J=1+INT(100*RND)
    SWAP PA(I),PA(J)
    NEXT I
```

The first loop simply fills an array PA( ) with its own subscripts, thus creating a pointer array. The second loop shuffles PA( ) by exchanging each pointer at least once with some other randomly selected pointer. The second loop randomizes the pointer array, yet still guarantees a perfect distribution of 100 pointers without duplication or omission.

And finally, to finish the chapter with a happy ending, a program for your amusement. As a silly example of random selection from parallel arrays, here is a program based on the old joke of simulating bureaucratic nomenclature by taking one random term from column A, one from column B, and so on. I vary the theme by using familiar quotations of the type "A soandso is a (or does) suchandsuch." The soandso phrases are stored in one string array H1$() and their corresponding suchandsuch phrases are stored in a parallel array H2$(). The program simply picks two random halves and prints them as one (fractured) cliche. Supplied with enough material, it can yield some street-smart combinations:

```
+---------------------------------------------------------------------+
: ^CLICHE.PRE^                                                        :
:   ' Program to print fractured sayings          2-11-85             :
:   DIM H1$(100), H2$(100)         ' the parallel arrays              :
:   ON ERROR GOTO ^+2^          ' continue at end of data             :
:   WHILE 1:READ H1$(N),H2$(N):N=N+1:WEND   ' read data               :
:   WHILE 1                                                           :
:       PIN=INT(N*RND)            ' random pin from 0 to N-1          :
:       PRINT:PRINT H1$(PIN); H2$(PIN)        '    display            :
:       SOUND 32767,30                       ' delay                  :
:       WEND                                                          :
:                                                                     :
:   DATA "A good man ","is hard to find"                              :
:   DATA "A pretty girl ","is like a melody"                          :
:   DATA "A rolling stone ","gathers no moss"                         :
:   DATA "A stitch in time ","saves nine"                             :
:   DATA "A thing of beauty ","is a joy forever"                      :
:   DATA "An apple a day ","keeps the doctor away"                    :
:   DATA "An idle mind ","is the devil's playground"                  :
:   DATA "Charity ","begins at home"                                  :
:   DATA "Half a loaf ","is better than none"                         :
:   DATA "Happiness ","is just a guy named Joe"                       :
:   DATA "History ","is bunk"                                         :
:   DATA "Ignorance ","is bliss"                                      :
:   DATA "The love of money ","is the root of all evil"               :
:   DATA "The pen ","is mightier than the sword"                      :
:   DATA "The rain in Spain ","falls mainly in the plain"             :
:   DATA "Virtue ","is its own reward"                                :
+---------------------------------------------------------------------+
```

The Chain

6

In Chapter 3, we saw how data objects are constructed by linking scattered data items together through the use of pointers. If you skipped that chapter, now would be a good time to review that material. (*See* Section 3.4.)

This chapter focuses on the chain. It provides details on how to implement and perform elementary operations on the chain in BASIC. In later chapters, we will use the chain again and again as the basic building block for various linked data objects.

6.1 Properties of the Chain

The key feature of the chain is that its data items are not stored next to each other and need not be physically related in any way. The advantage is that you can use the chain to organize and structure scattered data into a single data object *without* having to move the data. In fact, quite often the only reason we use a chain is because our data are scattered all over the computer and we don't have time or space to collect them into a contiguous data object such as an array. Instead of moving the data, we install a chain of pointers through them, like threading a string of pearls without moving any pearl (Figure 6-1).

The logical connection between data items of a chain is achieved by storing with each data item a "pointer" or "link" that connects the data item to the next data item in the chain. A pointer is the location of a data item, such as a memory address, an array subscript, or a file name.

For an example of a chain, consider the first paragraph of this chapter. Using the words "Section 3.4" as a pointer, it refers you (that is, points you) to material in another section. Having said that, note that this very paragraph you are reading points to the

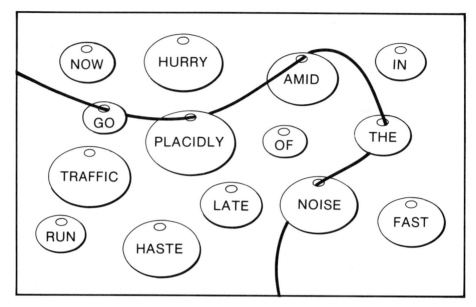

Figure 6-1. A chain threaded through selected nodes in memory.

first paragraph of this chapter. We have constructed a little chain from this paragraph to the first paragraph to Section 3.4.

Each data item and its associated pointer are called a "node" in the chain. Each node of a chain may be stored as one contiguous record, or it may be scattered with links to connect it, depending on the application. For example, an index to a large random disk file is often kept in memory as a chain.

The first and last nodes of a chain are called its "head" and "tail" nodes, respectively. The pointer of the tail node always contains a value not used for any other purpose, such as 0 or −1, that signals the end of the chain.

A chain is processed (or "traversed") by starting with the head node and following the pointers from node to node until the tail node is reached. This process gives the chain a "forward" direction: from head to tail. From any given node, a program can only go to the next node. There is no way back, unless the program keeps separate track of the location of previous nodes. To be able to traverse the data in the opposite direction, we must first thread a second chain through the data set in the reverse direction, creating what is called a "doubly linked list."

A final word on nomenclature. Theoretically, there are two classes of stored data lists: contiguous lists and linked lists. Contiguous lists store data into physically adjacent slots; for example, the string and the array. Linked lists (also called "threaded lists") store data into scattered slots and connect them with pointers.

In practice, many applications involve the use of several chains through some or all of the nodes of some data object: backward chains, sorting chains, subset chains, safety chains, chains of head nodes of chains, and so on. Some chains include all the nodes of the data object, others only include selected nodes. Some define a path through a network or a tree, others only highlight spots of interest.

Moreover, in many programming contexts, the word "chain" used as a verb means "go somewhere else to continue." Thus we have the CHAIN command in BASIC that continues execution with a program currently stored on disk, an excellent example of the chain concept in the time domain. Again, DOS does not store files contiguously on disk—this would cause great difficulty when a file increases in size. Instead, it uses chained blocks or sectors to store the file.

For practical use then, it is less confusing to think about following a specific chain through the maze. Therefore, I use the word "chain" to mean the set of nodes along one single path through a linked data object (Figure 6-1). For example, a doubly linked list has two chains: one forward and one backward.

Another important property of the chain is one that all linked data structures have: the chain links are themselves data that the program can manipulate. The program controls not just the data but also the structure of the data. It can build and break up chains by changing the appropriate pointer values. It can insert a new data item into the middle of a chain, or delete another, without leaving empty spaces or having to shift other items aside to make room. Moreover, the chain is a recursive data structure: when you break a chain apart, you end up with two chains. This means that the same chain subroutines can be used on any chain at any level of detail.

6.2 Using the Chain

To use the chain effectively, we must promise to distance ourselves a little from the array concept we learned as our first data structure. This is not easy. Our world is three-dimensional, and three dimensions are conveniently divided into rectangular cubicles, each filled with a single object, like so many pigeonholes. After years of exposure to this, our brains tend to assume that the real world somehow comes digitized, pixelated, and diced. For example, the popular spreadsheet programs can be successfully applied to many problems—as long as the problems involve data values that can be neatly arranged into rows and columns. But they are not practical for such real-world structures such as human anatomy, a traffic circle, a river delta, a beehive, a highway network, galactic clusters, a flower arrangement, the plotlines for a novel, a Chinese Checkers board, or the double helix of DNA.

The programmer who uses an array has to wedge data into a rigid space mold, cutting off toes here and there to fit the foot into Cinderella's cubical glass slipper. The chain programmer, on the other hand, selects space and molds it around the data, like Goldilocks selecting the bed that fits best. With chains; the logical sequence and interconnection of data can be preserved, no matter how complex it is. In effect, the chain acts as an agent that collates intelligence.

The difference between arrays and chains is that arrays are immutable space structures that the program has to live with, whereas chains are themselves data objects that can be manipulated by the program. This gives the program power to change the very form and fabric of the data. It can now manipulate structures that twist and branch and double back, that grow and shrink and move and interact. It can detect new relationships and freeze them for later use, it can dynamically define new structures and destroy old ones.

Chains are a higher order of structure than arrays. Chains are logical; arrays are physical. In effect chains let us dimension new arrays while running, to redimension arrays dynamically, to suddenly explode a single cell of an array into a subarray, to delete a range of cells from an array, to let one cell belong to two or more arrays; in short, to cut and paste arrays to suit our needs.

At the simplest level, a chain might merely identify a list of data items as one set to be tracked or processed. More often, we use chains as a vehicle for implementing still other data structures like queues, rings, stacks, trees, networks, and networks of networks. When we need a data set in several sort orders, we run several chains through it in different sequence. When we want to identify a subset of data in a chain, we simply "subchain" through the desired nodes.

Chains can be used in other spaces. In Chapter 7, we will see a chain of record pointers inside a random disk file. You can also invent your own structures, such as the "bookshelf"—an open-ended structure to which you can add and from which you can remove any number of items anywhere at any time. Or a "can of worms"—an array of head pointers to hundreds of parallel chains that snake their way through some vermiculate data base.

6.3 Implementing the Chain

Before we plunge into programming with chains, let's summarize their nomenclature. This is mostly intuitive, taken from the analogy to real-world chains. A chain (or linked list) is a set of nodes that have been connected (or linked) into a single sequence. The first node is the head; the last is the tail. The forward direction is from head toward tail, and a node following another is its successor (or the next node, behind it, following it, and so on). From the tail toward the head is the backward direction, (and preceding, before, prior). A node (or chain item, or chain element) is a structural unit of one or more values. A pin (or pointer, address, link, subscript) is a value that identifies the location of a node in the storage space. A chain is typically processed (or passed, or traversed) by starting with the head node and visiting each node in sequence until the tail node has been processed.

In the following sections, we develop some tools needed to work with chains. The BASIC statements given are by no means complete programs; they are simplified fragments intended to illustrate the heart of each operation. They assume a normal chain, they do not check for special cases, and they freely use variable names that help to illuminate each case.

The building block of every chain is a data node (Figure 6-2): a

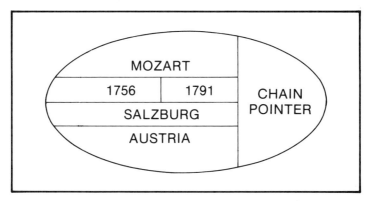

Figure 6-2. A node consisting of data and a pointer.

local data group that contains normal data values of all kinds *plus* a special value: a pointer to the location of the next element in the chain.

When values are stored into a set of data nodes, the nodes form a logical chain (Figure 6-3). Each node can be visited in turn, following the pointer from node to node. To visualize chains, we typically use a circle or a rectangle to represent the node and an arrow to show where the pointer is pointing to. The sequence of arrows from node to node is really the chain.

Operations on chains essentially consist of adding and removing nodes (Figure 6-4). They can be pictured in terms of breaking the chain at some convenient point to admit a new node or to bypass a node that no longer belongs to the chain. A new node is inserted into a chain by changing pointer values in two nodes. A node is removed from the chain by changing one pointer. No data items are moved; the rest of the chain does not know that an item has been inserted or deleted.

If you are wondering where these nodes to be added come from and where the deleted nodes go, the answer is: unused nodes are kept on a free chain. (*See* Chapter 7 for several methods of keeping track of small pieces of storage space.)

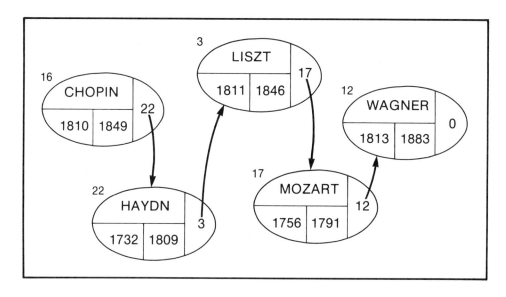

Figure 6-3. A chain is formed by connecting nodes with pointers.

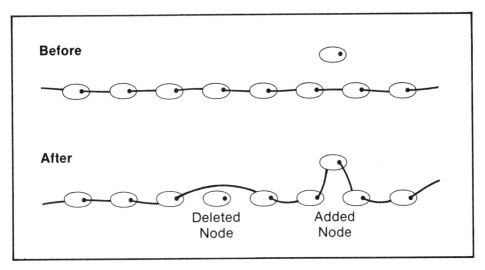

Figure 6-4. Nodes are added and deleted by manipulating the pointers of some nodes.

6.4 Setting Up a Chain

Another nice aspect of the chain is that it is a very unassuming data structure. It does not require special higher level language syntax, or a special compiler, or a special data type definition. Given a bunch of data items, all you need to build a chain through them is a place associated with each data item where you can store a pointer. If the data are stored as an integer array, you might define a parallel pointer array for this purpose (*see* Chapter 5). If the data are given in the form of a string array, you might steal the first 2 bytes of each string element as a pointer field. If the data are records in a file, you might add a field to each record, or redefine some other fields to give you 2 bytes for a pointer.

For the examples that follow, the data are in a string array INFO$( ), and the pointers are in the integer array LINK( ). INFO$( ) and LINK( ) are parallel arrays: one subscript identifies the same node in each array. For example, node 27 consists of the element INFO$(27) and the element LINK(27). (These arrays are only used to illustrate the inner workings of chain operations in some detail; their names and dimensions have no permanent importance.)

How should we identify the head node? Do you think it would be a good idea to make node 1 always be the first node? If you do, then your brain is still in the old array mode. To be a chain programmer, cast off your acquired urges to know anything about the specific location of a data item. Never again will you "know" where a chain starts or finishes or meanders through space. You will think of a chain as a single giant variable, and—as with all variables—you will give it a variable name.

For my examples here, I will use the variable FIRST to point to the first node. If FIRST is zero, then there is no chain. If FIRST contains some number from 1 to 100, that is the subscript of the first node in the chain. If FIRST contains a number greater than 100, something has gone horribly wrong somewhere: a pointer can only point into the available data space.

```
' initializing an empty chain
    DIM INFO$(100), LINK(100)
    FIRST=0
```

Chains are built by connecting nodes into the desired sequence. We start with an empty chain (FIRST=0) and keep adding nodes one at a time until we have the nodes we want on the chain. Two nodes are linked when the predecessor node P points to the successor node S. To do that, we store the address S into the link field of P:

```
            connecting two nodes
                LINK(P)=S
```

This code stores the value S into the link field of node P. This means that any program processing the chain from the beginning to node P will see node S as the node following P. Node S has been (logically) connected behind node P (Figure 6-5). Note that there is no physical connection between nodes P and S.

Please pause here an extra moment and ponder figure 6-5. You are looking at one of the roots of artificial intelligence! Consider that there is no physical connection between nodes P and S, yet they are "obviously" connected as indicated by the arrow. The program is taught not to treat the value S as data but as a pointer to data somewhere *else*. If there is intelligence embodied in data structures, it must start this way. Anyone who has trained a dog knows how difficult it is to get the dog to look in the direction in which you are pointing. Inevitably, the dog looks at your index finger.

Incidentally, the other root of intelligence can be found in the GOTO statement, which is the time-domain equivalent of the node

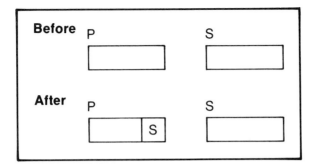

Figure 6-5. Two nodes before and after connection.

pointer. The GOTO statement is the index finger that points the program somewhere else to continue processing. Without a GOTO (or its equivalents such as GOSUB, WHILE, WEND, FOR, NEXT, RETURN, and RESUME) you cannot write intelligent programs at all. Ironically, due to its very power to give a program "free will", the GOTO statement fell on hard times in the late sixties. In a pathetic replay of the fall of Adam and Eve, the GOTO statement was literally driven out of some languages and replaced with euphemisms like BREAK, EXIT, and LEAVE.

To form longer chains, the idea is repeated. To connect another node K behind node S we write LINK(S)=K. If node K is to be the tail of the chain, we write LINK(K)=0; the zero pointer is always reserved to flag the end of a chain.

Here is a sample program to put the whole thing together. The program sets up a chain of trucks available for rental. The trucks' license numbers are stored as DATA statements. The order in which trucks are rented does not matter, so we may create the chain in any order we like:

```
' Building a chain out of data statements.
      DIM INFO$(100) , LINK(100)
      READ N            ' read number of trucks
      FOR I=1 TO N      ' read N data
          READ INFO$(I)
          LINK(I)=I+1
          NEXT I
      FIRST=1           ' node 1 is first
      LINK(N)=0         ' node 8 is last
      END
      DATA 8
      DATA NFR-226,EEF-835,CGW-443,DUY-623
      DATA VPD-553,ABW-746,CPO-463,CPX-334
```

The chain is now set up. This little data structure works well to support a truck leasing program. If a truck is rented out, it is deleted from the chain and added to another "rented-out" chain. When the truck is returned, it is deleted from the "rented" chain and pushed back onto the "available" chain.

6.5 Adding and Deleting a Node

To add a new node N in front of a chain, we point node N to the first node and point the variable FIRST to N, since N is now the first node.

```
+---------------------------------------------------------------------+
:      ' Add node N in front of a chain                               :
:      LINK(N)=FIRST                                                   :
:      FIRST=N                                                         :
+---------------------------------------------------------------------+
```

This code stores the pointer to the head node (in FIRST) into the link field of node N, so that N points to the head node. Then it stores N as the head node into FIRST, making N the new head node (Figure 6-6). Only two values change: FIRST and N's link field.

To insert a new node N into the middle of a chain, behind node M, we open the chain behind node M and relink it to include the new node:

```
+---------------------------------------------------------------------+
:      ' Add a node N to the middle                                   :
:      LINK(N)=LINK(M)                                                 :
:      LINK(M)=N                                                       :
+---------------------------------------------------------------------+
```

The new node N is set to point to what was M's successor, and node M is pointed to node N (Figure 6-7). The code only involves nodes M and N, the given nodes. The address of node S is manipulated indirectly, as the expression LINK(M).

As an aid to learning to write these add operations, note that the code to insert always starts by setting the link of the new item. This makes sense, because that pointer is "fresh," and we cannot be destroying anything we need later. The second part of an insertion consists of setting one or more chain links to include the new node.

Adding a node at the end of a chain is simple if we know the address T of the tail node. We point the tail node T to N and point the new node N to zero, to make it the new tail:

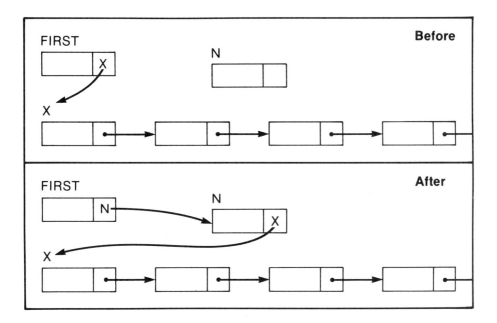

Figure 6-6. Adding a node in front of a chain.

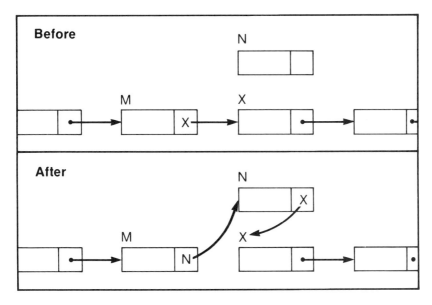

Figure 6-7. Inserting node N into the middle of a chain, behind node M.

```
+----------------------------------------------------------------+
:         ' Add a node to the tail                               :
:         LINK(N)=0                                              :
:         LINK(T)=N                                              :
+----------------------------------------------------------------+
```

If we do not know the pin of the tail node, we have to first find it (*see* Section 6.6).

To delete the head node of a chain we must point the variable FIRST to the second node in the chain. This is easy: we simply copy the link field of the head node into the FIRST variable:

```
+----------------------------------------------------------------+
:         FIRST=LINK(FIRST)   ' Delete the head node            :
+----------------------------------------------------------------+
```

To delete the last node of a chain, find the predecessor P of the last node and then set P's link to zero:

```
+----------------------------------------------------------------+
:         LINK(P)=0   ' Delete the last node                    :
+----------------------------------------------------------------+
```

Deleting an item from a chain involves disconnecting it from the chain and closing up the chain around it:

```
+----------------------------------------------------------------+
:         ' Delete a node in the middle                         :
:         LINK(M)=LINK(LINK(M))                                 :
+----------------------------------------------------------------+
```

This code puts the successor of the successor of M into M and short circuits the chain around the successor of M, effectively detaching it (Figure 6-8).

Note that we reference the link of X as LINK(LINK(M)) without ever knowing the actual value of X. This method of referring to linked data is called "indirect addressing." It is an important

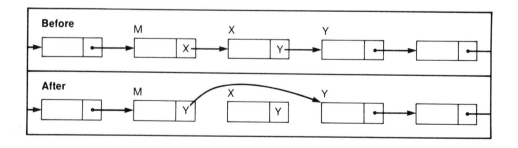

Figure 6-8. A node is deleted from a chain by moving a single pointer.

technique because it represents a crossover from the data domain to the process domain. The data actually drive the program by telling the program where the nodes to be deleted are located. Many computers have indirect addressing built into them as a machine language command, and it is used freely in assembly language programs.

6.6 Various Chain Operations

A chain is typically processed (or "traversed") by starting at the head node and visiting successive nodes until the process is completed or the end of the chain is reached. To avoid disorientation, it is helpful to adopt a mental image that the nodes are scattered throughout memory, and the program is making its appointed rounds through rain and sleet and dead of night, from node to node to node. Data items that are not on the chain are completely transparent to the process, regardless of their physical proximity to the chain nodes. Thinking of it this way will also be helpful later, when we have various chains threading their way through hundreds of nodes.

Note that chains are variable-length data objects. There is no defined end. In the chain Wonderland, we do well to follow Alice's advice: "Begin at the beginning and go till you come to the end. Then stop."

```
+----------------------------------------------------------------+
:     ' Template for processing a chain                          :
:     M=FIRST          ' M is the node being processed           :
:     WHILE M>O        ' as long as have a node M                :
:         .....            ' process node M                      :
:         .....            ' process node M                      :
:         .....            ' process node M                      :
:         M=LINK(M)        ' advance to next node                :
:     WEND                                                       :
+----------------------------------------------------------------+
```

As a first example of processing a chain, let's count the nodes in a chain:

```
+----------------------------------------------------------------+
:     ' Count the nodes of a chain                               :
:     COUNT=0            ' count                                 :
:     M=FIRST            ' first node                            :
:     WHILE M>O          ' as long as have a node M              :
:         COUNT=COUNT+1    ' count a node                        :
:         M=LINK(M)        ' advance to next node                :
:     WEND                                                       :
+----------------------------------------------------------------+
```

As our next example, let's find the tail node of a chain. By definition, the tail node of a chain contains the link zero, so that is what we look for. If the chain is long, this can be a time-consuming process. If we do it a lot, we may want to keep separate track of the tail node in some variable like LAST:

```
' Find the tail node T
T=FIRST
WHILE LINK(T)>0    ' as long as link is not O
    T=LINK(T)      ' advance to next node
    WEND
```

Now, let's find the *n*th node of a chain. Given a chain FIRST and an ordinal number N, this code finds M, the location of the *n*th node. We watch for the case where there are less than *n*th nodes in the chain to begin with:

```
' Find the Nth node M
M=FIRST
WHILE N>1 AND M>0   ' as long as have N and chain
    N=N-1           ' count a node
    M=LINK(M)       ' advance to next node
    WEND
```

Sometimes we need to find the predecessor P of some node M. To do this, we have to search the chain until we come to a node that points to M. That must be the predecessor, since any given node can only appear once on a chain. (Again, if the chain is long we can speed up the program if we keep track of the predecessor in some variable such as PRIOR.)

```
' Find the predecessor P of node M
P=FIRST
WHILE LINK(P)<>M
    P=LINK(P)
    WEND
```

As a final example of chain processing, assume we have a chain H with N nodes, and we want to find the center node of the chain. We'll write this as a subroutine so we can use it in a later section. It returns both the pointer P to the central node and the count C to node P. In other words, it finds the Cth node P, at or just past the center of the chain:

```
+------------------------------------------------------------------+
:  ^FIND MIDNODE^    ' Sub to find chain center                    :
:     ' Given a chain H with N nodes (N>0)                         :
:     ' Return pointer P to middle node                            :
:     '           and count C to node P                            :
:                                                                  :
:     P=H : C=1                                                    :
:     FOR I = 1 TO N\2 : P=LINK(P) : C=C+1 : NEXT I                :
:     RETURN                                                       :
+------------------------------------------------------------------+
```

6.7 Reversing a Chain

Since a chain only has one direction, and since Murphy's law also operates with chains, you will sometimes find a given chain is linked in the wrong direction. You need to reverse the chain.

Given chain H1, we reverse it by defining empty chain H2. Then we write a simple loop that peels an item off chain H1 and adds it in front of chain H2. At the end, H2 contains the reversed chain and chain H1 is empty. Here is the code

```
+------------------------------------------------------------------+
:  ' Reverse chain H1 into chain H2                                :
:  H2=H1              ' start chain 2 with head of chain 1         :
:  H1=LINK(H2)        ' drop head of chain 1                       :
:  LINK(H2)=0         ' chain 2 starts with one item              :
:  WHILE H1>0         ' as long as nodes left on chain 1          :
:     T = LINK(H1)        ' save second node on chain 1           :
:     LINK(H1)=H2         ' move node to chain 2                  :
:     H2 = H1             ' make node new head of chain 2         :
:     H1 = T              ' new head of chain 1                   :
:     WEND                ' repeat until no more chain 1          :
+------------------------------------------------------------------+
```

The explanation of the code is difficult in words but is greatly aided by a picture. This is typical with chain processing. We often need a picture of each step to appreciate what is going on. Let's repeat the code, accompanied by a picture this time (Figure 6-9).

Figure 6-9 illustrates two important points. First, chain processing takes place in a step-by-step manner just like a standard program. Second, to write a program involving chains, it helps to draw a picture. Without a picture, the need for the temporary variable T is not obvious. With the picture, we see at once that the statement LINK(H1) = H2 momentarily disconnects head 1 from its chain. Variable T saves the chain from being lost.

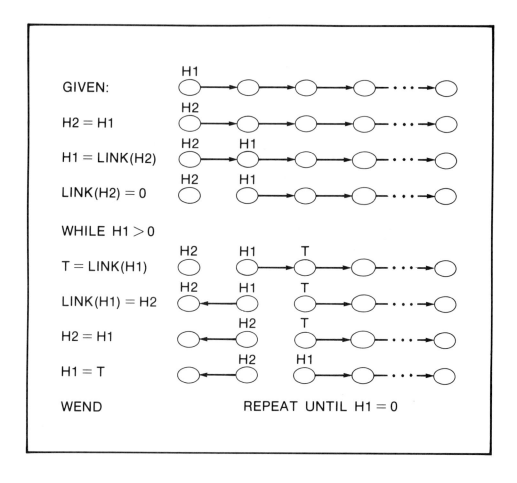

Figure 6-9. Reversing chain H1 into chain H2. Each iteration of the WHILE-WEND loop pops a node from H1 and pushes it to chain H2.

6.8 Searching a Chain

Much of our effort of designing data objects is spent on storing data in such a way that we can find them quickly later. This involves sorting data into desirable sequences as well as searching for data that have specific values, so much so that searching and sorting have been called the foundation of data processing. This book is not the place for a detailed presentation of this massive topic. All we do here is see how we might sort and search chains in a very simple manner.

First the simplest search of all: a sequential search of a chain. To find a node containing a specific data value (called a "key") in the chain, we traverse the chain and compare each node to the key. We will either find the matching node or run out of chain. In this example, the chain is a collection of classic film titles, and the program wants to find "SHANE":

```
+------------------------------------------------------------+
:       ' Sequential search for a key K$                     :
:       K=FIRST : K$="SHANE"                                 :
:       WHILE K>0 AND INFO$(K)<>K$                           :
:           K=LINK(K)                                        :
:           WEND                                             :
+------------------------------------------------------------+
```

This little search is perfectly useful if the chain is reasonably short, if we don't search too often, or if speed is not important, and so on. On the other hand, if the chain is stored on disk and contains 23,000 film titles, you would soon look for a better algorithm. That's when you head for sorted and indexed data that help to speed up the search.

6.9 Searching a Sorted Chain

In doing the simple sequential search just shown, we traverse the chain and compare each node to the given key. This is what takes most of the time, because comparing two values requires many detailed steps behind the scenes. More important, quite often the data are physically separated from the chain itself. For example, the data may be large records on a random disk file, whereas the chain is stored as an integer array in memory. Like "fast forward" on a cassette player, we can traverse the chain much faster if we don't have to stop to read every data item from disk and compare it to the given key.

There is indeed a search method that ignores most of the data! If a chain is in sorted order, it can be searched with the classic binary search method. A binary search first looks at the central item of a list. If that item matches the key, the search is over. If it does not match, the search is repeated with the left or right half of the list, depending on whether the key compared less or greater than the central item. Like a well-played game of 20 questions, the binary search eliminates one-half of the list to be searched at every step, thus using only one comparison per step.

The binary search method is usually associated with contiguous data structures such as the array, since the major time saved comes from the ability to quickly compute the location and compare the central item of the list at each step. A chain must be traversed sequentially, and so binary search loses some of its advantage. But there are some good uses for binary searching a chain.

One example occurs when the chain is long and each node is bulky, perhaps partly or entirely stored as records in a file. Using the parallel array implementation we use here, the LINK() is often small enough to be entirely in memory, and this is all that has to be traversed to find a given node. Another good use is when the comparison operation is complicated and involves special calculations. The binary search only requires comparison of the central node; the links can be traversed quickly and without stopping to compare data values at each step. This can offer significant improvement over linear search.

Another reason for presenting the binary chain search here is to show in some more detail how chain operations are used to write a program. We will see two important chain tricks: working with subchains and working with the head node plus a node count.

Incidentally, the word "binary" as used here has nothing to do with computer memory bits. It means "two valued" or "paired" as in binary star or binary fission. The method could equally well have been called "bisecting search," since—at each step—the list remaining to be searched is halved. Thus, 16 items can be searched in 4 steps, 64 can be searched in 6 steps, 32768 in 15 steps, and over one million in 20 steps. In fact, any human being on earth could be uniquely identified in just 32 steps—if we could ever get them lined up in some sorted order!

The following routine is given a sorted chain H with N nodes and a key value K\$. The routine binary searches the chain for the first matching node and returns pointer P to it. The pointer P will be 0 if the chain is empty or if the key value is less than the value of the first node, that is, less than the entire chain. If no node matching K$ is found in the chain, the subroutine returns −P, pointing to the insert point, that is, the node behind which the node K$ should be inserted. This makes it a a very useful routine for generating a sorted chain, and we will use it for that in the next section.

```
+---------------------------------------------------------------+
:  ^BINARY SEARCH CHAIN^    ' Sub to search a chain             :
:     IF N<1 OR K$<INFO$(H) THEN P=0:RETURN  ' low key          :
:     WHILE N > 0                                               :
:        GOSUB ^FIND MIDNODE^  ' find Cth node P at center      :
:        IF K$ = INFO$(P) THEN RETURN  ' center equal           :
:        IF K$ < INFO$(P)                                       :
:           -- THEN N=C                      ' center high      :
:           - ELSE N=N-C : H=P               ' center low       :
:        WEND                                                   :
:     P = -H      ' key not in chain; P is insert point         :
:     RETURN                                                    :
+---------------------------------------------------------------+
```

This routine uses a moving subchain starting with node H and containing N nodes. When we start, chain H is exactly the given chain of N nodes. We find the middle node P and compare it. If it matches K$ then we have found the item and return the pointer P. If it does not match, then it is either less or greater than node P. If K$ is less than node P, we adjust our subchain to the left half, that is, from H for C nodes and try again. If the key is greater than node P, we adjust our subchain to the right half of the chain H, that is, starting at P and N-C nodes long, so that the old middle node P becomes the new head node H.

As is true quite often with chain processing, the whole thing is easier done than said. Figure 6-10 gives a picture of the process.

6.10 Sorting a Chain

The binary search algorithm just shown assumed that we had a sorted chain to begin with. Now is the time to bite that bullet and actually sort a chain. Again this is *not* a book on sorting, and the focus of this section is on learning to manipulate chains, not on developing the world's best sort routine.

We saw earlier that binary searching with chains pays a small penalty because we cannot compute the location of the central node as fast as we could with a contiguous data structure. But

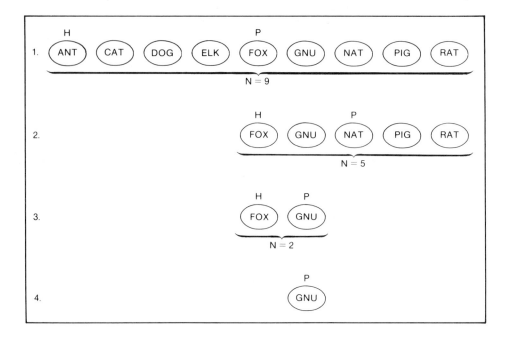

Figure 6-10. Four steps of a binary search for the key "GNU". The initial chain contains nine sorted animal names and is repeatedly halved until the node containing GNU is isolated.

when it comes to inserting new items into an existing data object, chains have the advantage. It is so time consuming to insert a new item between existing ones in an array that it is almost never done. With chains, arbitrary insertion and deletion is a matter of moving two pointers.

In the following sort routine, we take advantage of this property of easy insertion. Given a chain FIRST to be sorted, we leave the first node on it as a starter and treat the rest of the chain as unsorted chain UNSORT. Then we loop until we run out of unsorted chain by peeling a node off the unsorted chain and inserting it in sort order into the sorted chain. The routine sorts in ascending order.

Subroutine INSERT NODE searches for the insert point (using the binary search algorithm discussed earlier) and then inserts the key node. If the key value already exists in the sorted chain, the new node will end up at the end of the subchain of duplicates. This is called a "stable" sort because duplicate keys maintain their original order. In many applications this is extremely important. Unstable sorts may be smaller and faster; but whenever I have used them, I have sooner or later regretted it.

```
^CHAIN SORT^      ' Sub to sort a chain   2-11-85
    ' Enter with  FIRST = head of unsorted chain
    ' Return with FIRST = head of sorted chain

    ' if chain is empty, there is nothing to sort
    IF FIRST=0 THEN RETURN
    ' treat the first node as sorted
    COUNT = 1
    ' start the unsorted chain with the second node
   .UNSORT=LINK(FIRST) : LINK(FIRST)=0
    ' now sort the chain UNSORT until it is empty
    WHILE UNSORT>0
        ' peel off an unsorted node as key node K
        K=UNSORT : UNSORT=LINK(UNSORT)
        ' if key is less than head
        IF INFO$(K) < INFO$(FIRST)
            ' then insert in front
            - THEN LINK(K)=FIRST : FIRST=K
            ' else insert with binary search
            - ELSE H=FIRST : N=COUNT : GOSUB ^INSERT NODE^
        COUNT=COUNT+1
        WEND
    RETURN

^INSERT NODE^   ' Sub to find insert point for key
    ' Enter with a chain of N nodes starting with node H
    '           and a key node K to be inserted stably
    '           somewhere AFTER node H
    ' Return with node inserted
    ' Note: Duplicates are inserted at the end (stably)

    ' find center node C of chain H
    WHILE N>1
        C=H:FOR I=1 TO N\2:C=LINK(C):NEXT I
        IF INFO$(C)<=INFO$(K)
            - THEN H=C : N=N-N\2
            - ELSE N=N\2
        WEND
    ' insert node K behind H
    LINK(K)=LINK(H):LINK(H)=K
    RETURN
```

As a test program, here is a program that sorts ten names. It first reads the data into a chain. Then it sorts the chain. If you look closely at the output, you will see that the sort is, in fact, stable: the two names STRAUSS will be in the same order they were in the unsorted chain.

```
^CHAIN SORT TEST^
   DEFINT A-Z
   FOR I=1 TO 10          ' create unsorted chain
      LINK(I)=I+1 : READ INFO$(I) : NEXT I
   LINK(10)=0             ' mark the end of the chain
   FIRST=1 : GOSUB ^CHAIN SORT^  ' sort the chain
   P=FIRST                    ' print the chain
   WHILE P : PRINT P,INFO$(P) : P=LINK(P) : WEND
   END

DATA    BRAHMS, STRAUSS, LISZT, BARTOK, BEETHOVEN
DATA    STRAUSS, LEHAR, VERDI, MOZART, CHOPIN
```

The sort routine is also available as a generalized library subroutine (*see* Chapter 13).

6.11 Commencement

In this chapter we have seen how to create the chain and how to work with it. Surprisingly, the basic chain operations turn out to be relatively simple once you get used to the idea of building structure by storing pointers. We even developed simple chain search and sort routines.

We have seen the one great advantage of the chain over other data structures: its ability to work with the data in the space they occupy. With chains, you are much less restricted by the limitations of the space in which the data are stored. You are free to arrange a data set in one or more logical sequences without moving them.

But we have miles to go. More than any other mechanism, the chain opens the doors to a new world of fanciful data structures and exotic processes.

Dynamic Space Management

One important concern of every program is how to allocate memory and disk storage space to data. Advanced programs often process several competing data sets whose total volume far exceeds the available memory. The only way they can be handled is by sharing the available memory among them. A related problem exists with respect to disk file space. Given only the typical random access file with fixed-size records, it is difficult to manage files whose record sizes vary significantly from record to record (that is, real-world data).

System programmers have always used dynamic space allocation behind the scenes, but few programming languages offer this important feature to application programmers. Once again, we have to develop our own if we want one.

In this chapter, we develop dynamic space management (DSM) schemes for fixed-size, variable-size, and file space management. If you will invest a little time in the techniques presented in this chapter, you will be able to manage both memory and file space with flair.

7.1 The Need for Dynamic Space Management

We all manage our real-world space dynamically. Consider the typical house. Its floor space is subdivided with walls into a number of rooms. This represents static space, space that cannot be changed on a moment's notice. The space within each room, on the other hand, we use in a more dynamic fashion. Compared to the fixity of the walls, this is dynamic space. Within minutes, we can shift the furniture around for a party or for a home seminar or for our teenager's demonstration of break dancing.

Computer storage space also comes in these two flavors: Static and Dynamic. Static space is space that is occupied by the program itself and by those data arrays and variables that have a permanent, fixed size. Static space is analogous to read-only memory (ROM): cast in concrete for the life of the program, no matter how many times it is executed. It is managed by the BASIC interpreter (or compiler or linker) that decides what shall be stored where. The program has no choice in the matter.

Static space management saves time but wastes space. You save the time needed to search for dynamic space and to assign it; but you waste space because you are forced to allocate the maximum space you will ever need, regardless of your actual needs. As long as data volume is small and there is plenty of memory and disk space, static space management is an acceptable approach. But as programs and data size increase, as data structures become more complex, as files become larger and larger, you can run out of space even though there is enough total storage space. You need dynamic space management.

Dynamic space is space that is managed by the program itself, as it runs. Dynamic space is used to store data objects whose size is unpredictable or changes during execution, such as file buffers, strings, and string arrays.

The ordinary string is an example. Since the number of bytes in a string can vary from 0 to 255 (32767 in compiled BASIC), no permanent memory location can be assigned to it. The program must wait until it knows how many bytes are to be assigned to the string—then it can assign a memory location to it. This is what the word "dynamic" means in this chapter: as the program is executing, it searches its memory to find a suitable location for the variable A$. And every time A$ changes during execution (that is, dynamically) this process is repeated.

Another example of DSM is the FIELD statement. When a file is opened, a static area of memory is assigned as a buffer between the program and the disk file. The FIELD statement now maps program variables over this buffer area. Thus

```
FIELD #1, 2 AS A$, 3 AS B$
```

maps A$ to the first 2 bytes and B$ to the next 3 bytes of the buffer. This is dynamic allocation, because the program can change the mapping at any time:

```
FIELD #1, 2 AS B$, 1 AS A$, 2 AS C$
```

Space is nice and linear and orderly and well behaved. It is neatly divided into 8-bit bytes, each byte with its own precise integer address. Data, on the other hand, often come in awkward blobs and bundles and bunches, hard to predict, usually unclean, and often downright intractable. Data burst in on your neat arrays like drunken rowdies, demanding instant attention, taking up whatever space they want, and causing nasty errors like "disk is full" or "subscript out of range" or "overflow." Space is a fixed resource; data can be highly variable.

Quite often the total data volume is so large that not enough space exists to simply allocate the maximum required for each data set. Sometimes you don't even know the size of the data sets you will have to process or their time of arrival in the system. Most often, the data set changes as the program runs; you want to add and delete and change the data. Parkinson's Law applies here, too: data volume grows to fill the available space. If you have no problem this week, you can be sure you will have one next week.

Dynamic space management (DSM) can help to alleviate these headaches. With DSM, the program is in charge of how space is allocated. It can shape its storage space to suit the needs as they develop and change at run time. This flexibility lets the program adjust its environment to the data—a powerful feature and an important tool for advanced applications.

7.2 The Dynamic Space Management Mechanism

Managing space dynamically is much like running a hotel. Initially, a large storage space is set aside for dynamic allocation (Figure 7-1). The space might be a large string, an integer array, all of the available memory, or even a large random access disk file. Let's call this dynamic storage space the DSS. The DSS is analogous to the entire hotel, with numbered rooms ready to receive guests.

As the program runs, it uses the DSS to allocate various chunks of space to various data sets. Whenever it needs some space, the program examines the DSS and finds an area large enough to hold the data. It then allocates that area to the data, so that no

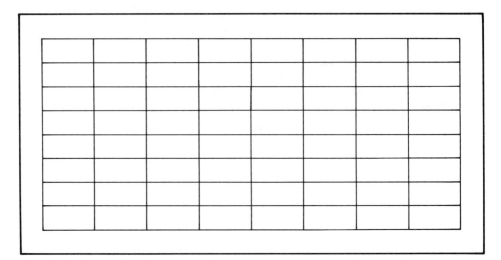

Figure 7-1. The dynamic storage space before it is used.

other data can use it for the time being. This is analogous to the hotel desk clerk assigning a suite of rooms to some rich visitor. The suite of rooms is allocated to the visitor and will not be assigned to anyone else for the time being.

Note that the program must be prepared to handle the case where there is "no room at the inn." That is, DSM includes the need to dynamically handle temporary space shortages.

When the visitor checks out, the space is no longer needed and can be released. After a while, this constant reserving and releasing of space causes rooms to be available here and there in random groups (Figure 7-2).

A note on nomenclature. DSM is variously called "dynamic storage allocation," "dynamic space allocation," "dynamic storage management," and so on. The DSS is called "free space" or "free list" or "available space." Reserving space is called "allocating" or "marking it busy," and releasing it is "freeing" or "making it available." Released space is "garbage" until it is cleaned and recycled as available space.

In some DSM methods, garbage is held in a limbo state until the program takes time out to consolidate all of it at once. This is called—you guessed it—"garbage collection." You can see it in action on the **IBM PC**, where the **BASIC** interpreter uses it to collect available string space. On machines with large memories, a program may stop mysteriously for more than one minute.

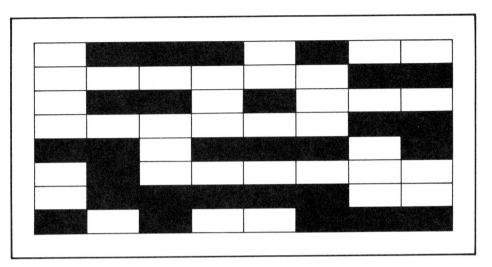

Figure 7-2. After it has been used a while, the dynamic space contains a random pattern of reserved and released subspaces.

The DSM algorithms developed in this chapter were designed *not* to require garbage collection because unpredictable program halts would seem to be unacceptable practice. (How would you like to be a patient hooked to a heart–lung machine whose program decides to go away for 2 minutes)? Our DSM mechanisms mark released space as "available" at once, and consolidate it with the other available space. We collect garbage while we search for space to satisfy a request. This slows each request down a little but it never accumulates a large amount of unprocessed garbage. You might say that "we collect garbage on the fly!"

Many algorithms have been published that optimize one or the other of these aspects. For our introductory purposes in this book, there are three mechanisms that should serve our beginning needs. The first allocates space in small, fixed-size chunks. It is simple and fast, but it can waste a lot of space. The second mechanism allocates space in variable-size blocks and can, therefore, reserve the exact amount of space requested. It saves space but is necessarily somewhat slower. The third mechanism is a modification of the second mechanism for dynamic disk space management.

The dynamic space is typically a large contiguous space, such as an array, that must be defined and filled with initial values to accommodate the particular DSM scheme employed. Initializing the space is never a problem, but reserving and releasing space present considerable design problems. The major challenge is to design a mechanism that is very fast, uses little overhead space, and usually finds space to satisfy a request if at all possible.

The rest of this chapter develops three DSM methods or mechanisms under these headings:

1. Fixed Blocks
2. Variable Blocks
3. V-Files

7.3 Dynamic Space Management with Fixed Blocks

The simplest way to manage space dynamically is to always allocate it in blocks of the same size. This method can be used in situations where the dynamic requests are roughly for the same size. The block size is then fixed to accommodate the largest data set to be managed, and all requests for space are for one block of space. If a data set is smaller than the block size, there will be some wasted space; but this is compensated for by the simplicity and speed of the method.

We start by considering the DSS space that we are supposed to manage. It has to be a simple contiguous space, such as an array or a random file, with elements or records that can be uniquely addressed with a subscript or a record number. We partition this space into blocks of equal size and run a linked list through these blocks from beginning to end of the space by using the first cell of each block to point to the next block. (*See* Chapter 6 for more details.)

As presented in this chapter, the DSM mechanism manages a single integer array. In many cases, this DSS array is sufficient to store variable-length integer data. If you need to dynamically manage strings and floating-point numbers, simply declare them as arrays parallel to the DSS array. Then, as DSM allocates space to you, you use the parallel space in the string and floating arrays to store the data. In other words, the DSS array is merely an index to the allocated space. Other data type arrays and even parallel random files can then be allocated as parallel structures. (*See* Chapter 5 for details.)

7.4 Code for Fixed Blocks

Setting up a shared space for fixed-block **DSM** basically requires that you subdivide the space into fixed-size blocks that you can then reserve and release. You do this by creating a linked list of fixed-size blocks inside the DSS (Figure 7-3).

The code to initialize the DSS follows. Assuming **MAX** is the maximum number of blocks and **SIZE** is the size of each block to be allocated, we use a loop to set up the first cell of each free block to point to the next free block. Then we fix up the last cell of the chain. Cell 0 is set to 0 because this simplifies chain processing. Cell 1 always points to the beginning of the chain of free blocks. The head of the chain is in cell 2, and the tail of the chain will be the last full block. Since a FOR-NEXT loop exits with the loop

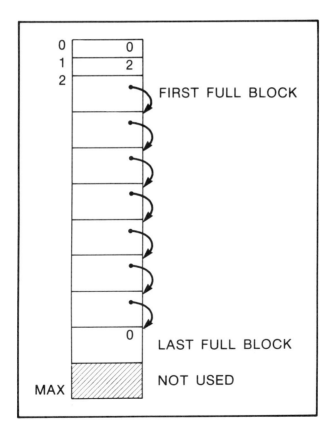

Figure 7-3. To set up the DSS array, it is divided into blocks of equal size.

variable set to the first value beyond the MAX, we subtract SIZE twice to find the last whole block. This we set to 0 to identify it as the last block:

```
'   Initializing for fixed block dsm
DIM DSS(MAX)                ' dynamic shared space
DSS(0) = 0                  ' always 0
DSS(1) = 2                  ' point to free chain
FOR S1 = 2 TO MAX STEP SIZE ' the free chain
    DSS(S1) = S1 + SIZE     ' point to next block
    NEXT
DSS(S1-SIZE-SIZE) = 0       ' the last full block
```

Reserving a block consists of finding the next available block, detaching it from the chain of available blocks, and giving its address or subscript to the user. Since cell 1 always points to the head of the chain of free blocks, DSS(1) is the address (that is, the subscript) of the next available block. We detach the first block of the chain and save its address in S0. Then we set DSS(1) to the block following the block S0:

```
'   reserving a fixed block S0
      S0 = DSS(1)
      DSS(1) = DSS(S0)
```

This operation is fast and simple. If S0 turns out to be 0, then there are no more blocks, and the request was rejected. Otherwise, S0 is the dynamic block where we can store our data.

Releasing a block is the reverse operation of reserving it. Given the address of the block S0 to be released, we add the block to the chain of free blocks. All blocks are alike; we don't need to keep them in order, and so we simply add the block to the front of the chain:

```
'   releasing a block
      DSS(S0) = DSS(1)
      DSS(1)  = S0
```

The first statement sets the first cell of the released block to point to the beginning of the free chain. The second statement then points cell DSS(1) to the newly released block. As a result, we have included the released block in the chain of free blocks, so that it will again be allocated. In fact, the way we have released it here, the last block to be released will be the next block to be allocated. Note that after a while, the chain of free blocks will be totally jumbled. Nevertheless, cell 1 will always point to the beginning of the chain (Figure 7-4).

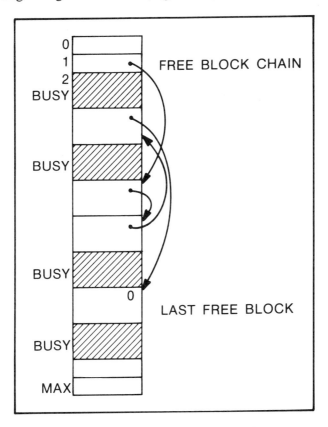

Figure 7-4. The DSS array after it has been used a while.

7.5 Dynamic Space Management with Variable Blocks

Fixed-size DSM is fast and clean, but it does have one great drawback: the block size has to be defined large enough to accommodate the largest possible request. If the request size cannot be predicted, or if they vary widely, then fixed-size blocks will waste much space. In that case we turn to variable-size allocation.

Variable-size data objects are the stepchildren of programming. Most programming languages don't support them, and, as a result, most programmers avoid them. IBM PC BASIC is more advanced in this respect, since at least it offers the variable-length string. But it, too, requires static allocation of arrays and fixed-size record length in random files.

(The interpreter will actually let you dynamically dimension an array, as in N=200 : DIM A(N) and will let you delete the array with the ERASE statement. But compiler BASIC does not support either dynamic dimensioning or deletion. This is a typical example of why I call them stepchildren.)

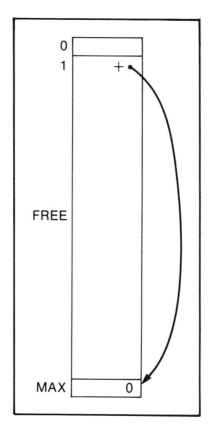

Figure 7-5. The DSS array set up for dynamic space management with variable-size blocks.

Handling variable-size data sets is no more difficult than many others handled by programmers as a matter of course. Again, the key to handling them lies in the linked list or chain data structure. Here's the plan: First, we initialize the entire DSS into one large free block (Figure 7-5).

Every time we get a request for a block, we now lop off a suitable chunk of the free block and create a new block. We mark each block as busy or free, and we keep them all on one chain. When a block is released, we simply mark it "free." As blocks are allocated and released, this will end up in a mix of free and busy blocks of variable sizes (Figure 7-6).

What we have done is created a chain of blocks of two types (free or busy), completely intermingled. To collect garbage, all we have to do is merge adjacent free blocks into single free blocks. We do this in the next section.

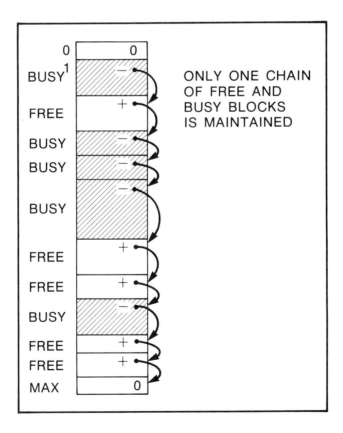

Figure 7-6. The DSS array after some use.

7.6 Code for Variable Blocks

To initialize the DSS, we simply set it up as one large free block. DSS(0) again contains 0 to simplify handling the end of the chain. But this time, the chain can start in cell 1 because blocks will always be in increasing address order, so the first block will never move.

```
'  initializing fixed block dsm
      DSS(0)=0
      DSS(1)=MAX            ' first free block
      DSS(MAX)=0            ' end of chain
```

To reserve a block of *n* cells, all we have to do is search down the chain for the first free block that is large enough. If we don't find

```
^RESERVE.LIB^   ' Sub to reserve dynamic space   10-11-84
   ' Reserves a variable-length block of cells in DSS().
   ' Uses linked list of free and busy blocks.  Cell 1
   ' is first block.  Link is negative if block is busy.
   ' To initialize, dimension DIM DSS(max), then
   '               DSS(0)=0:DSS(1)=max:DSS(max)=0

   ' Enter with  S0 = n = number of cells requested
   ' Return with S0 = address of block of n+1 cells
   '                 (0 = no space found)
   '        cells S0+1 thru S0+n are now available
   '        to release:   DSS(S0)=-DSS(S0)

   S1=1           ' S1, S2, and S3 are 3 successive blocks
^RESERVE.LIB 1^
   ' find first free block S1
   IF S1=0 THEN S0=0 : RETURN     ' out of space
   S2=DSS(S1):IF S2<=0 THEN S1=-S2:GOTO ^RESERVE.LIB 1^
   S3=DSS(S2)    ' free/busy flag of block S2
               ' S1 is a free block and S2 follows it
   ' while S2 is also free, merge S2 into S1
   WHILE S3>0 : DSS(S1)=S3 : S2=S3 : S3=DSS(S2) : WEND

   ' if free block S1 is too small, try next block
   IF S2-S1<=S0 THEN S1=-S3 : GOTO ^RESERVE.LIB 1^

   ' carve new busy block S0 out of free block S1
   S0=S2-S0      ' compute address of new busy block
   DSS(S1)=S0    ' link block S1 to S0 and flag it free
   DSS(S0)=-S2   ' link block S0 to S2 and flag it busy
   RETURN
```

one, we reject the request. If we do find one large enough, we cut it into two blocks and mark the second one "busy."

One refinement is needed for this to work. As mentioned earlier, we want to collect garbage as we go. This means only that we have to consolidate adjacent free blocks before we carve out a new busy block from them. Otherwise our DSS will fracture into smaller and smaller free blocks as users request and release blocks at random. In the end, our DSS will look like Swiss cheese, and requests for larger blocks will be rejected even though the required space is available if adjacent free blocks were merged.

If we merge adjacent free blocks as we go, this problem is alleviated. Before we cut up a free block to satisfy a request, we first look at the block immediately following. If both blocks are free, we merge them into one free block and repeat the test. In other words, each request causes the leading free blocks to be merged until it finds a suitable block.

Releasing a block is utterly simple: all we have to do is change the block's busy flag from "busy" to "free." In our implementation, we use a positive link for free blocks and a negative link for busy blocks. If the address of the block to be released is S0, then the code to release the block simply changes the sign of the first cell:

```
+-----------------------------------------------------------------+
:            '    releasing a variable block                      :
:                 DSS(S0) = -DSS(S0)                              :
+-----------------------------------------------------------------+
```

This easy release mechanism is significant not only because it is very fast but also because the process that requested the dynamic space can release it directly, without having to call a library routine. All of the DSM work of merging, allocating, and enchaining is done by the RESERVE mechanism at request time.

As a first example of using DSM, here is a program that randomly reserves and releases blocks of random sizes from 1 to 50 cells in a dynamic space of 2000 cells. The program does nothing with these blocks except plot them on the screen. Busy blocks appear as asterisks; free cells appear as blanks. The program tests our DSM mechanism and provides an interesting illustration of dynamic space management in progress. It lets us observe the Swiss cheese pattern I mentioned, and shows how small adjacent blocks are merged as they are freed.

The program is very simple. First it fills the entire dynamic space with busy blocks of random sizes from 1 to 50 cells. Then it loops forever, alternately reserving and releasing one block at random.

```
+------------------------------------------------------------+
:  ^DSM SIMUL.PRE^          ' DSM Simulator      2-11-85      :
:    DEFINT A-Z : CLS : DIM DSS(2000)                         :
:    DSS(0)=0 : DSS(1)=2000 : DSS(2000)=0                     :
:                                                             :
:    ' set up for monochrome or color adapter                :
:    GOSUB ^VIDEO.LIB^                                        :
:    VIDRAM! = S!              ' start of video RAM           :
:                                                             :
:    ' fill dynamic space with random busy blocks            :
:    DEF SEG=VIDRAM!                                          :
:    SO=1+INT(50*RND) : GOSUB ^RESERVE.LIB^                   :
:    IF SO THEN S$="x" : GOSUB ^SHOW^ : GOTO ^-1^             :
:                                                             :
:    WHILE 1  'loop forever, releasing and reserving          :
:       ' find a busy block                                   :
:       SO=1+INT(2000*RND) : IF DSS(SO)>=0 THEN ^+0^          :
:       ' release it                                          :
:       DSS(SO)=-DSS(SO)   : S$=" " : GOSUB ^SHOW^            :
:       ' reserve a block                                     :
:       SO=1+INT(50*RND) : GOSUB ^RESERVE.LIB^               :
:       IF SO THEN S$="x" : GOSUB ^SHOW^                      :
:    WEND                                                     :
:                                                             :
:  ^SHOW^          ' sub to display block SO on screen        :
:    DEF SEG = VIDRAM!                                        :
:    FOR I=SO+1 TO ABS(DSS(SO))-1:POKE 2*(I),ASC(S$)          :
:       NEXT I                                                :
:    RETURN                                                   :
+------------------------------------------------------------+
```

7.7 Dynamic Space Management with V-Files

Random access disk files require each record to be of the same size. This poses one of the more vexing problems for the applications programmer: data of the real world seldom come packaged in neat fixed-length records. Students have variable-length names, houses have variable-length addresses, text files have variable-length paragraphs, numbers have variable-length precision, and taxpayers have a variable number of dependents.

Fortunately, the concept of dynamically managing space can be used for any storage space whose elements can be individually addressed. Since a random file is more or less a string array stored on disk, we can manage it dynamically, too. To do this, let's invent a new file type called a "v-file" (Figure 7-7). A v-file is nothing but a standard random access file whose fixed-length "records" we lump into variable-size "blocks" that we then reserve and release on request, chaining them together very much as we just did with the variable-length memory array.

A typical block (variable length) is composed of one or more records (fixed length). Bytes 1 and 2 of the very first record are

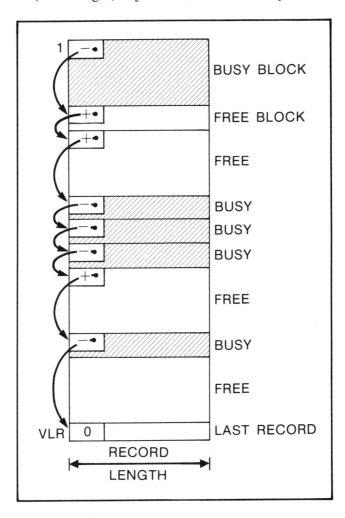

Figure 7-7. A v-file after some use. Compare this to Figure 7-6: The same idea is applied to memory and to file space.

used as a link field to point to the next block. They are overhead space and are never used to store user data. The rest of the first record and all the remaining records in that block are available for user data.

Note that, in this section, all we develop is the bare mechanism for reserving and releasing variable-length file space. We make no provisions for segmenting the user data into the individual records or for writing them out. Since a v-file contains variable-length user data, it cannot be fielded with fixed-length fields. Therefore, you will have to use some other method of identifying the fields within the blocks. In a later section, we develop a v-file test program that packs user records into blocks. For other suggestions on packing data into strings, *see* Chapter 4.

For the variable-length array, we again use the block pointers both to compute the length of the block between them and to determine if the current block is free (positive pointer value) or busy (negative pointer value). Again, all the pointers form a single chain running from block 1 to the end of the file.

Since a random file can contain up to 32K records and a record can be up to 32K bytes long, you can theoretically manage over one billion bytes of disk with a v-file. Note also that the v-file is permanently recorded and can be kept between sessions. This makes it a valuable data structure for many applications that need to store variable-length data permanently.

Four DSM operations apply to v-files: create, open, reserve, and release. Creating a v-file involves extending it to its maximum length by writing the first and last records to set their link fields. The file space is fully extended to hold all the anticipated data at the start. If this is inconvenient because the maximum is not known or the file space is not yet available, simply open a smaller file and later copy it to a larger one.

Creating a file requires some consideration regarding the record size to be used. As a rule, smaller record sizes waste less space but require more time to read and write a full block. The minimum record size is 2 to accommodate the link fields. If time is not critical, try using this for your first v-file; but note that it limits you to a total file space of 64K, since there can only be 32K records in a random file. If you need more file space than 64K, use slightly larger record lengths that don't waste much space but let you store all of the data. For example, to fill a floppy disk with room for 360,000 bytes, a record size of 11 would handle 32,727 records.

Reserving a block is done exactly as for the memory array just discussed, except that now you ask for space in terms of records instead of array elements (Figure 7-8). You must, of course, add 2 bytes for the link in your request. For example, if you need 2400 bytes to store some data, and the record length is 100, you have to reserve 25 records to accommodate 2402 bytes. (Note that this means you have to use 2500 bytes to store 2400 bytes. This waste is unavoidable with the underlying fixed-length records; but it is minimized by making the record length as small as possible).

Releasing is done exactly as it was for the memory version of DSM shown earlier. Again the key is that a busy block is identified by a negative link field. Therefore, to release a busy block, all you need to do is change the sign of its link field to positive. This may leave the block unconsolidated with its neighbors for the moment, but that is all right; when the next reservation request passes through here, it will consolidate the block. We consolidate, but only when we need the space.

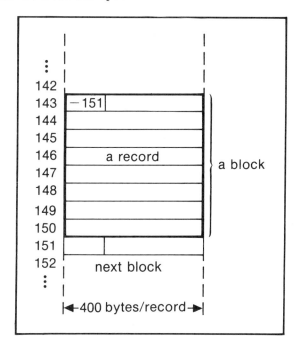

Figure 7-8. A typical v-file block.

Because the link field is negative, the block is currently reserved. The link points to record 151 as the beginning of the next block. Therefore, the length of this block is 151 − 143 = 8 records. Each record is 400 bytes long; hence, the block contains 8 times 400 = 3200 bytes. Since two bytes are reserved for the link field, 3198 bytes are available for user data.

7.8 Code for V-Files

Here, then, is library routine VFILE.LIB to support DSM for a file space. It can perform four operations or functions: Function 1 opens and initializes a new v-file from scratch. Function 2 opens an existing v-file. Function 3 reserves a block of records; it returns the block number or 0 if not enough space could be found. Function 4 releases a previously reserved block.

To make the concept as clear as possible, the routine is written with hardcoded user-variable names VB$, VF$, and so on. As a result, you can only use the routine as is to manipulate one v-file. For additional v-files in the same program, you will have to make a copy and alter the hardcoded variable names slightly, such as from VB$ to V2B$.

In the setup, the routine uses its own error handler to capture the many errors that can arise when opening files. It simply passes these back to the user without comment. The open functions 1 and 2 use two FIELD statements, one to establish the buffer VB$ and the other to define the link field VL$. These fields are then used by the routine to transfer data and to manipulate the block linkage. The space reservation function is adapted directly from the RESERVE.LIB routine given earlier. It works much the same, consolidating free blocks as it searches for space.

```
+-------------------------------------------------------------------+
:  ^VFILE.LIB^     ' Sub for random file DSM      10-12-84      :
:     '. Provides 4 functions for sharing random file space.  :
:      ' Uses linked list of free and busy blocks.            :
:      ' Every block starts with 2-byte link field. Link is   :
:      ' minus if block is busy; plus if free; 0 if last.      :
:      ' Record 1 is first block.  VLR is last block.          :
:      ' Handles errors by returning error code in S(S).       :
:      ' Fields VB$ as buffer for user's convenience.          :
:      ' Uses hardwired parameters:                            :
:      '      VB$           file buffer                        :
:      '      VF$           file name                          :
:      '      VL$           link to next record                :
:      '      VCH           channel                            :
:      '      VRL           record length                      :
:      '      VLR           last record number                 :
:      ' Enter  with S(S) = function code                      :
:      '               and parameters as shown for function    :
:      ' Return with S(S) = 0=normal;   >0=error code          :
:      ' Function:                                             :
:      '         1 = Create and open new file                  :
:      '             uses   VF$, VB$, VL$, VCH, VRL, VLR        :
```

```
 :      ’      2 = Open an existing file
 :      ’           uses   VF$, VB$, VL$, VCH, VRL
 :      ’      3 = Reserve a block of S0 records
 :      ’           uses   VL$, VCH
 :      ’           returns S0=record address or 0
 :      ’      4 = Release block S0
 :      ’           uses   VL$, VCH
 :    ON ERROR GOTO ^+4^
 :    ON S(S) GOSUB ^VFILE.LIB 1^,^VFILE.LIB 1^,
 :              - ^VFILE.LIB 3^,^VFILE.LIB 4^
 :    S(S)=0
 :    ON ERROR GOTO ^GLOBAL ERROR HANDLER^ : RETURN
 :    S(S)=ERR : RESUME ^-1^      ’ local error handler
 : ^VFILE.LIB 1^    ’ create or open
 :    OPEN "R",VCH,VF$,VRL
 :    FIELD #VCH, VRL AS VB$ : FIELD #VCH, 2 AS VL$
 :    IF S(S)=2 THEN RETURN    ’ open only
 :    LSET VL$=MKI$(VLR) : PUT #VCH,1
 :    LSET VL$=MKI$(0)   : PUT #VCH,VLR
 :    RETURN
 : ^VFILE.LIB 3^     ’ reserve a block of S0 records
 :    S1=1            ’ start looking at this block
 : ^VFILE.LIB 3b^
 :    IF S1=0 THEN S0=0 : RETURN     ’ out of space
 :    GET #VCH,S1 : S2=CVI(VL$)
 :    IF S2<=0 THEN S1=-S2 : GOTO ^VFILE.LIB 3b^
 :    GET #VCH,S2 : S3=CVI(VL$)
 :    WHILE S3>0     ’ merge free blocks
 :       GET #VCH,S1 : LSET VL$=MKI$(S3) : PUT #VCH,S1
 :       S2=S3 : GET #VCH,S2 : S3=CVI(VL$)
 :       WEND
 :    IF S2-S1<=S0 THEN S1=-S3 : GOTO ^VFILE.LIB 3b^
 :    S0=S2-S0       ’ allocate; S0 is new busy block
 :    GET #VCH,S1 : LSET VL$=MKI$(S0)  : PUT #VCH,S1
 :    GET #VCH,S0 : LSET VL$=MKI$(-S2) : PUT #VCH,S0
 :    RETURN
 : ^VFILE.LIB 4^    ’ release block S0
 :    GET #VCH,S0
 :    LSET VL$=MKI$(ABS(CVI(VL$)))
 :    PUT #VCH,S0
 :    RETURN
 +------------------------------------------------------+
```

7.9 A V-File Tester

Here is a simple program for testing v-file commands and subroutines. It accepts variable-length lines from the keyboard and stores them into a v-file. You can dynamically add and delete lines, and watch where they are stored. You can list the entire file or list only lines containing a specified quote.

The program is intended to be an exerciser for the v-file concept and as a tutorial for the v-file techniques. Error handling is minimal here: the error is displayed, and the program stops cold. If you run it interpretively, you can examine variables and records directly from the keyboard.

The subroutines are arranged in alphabetical order by label. The commands are:

A Add a new line to the file. After the line L$ is input, the number of records needed to store L$ as a v-block is computed. We need a block of 2+LEN(L$) or more bytes to store the link field plus the line itself. We divide this by VRL to convert it to records and round it up to the nearest whole record with the INT function. The count required is S0 = −INT(−(2+LEN(L$))/VRL). Note also that the link field is prefixed to the line so that it will appear as the first two bytes of the block.

C Creates and initializes a new v-file from scratch.

D Delete a line from the file. You have to enter the block number to be deleted. In real applications, this number represents the key to where the data are stored in the v-file, and it is usually stored in an array or another v-file that serves as an index.

F Find lines by content. This command uses subroutine NEXT-LINE to search the v-file and list only lines that contain a given quote. In real applications, it could be modified to extract a subset of data from one v-file to another.

L List lines in the v-file. This command uses the subroutine NEXT-LINE which skips forward to the next busy block and reads it into line L$. Note that lines will appear to be listed in the reverse order that they were entered at the keyboard. The v-file mechanism allocates new blocks from the end of the free space, to speed up allocation. After you add and delete for a while, the lines are stored in random order in the v-file.

O Open an existing v-file.

Q Quit. This command is essential when using DSM to allow the program to close files, save indexes, and report v-file counts.

```
+------------------------------------------------------------------+
:   PRINT "Welcome To V-FILE TESTER"                               :
:   ON ERROR GOTO 'GLOBAL ERROR HANDLER'                           :
:   DEFINT A-Z : CLS                                               :
:   VCH=1          ' file channel                                 :
```

```
:  VRL=8         ' record length                            :
:  VLR=100       ' last record                              :
:  ' VB$ is v-file buffer, fielded in VFILE.LIB            :
:  ' VL$ is link field,    fielded in VFILE.LIB            :
:                                                           :
:  WHILE 1      ' main loop                                 :
:     LINE INPUT "Enter Command (ACDFLOQ)  "; C$           :
:     ON INSTR("ACDFLOQ",C$) GOSUB                          :
:        - ^ADD^,^OPEN^,^DEL^,^FIND^,^LIST^,^OPEN^,^QUIT^   :
:     WEND                                                  :
:                                                           :
: ^ADD^    ' add line to file                               :
:   LINE INPUT "Enter the line to be stored  "; L$         :
:   SO=-INT(-(2+LEN(L$))/VRL)     ' block size needed      :
:   S(S)=3 : GOSUB ^VFILE.LIB^     ' find a block          :
:   IF SO=0 THEN PRINT "No Room Found" : RETURN            :
:   PRINT "Stored at block"; SO   ' report block address   :
:   L$=VL$+L$                     ' prefix link            :
:   FOR I=1 TO LEN(L$) STEP VRL   ' break L$ up            :
:      LSET VB$=MID$(L$,I,VRL)    '   into records         :
:      PUT #VCH, SO : SO=SO+1     '   and write them out   :
:      NEXT I                                               :
:   RETURN                                                  :
:                                                           :
: ^DEL^   ' delete label from file                          :
:   INPUT "Enter Block Address To Be Deleted  "; SO        :
:   S(S)=4 : GOSUB ^VFILE.LIB^                              :
:   RETURN                                                  :
:                                                           :
: ^FIND^    ' list records containing quote                 :
:   LINE INPUT "Enter Quote  "; Q$                         :
:   CB=1                     ' current and next block       :
:   WHILE 1                  ' loop until end of file       :
:      GOSUB ^NEXT-LINE^     ' get next line                :
:      IF NB=0 THEN RETURN   ' CB is last block             :
:      IF INSTR(L$,Q$) THEN PRINT CB;L$  'list if matches   :
:      CB=NB                 ' advance to next block         :
:      WEND                                                 :
:   RETURN                                                  :
:                                                           :
: ^GLOBAL ERROR HANDLER^                                    :
:   PRINT "Error"; ERR; "at line"; ERL                     :
:   STOP                                                    :
:                                                           :
: ^LIST^    ' list v-file on screen                         :
:   CB=1                     ' current and next block       :
:   WHILE 1                  ' loop until end of file       :
:      GOSUB ^NEXT-LINE^     ' get next line                :
:      IF NB=0 THEN RETURN   ' CB is last block             :
:      PRINT CB; L$          ' list block and line          :
:      CB=NB                 ' advance to next block         :
:      WEND                                                 :
:   RETURN                                                  :
```

```
:  ^NEXT-LINE^    ' Sub to read nearest line            :
:    ' Enter with  CB = current block                   :
:    ' Return with CB = nearest busy block              :
:    '             NB = link of CB; if 0,  end of v-file :
:    '             L$ = data from block CB              :
:    GET #VCH,CB          ' current block               :
:    NB=-CVI(VL$)         ' next block                  :
:    IF NB<O THEN CB=-NB:GOTO ^-2^  ' free block?        :
:    IF NB=O THEN RETURN  ' return if last block         :
:    L$=""                                              :
:    FOR I=CB TO NB-1     ' for all records in block     :
:        GET #VCH, I      ' read record                  :
:        L$=L$+VB$        ' and add it to line           :
:        NEXT I                                          :
:    L$=MID$(L$,3)        ' strip link field             :
:    RETURN                                             :
:                                                       :
:  ^OPEN^    ' create or open old v-file                :
:    LINE INPUT "Enter name of V-File  "; VF$            :
:    IF C$="C" THEN S(S)=1 ELSE S(S)=2                   :
:    GOSUB ^VFILE.LIB^        ' open                      :
:    RETURN                                             :
:                                                       :
:  ^QUIT^   ' stop program                              :
:    CLOSE                                              :
:    END                                                :
```

The v-file tester can be put to several uses. It shows how v-files can be used in application programs. The start of the program shows how the hard-wired variables are initialized for the library routine VFILE.LIB. In the A command, you can see how to partition the variable-length data lines into fixed-length records and how to compute the required block size. The NEXT-LINE subroutine shows how to search for the next busy block and how to assemble the records into a line again.

The v-file tester also lets you test new DSM routines and new commands that use them. It is very difficult to debug programs with DSM if the supporting routines are not working properly. As will be discussed in later chapters on library routines, test programs are effective debugging time savers. The v-file tester is nothing but a cleaned-up tester for the VFILE.LIB routine.

Finally, the v-file tester can be used as a starter template for new applications that use v-files. After all, it contains the primitive routines needed in every application:

create and open
read and write
find and list
close and quit

You may find you can generate some very simple data base applications with this template. For example, you might use it to store names and addresses for a MAILING LABELS program. Or to generate a simple TAX RECORD v-file into which you throw tax data throughout the year.

7.10 Uses for Dynamic Space Management

Dynamic space management is not a beginner's concept. It requires some understanding of space and data structures and some extra energy to develop and operate the DSM mechanisms. Why do we bother? What's in it for us?

Our payoff for all this work is that we can free ourselves from the straitjacket of fixed-length data objects such as arrays and random files. We can now take any scarce storage or display resource and ration it out to demanding processes. Even the elementary DSM algorithms we have developed here can be used for managing any addressable space, whether an array, a screen, a random file, or even a byte string. They let us invent complicated data structures with unspecified extensions and variable substructures.

Never again do we have to establish some fixed scheme when we are writing a program, when we have no real idea of what the data look like. Now we can defer data structure decisions to the program itself. When the program runs, it decides dynamically what space it needs and uses the DSM mechanism dynamically to obtain it. This gives the program a whole new set of powers whose scope can only be sketched in this book:

- DSM allows several processes to share a common resource without interfering with each other. Example: Array, File, and String Space.
- DSM wastes less of a scarce resource because it only assigns the amount needed while it is needed. Example: memory, screen space.
- DSM with v-files, used on RAM disks, can be an effective extension of the BASIC data space to use all of the available memory.
- DSM saves you design time required to handle the dynamic space demand, the various maxima, and the possible overlap in demand. Example: Multiple Users, Multi-tasking, Integrated Applications.

- DSM lets data objects adapt themselves to their environment as needed. Example: Variable Record Fields, Windowed Screens.
- Ultimately, DSM is essential for designing programs that learn as they run, that configure themselves to match their environment. We can start to write intelligent programs that make their own decision.

The Queue

8.1 Introducing the Queue

A queue is a data object in which data items are arranged into a single line, one item behind the other (Figure 8-1). The queue has two ends: a front or head end and a rear or tail end. Data items are always added at the tail and always leave from the front, so that a given data item slowly advances from the rear to the front of the queue.

The queue is really a very simple mechanism, but it does have some special properties that distinguish it from other data objects. To help us distinguish the queue, and to get a better feel for its essential nature, let's look at four examples from the real world. Each of these is a lineup of "data" items of some kind. Only *one* of them is a queue:

1. A pearl necklace
2. A freight train
3. A telephone book
4. A car wash

A pearl necklace is a line of pearls with two ends, usually closed off with a clasp. The position and count of pearls on the necklace is fixed. Its main function is as a static collection of pearls for storage and display. This is *not* a queue, since it has no mechanism for adding and deleting data, and since the data do not move inside the queue.

A freight train is a line of boxcars. It has a front and a rear end, and it moves the cars from point A to point B. This is *not* a queue. Even though it involves movement of data in a forward direction, all of the cars move forward together. No matter how far a train travels, no boxcar advances one inch closer to the engine.

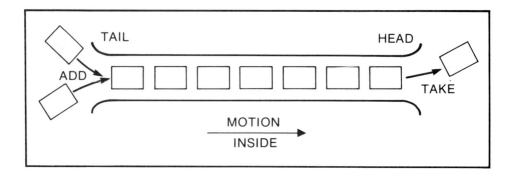

Figure 8-1. A queue.

A telephone book is a large data stream, arranged in a line, with a beginning and an end. It has a fixed number of data items, permanently stored in a fixed spatial order, with direct access to any item. There is no requirement to process the data in any particular order, much less in sequence. This is *not* a queue but an array. It illustrates well the essential difference between the fixed, direct access nature of an array and the dynamic, sequential processing nature of a queue.

A car wash is a device into which dirty cars disappear at one end and clean cars emerge from the other (Figure 8-2). While our car is inside the car wash, we cannot enter it or drive it away. We cannot pass other cars ahead of ours. We must wait until our car emerges from the wash line. This, at last, is an example of a queue. We have the essential requirements for a queue: a single line of data, a front where data are removed and a rear where data are added. Data inside the queue cannot be accessed; they must advance through the queue until they leave it at the exit end.

In fact, a car wash is an example of several queues lined up behind each other. When we peek inside the car wash, we see several stations. First the cars are wetted down, then soaped, rinsed, dried, and waxed. Several queues are arranged behind each other to process dirty cars into clean ones. This is a hint of why queues are so important to advanced programming: they let us pass data streams from one process to another, in assembly line fashion.

There is more. Note that the owners are separated from their cars at an early stage. While their cars go through the wash, the owners go to a cashier—a different queue entirely. After paying the cashier, the owners are again "merged" with their cars when they come out of the car wash. Here we have a network of queues,

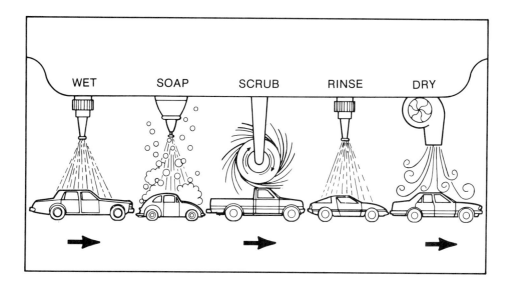

Figure 8-2. A car wash is an example of a queue.

cleverly designed into a system that performs a useful overall process.

Finally, note that queues and processes alternate. This is an invariant that applies to every system no matter how complex: programming involves data and processes. Every process requires input data and generates output data; every data stream is generated by some process and feeds into some process. You can consider each queue as sandwiched between two processes or each process sandwiched between two queues. For example, a print queue is a queue enclosed by a printing program on one side and a printing machine on the other (Figure 8-3).

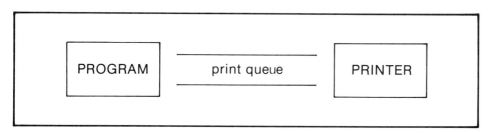

Figure 8-3. A queue serving as a data bridge between a generating program and a consuming printer.

On the other hand, it may be useful to view the printing program as enclosed between a raw data queue and a print queue (Figure 8-4).

The next step is to connect several of these sequences into larger series, until you build up entire applications (Figure 8-5). The queue then plays an important role as a kind of glue that connects individual data and processes into total data processing sequences.

This most useful view of the process–data relationship is often hidden from the beginning programmer, who crams data into static arrays and processes them in place. This is akin to the way a typical suburban homeowner washes a car: the car is stationary, and the soap, water, and wax are brought to it in turn.

In many advanced applications, it is relatively easy to separate the various data streams and to handle each stream individually as a sequence of one or more queues. Once you develop a few routines to set up and manipulate queues, the queue becomes an easy and natural tool. We explore this in depth in the next chapter, but first we need to develop some basic tools to manipulate queues.

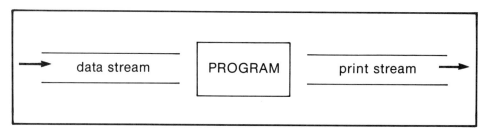

Figure 8-4. Two queues serving as data input and data output providers to a program.

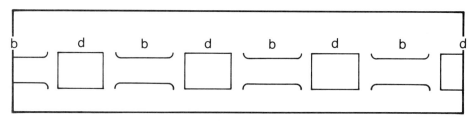

Figure 8-5. Alternating queues (q) and programs (p) form a processing sequence that looks much like the car wash in Figure 8-2.

8.2 Implementing a Queue

BASIC does not support the queue as a built-in data object, so we have to implement it ourselves. As we saw in the chapter on data objects, we need to define the physical space occupied by the queue and the operations we can perform on it.

No special technical terms are used for queue operations. An item is "added" to a queue or just "queued," and "taken" or "removed" from the queue. There is usually no ambiguity regarding which queue end is involved, since items are always added to the tail end and removed from the front end. A queue without items is "empty." If you try to remove an item from an empty queue you get a "queue underflow" condition. If the space allocated for the queue is full, trying to add an item to the queue generates a "queue overflow" condition.

We need at least three operations to manipulate a queue:

1. SET UP—initialize an empty queue
2. ADD—add a data item to the queue
3. REMOVE—take an item from the queue

A queue can be implemented in several ways, depending on the data types to be queued, the number of items in the queue, and the processing to be done with the queue. We'll certainly use a different mechanism to queue three files for printing than to manage a queue of 200 cars waiting to go through a toll booth or 40 million tax returns waiting to be processed by the IRS.

Each implementation also has different attributes that make it more or less easy to use in real applications. In this respect, we want to consider such things as ease of overflow and underflow handling, counting items in the queue, and accessing items in the middle of the queue.

Yes, I said accessing items in the middle of the queue! While that violates the theoretical definition of a queue, it is very handy sometimes to be able to pull a rowdy drunk out of the middle of a ticket line or to accelerate the boss's print job for immediate printing. I think one of the shortcomings of the data types built into programming languages is that they do not leave elbowroom to handle the exceptional situations. This is one of the great advantages of designing your own data objects with their own structures. If you design your own data structures, you can also design flexibility to accommodate the exceptions and the anomalies that you encounter in real applications.

8.3 Implementing a Queue in a String___

The string is an interesting space object for storing queues. It can be easily packed with data items of fixed or variable length, separated by suitable counts or delimiters. If you are using the BASIC interpreter, you are limited to a maximum of 255 bytes per string; but this restriction can be alleviated by using an array of strings, or it can be eliminated completely by compiling the program (most compilers have a maximum length of 32767 bytes per string).

To implement a string queue, treat the first byte of the string as the front of the queue and add new items to the queue by concatenating them at the end. The queued data items then advance inside the string, from right to left, until they are stripped off at the front (Figure 8-6).

Assuming that Q$ is a queue of 1-byte items and BYTE$ is a single byte of data, the operations for a string queue can be written in very simple statements. To add the item, we concatenate BYTE$ to the string. To take an item from the queue, we peel the first byte off the string and store it in BYTE$. Queue underflow can be detected by testing for Q$="" or LEN(Q$)=0 before taking a byte. Queue overflow is detected by testing the length of the string before adding a byte:

```
' SET UP the queue
Q$=""

' ADD an item to the queue
IF LEN(Q$)=255 THEN ^OVERFLOW^
Q$=Q$+BYTE$

' REMOVE an item from the queue
IF Q$="" THEN ^UNDERFLOW^
BYTE$=MID$(Q$,1,1) : Q$=MID$(Q$,2)
```

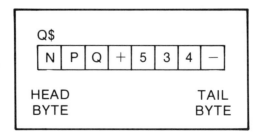

Figure 8-6. An ordinary string can be treated as a queue of bytes.

As a sample application, let's design a string queue to keep track of random records in memory. Many applications have random access files containing too many records to keep in memory at one time. By noting the order in which the records are accessed, the program can keep the most recently accessed ones in memory longer and reduce processing time.

Assume you have dimensioned a string array MEM$(100) in which you plan to hold the 100 latest records the program has read. The design problem is how to keep track of the sequence in which the program has read these records. Basically, you need to know which is the oldest record so you can throw it out to make room for a new record. (Assume the program does not change any records; it only reads them.)

As you consider the data objects you could use for this, you hit upon the queue. If you keep the record numbers in a queue, and if you always add the newest record at the tail of the queue, then the record at the head of the queue will automatically be the oldest record (Figure 8-7). The queue serves as the aging mechanism.

Here is the setup code. The file is opened on channel 1, and all records are 200 bytes wide. Since the program does not know which records the user will want, it simply reads the first 100 records into MEM$( ). Q$ is also set up to 100 bytes; the CHR$( ) function converts the MEM$( ) subscript into a single byte:

```
DIM MEM(100), MEM$(100)
OPEN "R",1,"FILENAME",200
FIELD #1, 200 AS BUFFER$
Q$=""
FOR I=1 TO 100
    GET #1, I : MEM$(I)=BUFFER$ : MEM(I)=I
    Q$=Q$+CHR$(I)
    NEXT I
RETURN
```

Here is the code to read a requested record R into memory. M, the MEM$( ) slot to be used, is taken from the front of the queue. The record is read and stored at MEM$(M), and its number is entered into MEM( ), which serves as an index to which record is stored in each slot of MEM$( ). Finally, M is added to the tail of the queue, reflecting the fact that it is the newest record.

```
^READ RECORD R^
    M=ASC(LEFT$(Q$),1)
    GET #1,R : MEM$(M)=BUFFER$ : MEM(M)=R
    Q$=MID$(Q$,2)+CHR$(M)
    RETURN
```

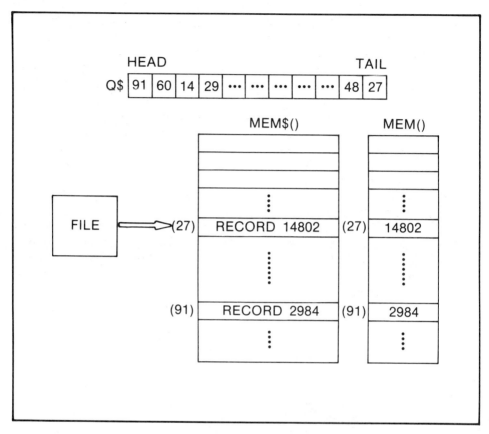

Figure 8-7. Q$ tracks the records in order of length of stay in MEMS(). Record 14802 was the latest one read from the file. It is stored in MEMS(27). The oldest record is 2984, in MEMS(91). This will be the slot used to read the next record.

8.4 Implementing a Queue in an Array ____

The simplest way to store a queue in an array is to store the first queue item into array element 1, the second item into element 2, and so on. In addition, a count variable is kept to indicate which is the last "live" element of the array. To add an item to the queue, the count is raised by one, and the item is stored into the element indicated by the new count. To remove an item from the queue, element 2 is moved into element 1, element 3 is moved into element 2, and so on. Then the count is reduced by 1. This design is acceptable for small queues or for queues that are seldom adjusted; but it cannot be recommended for general use. The time required to shift the entire queue down one element is usually too long. If several such queues are used, the program will run slowly and with unpredictable pauses.

The array is a fixed-length space object, and the queue is a variable-length data object. Unlike the string, there is no simple way to strip off the first element or to add an element to the end of the array. This presents a momentary design problem: how do you stuff a wiggly queue into an inflexible array? The solution is a common programming trick, almost a rule of thumb: DO NOT MOVE DATA—MOVE POINTERS. Programmers have an instinctive aversion to moving data around in memory, because simply moving data from element A to element B wastes time, wastes space, and does little or nothing to increase information content.

A better way to implement a queue in an array is to again store the queue items consecutively into the array, but this time carry two variables, say HEAD and TAIL, that point to the queue inside the array (Figure 8-8). Now we can drop the first item of the queue by simply adding 1 to the HEAD pointer! This is much faster than moving every item in the queue.

To set up the queue, dimension an array A( ) one element larger than the longest queue to be accommodated. (The extra element gives the HEAD pointer a place to point when the queue is full.) Store the array's dimension in a variable called MAXDIM for use in overflow testing:

```
DIM A(2000) : MAXDIM=2000
```

As an aside, most BASIC interpreters and compilers do not allow dimensioning an array with a variable. Some even require all dimension statements to occur physically in the program, before statements that reference the array. This simplifies the work of a handful of compiler designers; but it makes life miserable for thousands of application programmers. Curiously, these are often the same language designers who dare to lecture programmers about efficient programming!

The HEAD and TAIL pointers are integer variables that identify the limits of the queue. The natural impulse is to point the HEAD to the first and the TAIL to the last queue item. But this creates a problem when the queue is empty. Since HEAD and TAIL must always contain some value, we have no way to flag the empty queue except with a third variable, such as a count. In some applications, this approach is quite useful since the count of a queue is often valuable information.

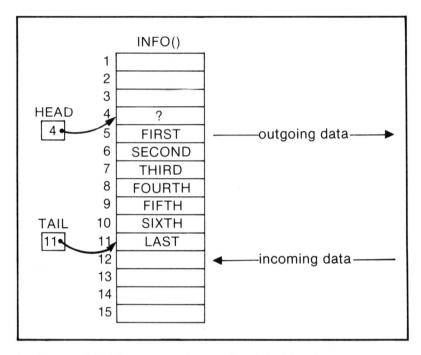

Figure 8-8. The queue is not fixed inside the array. Its current location is indicated by the HEAD and TAIL pointers.

The simplest way to solve the empty queue problem without using a count is to use one array element as a spacer, a dummy element that does not contain a data item. We keep this spacer just in front of the first queue item, as a "zeroth" item. It gives us an element to point the HEAD and TAIL to when the queue is empty. In other words, whenever HEAD=TAIL, the queue is empty. Now we can set up the empty queue:

```
HEAD=1 : TAIL=1
```

To add an item to the queue, increment the TAIL pointer to the next element and then store the item in A(TAIL). To remove an item from the queue, remember that the HEAD pointer always points to the dummy element in front of the queue, so increment the HEAD pointer first, then copy the element A(HEAD):

```
TAIL=TAIL+1   : A(TAIL)=ITEM     ' to add an item
HEAD=HEAD+1 : ITEM=A(HEAD)   ' to remove an item
```

Next, we have to provide for queue over- and underflow. Overflow occurs when the tail reaches the end of the array, that is, when TAIL=MAXDIM. When that happens, we go to code that handles overflow in some way, here represented by the label OVERFLOW. This code might simply issue a message or return a special flag from the subroutine trying to insert a new item. It might even try to compact the array by shifting the entire queue up, as we did for the very first array queue in this section.

Queue underflow, meaning the queue is empty, is detected when the TAIL points to the dummy element in front of the queue, that is, when HEAD=TAIL. Again, we go to label UNDERFLOW where we take some appropriate action such as flagging the condition and returning. One good idea might be to take this opportunity to set up the queue as brand new. This will reduce future overflows. Here, then, is the complete code to implement the queue in an array:

```
+----------------------------------------------------------------+
:   ^SET UP^    ' initialize the empty queue                     :
:      DIM A(2000) : MAXDIM=2000                                 :
:      HEAD=1 : TAIL=1                                           :
:      ...                                                      :
:                                                               :
:   ^ADD^    ' add ITEM to the queue                            :
:      IF TAIL=MAXDIM THEN ^OVERFLOW^                           :
:      TAIL=TAIL+1 : A(TAIL)=ITEM                               :
:      ...                                                      :
:                                                               :
:   ^REMOVE^    ' remove item into ITEM                         :
:      IF HEAD=TAIL THEN ^UNDERFLOW^                            :
:      HEAD=HEAD+1 : ITEM=A(HEAD)                               :
:      ...                                                      :
+----------------------------------------------------------------+
```

Incidentally, the variables MAXDIM, HEAD, and TAIL could easily be stored inside the array itself, as $A(0)$, $A(1)$, and $A(2)$, respectively. In that case, the queue would always start at $A(3)$. This would consolidate the queue as a single physical data object entirely inside the array $A(\ )$. But it would create problems if you want to store more than one queue in an array, or if you want to use dynamic storage management to manage the queue space.

That's all there is to implementing a queue in an array. Technically speaking, we have used an array as a space object to build an abstract data object called a queue, including three operations SETUP, ADD, and REMOVE. As just written, it is a useful mechanism; but two interesting improvements on the theme are possible. One follows here, the other is in the next section.

As just implemented, the queue uses the variable **HEAD** and **TAIL** to point to the beginning and end of the queue. This method works as long as we only have one queue. But in practice, we juggle dozens of queues, and we have to find a nice way to handle the many head and tail pointers. One way is to dimension a HEAD() and a TAIL() array, whose elements point to the various queues. This design is very attractive because it lets us give an integer number to each queue. Thus, queue 13 would be the queue identified in HEAD(13) and TAIL(13). Because each queue is independent of the others, we can still use one array to contain them all. The idea of multiple queues is more fully explored in the next chapter on Pipelines.

8.5 The Circular Queue

As we add items to the end of the queue and remove them from the front, the queue creeps farther and farther down the array until it hits the last element and causes queue overflow. Thus, a queue can overflow even though plenty of room remains in the array above the queue. In fact, even an empty queue can cause overflow on the very first insertion, if you set up the queue as HEAD = MAXDIM : TAIL = MAXDIM.

One way to solve this creeping problem is to shift the queue back up whenever it sags too far. But there is a more elegant design: the circular queue. We modify the queue implementation so that when the queue reaches the last array element, it continues at the top of the array (Figure 8-9).

```
^SET UP^    ' initialize circular queue
    DIM A(2000) : MAXDIM=2000
    HEAD=1 : TAIL=1
    ...


^ADD^    ' add item to circular queue
    IF TAIL+1=HEAD THEN ^OVERFLOW^
  ' IF HEAD=1 AND TAIL=MAXDIM THEN ^OVERFLOW^
    TAIL=TAIL+1 : IF TAIL>MAXDIM THEN TAIL=1
    A(TAIL)=ITEM
    ...


^REMOVE^    ' remove item from circular queue
    IF HEAD=TAIL THEN ^UNDERFLOW^
    HEAD=HEAD+1 : IF HEAD>MAXDIM THEN HEAD=1
    ITEM=A(HEAD)
    ...
```

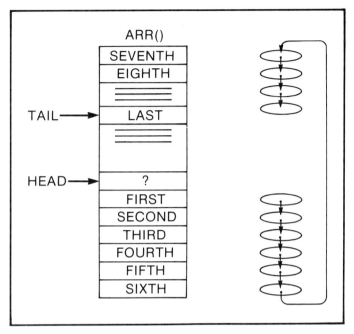

Figure 8-9. A circular queue installed inside an array. The tail chases the head round and round.

To build a circular queue, the operations are modified to let the queue wrap around from the bottom of the array to the top. Overflow now occurs only when the queue has used all of the array elements, so we test for TAIL+1 = HEAD. Removal remains the same, except that we allow the tail pointer to wrap when it reaches the end of the array.

With this final improvement, we have completed an acceptable implementation of the queue in an array. It uses the array space completely and without any overhead, and it requires no special housecleaning pauses.

8.6 Implementing the Queue as a Chain ___

In the chapter on chains, we developed the chain as a linked list whose data items are arranged into a single line with a head and a tail. This data object is a natural for use as a queue. All we have to do is provide pointers to the head and tail of the chain—the rest is handled by the chain operations (Figure 8-10).

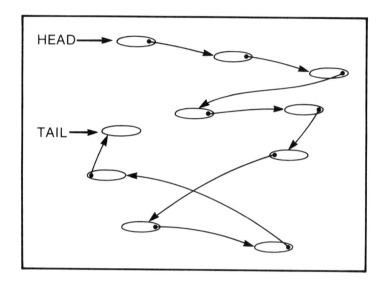

Figure 8-10. A chain with a tail pointer.

Assuming that you have a LINK( ) array that contains the pointers for each node, here is the code to insert an item into a chained queue. This time, we don't care where the data item is stored; all we need is its pointer I. The link of the old tail item is pointed to the new item, and the new item's link is set to 0 to identify it as the new tail item. Then we update TAIL to point to the new item:

```
+-------------------------------------------------------------------------+
:                      LINK(TAIL) = ITEM                                  :
:                      LINK(I) = 0                                        :
:                      TAIL = I                                           :
+-------------------------------------------------------------------------+
```

The major advantage of using a chained queue is that it is a linked data object. The queue is no longer constrained to a specific range 1 through MAXDIM of an array; it can jump around inside the array as needed to queue up items. Several queues can share the array, intertwining like ivy to trace their particular data items. In fact, the best use of chained queues is in conjunction with dynamic space management (*see* Chapter 7). If a single giant array is provided for all chains in the program, you can obtain an available cell with the RESERVE operation and add it to a specific queue. When an item is removed from a queue, its space is returned via the RELEASE operation. This approach shares space across the entire program and reduces queue overflow to those occasions where the entire data space is in use, not just one queue's array.

8.7 Implementing the Queue as a File

A file is essentially a data object stored on some medium like a disk or transmitted to a printer or even to another computer via a modem. To implement the queue as a disk file, we have very little to do because BASIC provides the sequential file as a built-in data object. (The random file, by contrast, is like a string array stored on disk.)

The sequential file is a queue of variable-length strings called "lines." Each line is terminated by the two characters 13 and 10, which are the ASCII command codes for "carriage return" and "line feed." Because of these two characters, the sequential file mechanism can only be used for text files, more precisely for files whose data do not contain the character 13 (end-of-line) or 26 (end-of-file).

Operations on files are provided as BASIC statements. A file is opened on some channel (called "file number" in PC BASIC) that connects the disk to the program. Lines are added to the file by "printing" them and are removed from the file by "inputting" them. Here are two sample programs to write and read a one-line file:

```
' to create and write a new sequential file
OPEN "O",#1,"FILENAME"    ' open file for output
PRINT #1, ITEM$           ' write a line
CLOSE #1                  ' close file

' to access an existing sequential file
OPEN "I",#1,"FILENAME"    ' open file for input
LINE INPUT #1, ITEM$      ' to read a line
CLOSE #1                  ' close file on channel 1
```

As a first example of using sequential files, here is a program to copy a file. Note how BASIC uses the end-of-file function EOF in place of a tail pointer:

```
^COPY FILE^
    OPEN "I",#1,"OLDFILE"
    OPEN "O",#2,"NEWFILE"
    WHILE NOT EOF(1)
        LINE INPUT #1, A$
        PRINT #2, A$
        WEND
    CLOSE
```

Here is a program to append file B behind file A. BASIC provides the append mode to open the file at the end. This mode was made necessary because there is no tail pointer to the file. It shows us yet another way to implement our queues with operations to test for end of queue instead of testing variables like TAIL.

```
^APPEND FILE^
    OPEN "I",#1,"FILEB"
    OPEN "FILEA" FOR APPEND AS #2
    WHILE NOT EOF(1)
        LINE INPUT #1, A$
        PRINT #2, A$
        WEND
    CLOSE
```

As a final example of the sequential file, here is a program to extract a subfile from a file.

```
^EXTRACT^
    INPUT "Enter source file name   "; SFILE$
    INPUT "Enter target file name   "; TFILE$
    INPUT "Enter line range  "; FLINE, TLINE
    OPEN "I",#1,SFILE$
    OPEN "O",#2,TFILE$
    FOR I=1 TO FLINE-1
        LINE INPUT #1, A$
        NEXT I
    FOR I=FLINE TO TLINE
        LINE INPUT #1, A$
        PRINT #1, A$
        NEXT I
    CLOSE
```

8.8 Using the Queue

The queue has many uses in programming. It is difficult to classify these in any one way because they overlap with other data objects and their uses. But here is a list of some problem types where the queue comes in handy.

Lining Up Data

One of the eternal problems of programming is to bring order to a disorganized data set. Data may come to a program from a number of sources, in a number of formats, with or without errors, in various shapes and sizes. Consider the volume and variety of data dumped on a program handling 45 automated teller stations for a bank or the program that handles the launch of a space shuttle. The image that comes to mind here is that of a herd of cattle, so let's track that example for a while.

A queue can be used as a simple linearizer, as a tool for arranging data into a single stream that can then be processed. To process a herd of cattle, cowboys (or cattlepersons, if you prefer) funnel the herd from a corral into a narrowly fenced channel, barely wide enough for one cow. At the end of this channel, they process each cow individually, perhaps inoculating or branding or washing it. Then they release the cow into a second corral. They have used the channel to form the herd into a single queue.

Preserving Arrival Order

A queue can be used to keep track of the arrival sequence of a data item. Since items inside a queue cannot pass each other, the queue preserves the order in which items are added. It tracks data in arrival order, "remembering" which item was added first. This time-ordering property of the queue is often used to process an otherwise disorganized data set in sequence. At the entrance to the queue, some process knows the order in which data should enter the queue. For example, given a dozen cows ready to be milked, some program with special dairy intelligence can use a queue to arrange the cows into the proper milking order.Another example comes from accounting, where you must keep track of *when* you bought a certain item for inventory and tax purposes; accountants used FIFO to mean "First In First Out" long before they used computers.

Delaying or Aging Data

Data cannot be processed while they are inside a queue. All they can do is inch their way forward to the head of the queue, to the serving process. Therefore, a queue can be used as a delay device that ages data items or delays their processing. Delay queues are often used as "buffers" to match processes with different speeds or formats or to intercept data items between processing for inspection, sampling, and so on. Many banks use a delay of several days before giving credit for a deposited check to allow checks to clear. In our continuing dairy example, some of the milk may be processed and stored in cool moist caves (delay queues) for months, slowly ripening into cheese in much the same order the cows were milked long ago.

Sorting

Sorting can be thought of as arranging data as a queue in which the value of some "key" data item increases or decreases along the queue. There are dozens of methods for sorting; many of them are designed to handle the problem of arranging data during the sort in some way that permits insertion of a new item between two items already sorted. We recognize this problem as one that we can solve by use of a chain queue. The chain simplifies the insertion of new items in the middle; the queue presents the final data set as a sequentially accessible data object.

Multiple Key Sorting

Queues can be used to sort data sets on several keys at once. We do this by using a different queue for each key sequence; but we slip in a powerful programming technique here. Instead of making a full copy of the data set for each key queue, we queue some number such as a subscript or a record number that uniquely identifies the data. We end up with one "main" queue that contains the complete data values plus several queues containing identification numbers arranged in various key orders. This technique saves space and, most important, avoids having to update the same data item in many queues when it changes.

Indexing Data

If we write the sorted key queues out as files, we create a design used in many data base programs: one main data file, usually a random access file, plus a number of index files that point to the main data in sequence by some key field. (*See also* Section 5.7.)

For example, the dairy may track age, weight, health, and milk production for each cow. It would create an index file for each of these key data fields. To generate a report by weight, it would follow the weight index file and print out data from the main file in that order.

Task Management

Quite aside from managing data, queues can be used for managing processes. One example of this is the common DOS batch file—a queue file that controls the sequence in which programs are called up. In operating system jargon, a task is any hardware or software unit that needs to gain control periodically to do its job. For example, the central clock is a task that needs control about 18 times a second to maintain the system time and data information. Application programmers call this a subroutine. The main difference is that a subroutine does not interrupt the main program and demand control. But we can simulate this with queues that demand service, and we do this in the next section.

8.9 Using a Queue to Manage Tasks _____

A queue preserves the chronological order of arrival of items requiring service. This makes it useful for arranging tasks demanding control of the computer into a line for processing. A typical example is a line of cars waiting at a traffic line or a line of people waiting at the supermarket checkout or at the bank. (In England such a line is in fact called a queue.) When you think about it, a program itself is merely a queue of statements waiting to get control of the computer.

If we view these cars or these people not as data objects that we manipulate but as tasks (with their own free will), then we get into the fascinating area of tasking and multitasking. The topic is much too large to cover in this book, but it is also too fascinating to omit entirely. I include only the barest hint here to show you that we can tackle even this sophisticated problem in BASIC, once we have developed our tools.

This section presents a very simple program that simulates the operation of a queue of customers waiting for service at a bank. Banks were one of the first businesses to organize their waiting lines so that customers stand in one queue that splits into several at the serving end (Figure 8-11). This put a merciful stop to the

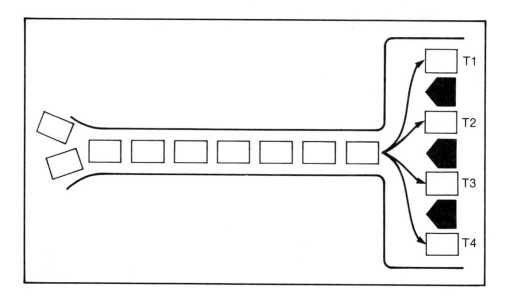

Figure 8-11. The multiserver queue simulated in program TELLER.PRE. Four tellers are serving a queue of waiting customers.

frustration of seemingly always selecting the one queue that absolutely did not move. The drawback is that now we often stand in a much larger queue that does not move!

We will now simulate such a "multiple server queue" to show how easy it is to code and how queue processing can simplify a rather complicated process. Assume a small bank with four tellers T1, T2, T3, and T4. At any given moment, each teller is either serving one customer or is waiting for a customer. Customers line up for service in a waiting queue called WQ$. We use a string queue for the waiting queue here because it is large enough to hold the waiting line and because we can print the queue directly on the screen.

The ARRIVE routine simulates random arrival of customers and adds a new customer to the waiting queue. It also randomly adds a few spaces behind each customer, so that we can see the queue advancing on the screen. The arrival queue is limited to 30 customers just so the display will look better. The DISPLAY routine simply prints the current status of the tellers and the queue.

NEXT is the routine to move a customer to one of the teller windows. In this demonstration, it assigns a customer to a teller after delaying for a random interval to simulate the time customers take with each teller. In a more realistic program, each teller would be a separate task that would demand service (that is, beckon for a new customer) when ready.

```
+---------------------------------------------------------------+
:  ^TELLER.PRE^                                                 :
:     CLS : PRINT "Teller"                                      :
:                                                               :
:  ^TASKER^    ' give control to tasks in turn                  :
:     GOSUB ^ARRIVE^:GOSUB ^DISPLAY^:GOSUB ^NEXT^               :
:     GOTO ^-1^                                                 :
:                                                               :
:  ^ARRIVE^   ' task to greet customers at the door            :
:     WHILE LEN(WQ$)<30 AND RND>.3                              :
:        WQ$ = WQ$+CHR$(65+INT(26*RND))+SPACE$(1+2*RND)         :
:        WEND                                                   :
:     RETURN                                                    :
:                                                               :
:  ^DISPLAY^     ' task to update the screen                    :
:     LOCATE 4,1    : PRINT 1; W1$                              :
:     LOCATE 8,1    : PRINT 2; W2$                              :
:     LOCATE 11,11  : PRINT STRING$(30,"-")                     :
:     LOCATE 12,10  : PRINT WQ$; SPACE$(30);                    :
:     LOCATE 13,11  : PRINT STRING$(30,"-")                     :
:     LOCATE 16,1   : PRINT 3; W3$                              :
:     LOCATE 20,1   : PRINT 4; W4$                              :
:     RETURN                                                    :
:                                                               :
:  ^NEXT^     ' task to move a customer to a teller             :
:     IF LEN(WQ$) = 0 THEN RETURN    ' is queue empty?          :
:     FOR I=1 TO 1000*RND : NEXT     ' simulate delay           :
:     NC$=LEFT$(WQ$,1) : WQ$=MID$(WQ$,2)                        :
:     IF NC$=" " THEN ^-1^    ' ignore spaces in queue          :
:     ON 1+INT(4*RND) GOTO  ^+1^, ^+2^, ^+3^, ^+4^             :
:     W1$=NC$ : RETURN    ' move next customer to teller 1      :
:     W2$=NC$ : RETURN                                          :
:     W3$=NC$ : RETURN                                          :
:     W4$=NC$ : RETURN                                          :
+---------------------------------------------------------------+
```

The example illustrates the first halting steps of a program that can process several tasks at the same time, that is, a multitasking program. We have here the teller tasks, the queue management tasks, and the display tasks. Each task represents some action or process simulated by the program. For actual use, we would not code our tellers as individual variables. Rather, they would become fairly sophisticated tasks that would interact with the customers in complex ways, including a dialogue of questions and answers.

The tasks are orchestrated into a working whole by the TASKER, who sees to it that every other task gets control to do its work. It would be simple to add other tasks such as LUNCH BREAK, CLOSING TIME, SICK TELLER, and even BANK HOLDUP to handle the various problems that arise in the bank world. Finally, if we code the TASKER itself as a task, we can build a hierarchy of tasks that represent some complicated system like a traffic intersection or a dairy farm.

In the next chapter, we return to working with the data queue, this time used in a structure of queues called a pipeline. We won't talk of tasks again, but it may be a good idea to keep the idea in the back of your mind. Someday you may run into the proverbial "can of worms," and it may turn out that it is most easily modelled as a can of task queues.

The Pipeline

In one of its early advertisements for the PC, IBM showed the Little Tramp as the owner of a bakery. At the beginning of the commercial, he stands at the end of a conveyor belt on which frosted cakes are emerging from a slot in a wall. His job is to pack each cake into a carton. As can be guessed, the cakes start to come at him too fast. He gets behind, and cakes are falling on the floor. His solution is to buy an IBM PC, presumably including IBM's famous Slow-Your-Belt software. At the end of the commercial, he is a computer expert, and his shop is running smoothly.

Computer programmers would have three comments:

1. Adding a computer to a business that is running into the ground will merely run the business into the ground faster.
2. Buying a computer does not turn a manager into a computer expert.
3. Removing an inept bum from the assembly line often improves its operation.

No matter how unrealistic the commercial is, it does serve to introduce a class of applications that tend to be very complex and difficult to program without some special techniques. Imagine the operation of this bakery behind the scenes. There is a bewildering stream of diverse materials such as sugar, flour, trucks, cakes, customers, eggs, money, milk, cartons, icing, and so on. This chaos has to be ordered, inspected, unpacked, stored, moved, prepared, counted, mixed, measured, paid for, delivered, and so on. It seems absolutely amazing that anything edible ever emerges from this jungle.

How can this chaos possibly be captured into a program? As always, modular programming comes to the rescue. If we divide the data stream into smaller and smaller substreams, until each small stream only undergoes one specific operation, we end up with a design like a manufacturer's assembly line, where each

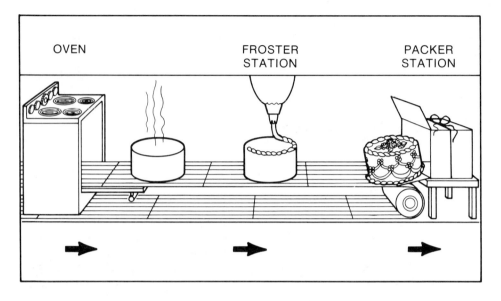

OVEN   FROSTER   PACKER
                        STATION   STATION

Figure 9-1. An assembly line.

workstation performs the same operation on every item moving
down the assembly line (Figure 9-1).

This chapter presents "pipelining" as a technique for programming the assembly-line type of application. Pipelining uses
queues to control and move the data from module to module.
Dynamic space management is used to share memory among the
modules, and a supervisor module controls the entire operation.

9.1 Pipeline Programming

Programmers use the words "piping" or "pipelining" to describe a system of processes connected in complex ways by pipes
(that is, data structures) that move materials from source to
destination. For example, the Alaska oil pipeline can be seen as a
very long pipe (queue), interrupted in many places by stations
(subroutines) for pumping, diverting, filtering, measuring, quality
control, and so on. This type of application can be a nightmare to
program as a conventional single-stream program. You need to
organize it and to consider several problems.

First of all, the modules have to cooperate, and the data must be
routed so that they mesh in just the right proportions at just the
right time. Having broken the problem into modules, we need a

supervisor module that knows how the modules fit together to manufacture the final product. To play a good game, a team of players need a captain to form a plan and call the signals.

Next, some way must be found to handle the many errors that can arise. Hardware breaks down, data contain typographical errors and mistakes, and even the finest programs have syntax and semantics errors. Every module must be allowed to report problems to its supervisor.

Finally, we need a way to stop or interrupt production. Because there is a time delay for each data item to work its way through the system, we must let some modules wait for others, until the last data item has worked its way through the system. We need some feedback mechanism to slow down modules when there is a problem (such as the Little Tramp) downstream.

9.2 The FILLER Program

To illustrate the use of queues for pipelining, let's write a word processing utility program called FILLER. FILLER will read text from an input file and format it into output lines that are filled with words to some specified margin. (The complete listing is also given in Chapter 13.)

"Filling" a line means adding words to the line until the next word would extend beyond the right margin. It is the first step in formatting an arbitrary text stream for typesetting into a book or magazine in its final form. Filling creates a flush left margin but leaves a ragged right margin. To align the right margin requires a subsequent formatting step called "justifying," in which blank spaces are judiciously inserted into the line to stretch it to the right length.

The FILLER utility takes a lump of input text and shapes it into a uniform stream of output lines. Each line is guaranteed to have enough words to fit inside the right margin (Figures 9-2 and 9-3). This stream can then be justified and typeset (by subsequent pipeline utilities) onto the pages of a book or magazine, as text, footnotes, or figure captions.

9.3 The Design

Let's visualize the filling process as an assembly line. A single conveyor belt moves text through the factory. At one end, raw text

Figure 9-2. A pastry chef's cake-decorating tool. The bag contains a frosting mix, and as the chef squeezes the bag, the frosting emerges from the funnel as a uniform stream.

lines are dumped onto the belt from some input file. As the text moves down the line, it is cut up into words that are then shaped into uniform lines. At the exit end, the uniform lines are written to an output file. This process will be implemented as four main subroutines:

READER	Reads the input file
WORDER	Chops lines into words
LINER	Fills words into lines
WRITER	Writes the output file

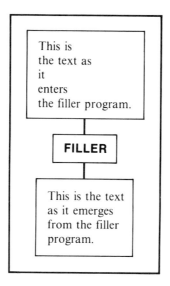

Figure 9-3. The FILLER program acts like a pastry chef's frosting bag.

Between these main subroutines, we will simulate the conveyor belt with three queues that move the text from subroutine to subroutine:

FILE 1   raw text
   READER PROGRAM   reads the input file
QUEUE 1   text lines
   WORDER PROGRAM   chops lines into words
QUEUE 2   words
   LINER PROGRAM   fills words into lines
QUEUE 3   filled lines
   WRITER PROGRAM   writes the output file
FILE 2   finished lines

The whole show will be controlled by a supervisor module called BOSS. Seen as a whole, the program will look much like the assembly line shown in Figure 9-1; the queues act as conveyor belts and the programs act as workstations.

The queue is the ideal data structure for pipelining. In Chapter 8, we saw a number of applications that could be piped: the car wash, the cows conducted from corral to corral (a corral symphony?), and the customers lined up at the bank. The queue streamlines the data nicely, it can be formatted in various ways, and it can easily be generalized so we can clone many queues of varying sizes and data types.

For our purposes here, the linked list or chain queue is best, because it supports variable-length queues and lets us share the memory space among various queues as needed. Therefore, we define our queue space as two large parallel arrays: a string array QDATA$() for the data and an integer array QLINK() for the links from item to item. This space will contain all of our queues, completely intermixed. For any given queue item X, the data will be in QDATA$(X), and QLINK(X) will point to the next item in the queue. We will use dynamic space management (*see* Chapter 7) to allocate the available space among the queues.

To separate the queues and to carry various control data about them, we define a set of arrays QH() and QT(). These are treated as parallel arrays, with the queue number as pin, so that the same element in each array belongs to the same queue. For example, QH(2) points to the head item of queue 2 in the queue space, and QT(2) points to the tail item (Figure 9-4). This is an open-ended design. If we later want to track additional information for each queue, we can simply add more parallel arrays.

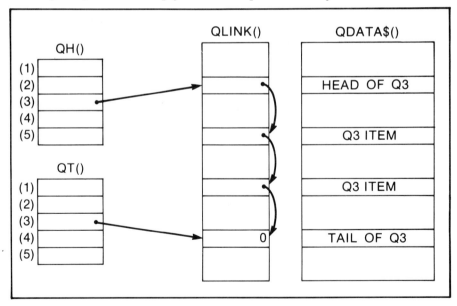

Figure 9-4. QLINK() and QDATA$() represent the dynamically managed queue space. QH() and QT() are auxiliary arrays to track the head and tail elements of each queue.

9.4 The Main Program

The FILLER program will be described in two sections. In this section are the BOSS and the main routines READER, WORDER, LINER, and WRITER. The supporting subroutines are described in the next section.

The BOSS is the driver routine for the entire program. It initializes arrays and enters the options from the keyboard. Then it gives control to each of the processing routines in turn, in a loop that ends when the last line of text has been entirely processed through all the queues and written to the output file.

One key to the design is that no one process keeps control for very long. Each subroutine does one small chore and returns control at once. Each iteration of the BOSS loop acts as a time increment during which each routine gets control once, so that the entire assembly line moves forward one small step. In effect, the BOSS loop slices time into discrete intervals, into tiny pauses between the tick-tock of the imaginary factory clock.

To keep track of the end of the text, the READER routine appends a special marker line containing ".EOTEXT." to the end of the input text. Each process uses a status variable to indicate whether or not it has processed this marker line. As the marker works its way through the queues, each process encounters it and sets its own status flag. After that, the process no longer works. When the status flag of the last process has been set, BOSS knows that the program is finished. It closes the files and stops.

```
: ^BOSS^                    ' Sub to supervise Filler program  :
:    DEFINT A-Z                                                 :
:    DIM QH(10), QT(10), QLINK(1000), QDATA$(1000)              :
:    QH(O)=1                   ' intialize dynamic space stack  :
:    FOR SO=1000 TO 1 STEP -1 : GOSUB ^RELEASE^ : NEXT SO       :
:    LINE INPUT  "Enter Source File Name  "; INFILE$            :
:    LINE INPUT  "Enter Target File Name  "; OUTFILE$           :
:    INPUT   "Enter text width  "; COLUMNS                      :
:    OPEN "I",1,INFILE$ : OPEN "O",2,OUTFILE$                   :
:    WHILE STOPWRITE=0     ' until WRITER detects text end      :
:       GOSUB ^READER^        ' read source lines from file     :
:       GOSUB ^WORDER^     ' break source lines into words      :
:       GOSUB ^LINER^           ' pack words into lines         :
:       GOSUB ^WRITER^             ' write lines to file        :
:    WEND                                                       :
:    CLOSE                                                      :
:    END                                                        :
```

The READER reads one line from the input file and appends it to queue 1. At the end of the file, it appends the ".EOTEXT." line to mark the end of the text for other routines. After that, it ignores all calls.

The WORDER routine breaks the text lines in queue 1 into individual words and writes them to queue 2. A word is defined as all text between blanks. Blank or empty input lines are passed on as null words (that is, as a null strings) in queue 2. This null word signals the end of a paragraph to the LINER routine downstream.

To simplify its work, WORDER reads each line into a temporary work string W$, which it then breaks into words. If it runs out of memory while breaking up a line, it returns control and continues processing the W$ string on the next call. (This technique of using a local private copy of data being processed is very useful in pipeline processing. It allows a routine to be interrupted at any point without having to worry about how to mark the exact processing place.)

This routine reads words from queue 2 and assembles them into lines in queue 3. One blank is inserted between each word.

```
+-------------------------------------------------------------------+
:  ^READER^                      ' Sub to read lines from file      :
:     IF STOPREAD THEN RETURN                 ' ignore calls?       :
:     IF QH(0)=0 THEN RETURN                  ' out of space?       :
:     GOSUB ^RESERVE^                   ' get an available slot      :
:     IF EOF(1)          ' on eof, set flag and force marker        :
:        - THEN STOPREAD=1 : QDATA$(S0)=".EOTEXT."                   :
:        - ELSE LINE INPUT #1, QDATA$(S0)       ' read a line       :
:     S2=1 : GOSUB ^APPEND^             ' append line to queue 1     :
:     RETURN                                                        :
:                                                                   :
:  ^WORDER^                      ' Sub to break lines into words     :
:     IF QH(1)=0 THEN RETURN                   ' out of lines?      :
:     IF QH(0)=0 THEN RETURN                   ' out of space?      :
:     IF W$<>"" THEN ^WORDER 2^           ' handle leftovers        :
:     W$=QDATA$(QH(1)):S1=1:GOSUB ^DROP^          'get a line       :
:     WHILE LEFT$(W$,1)=" ":W$=MID$(W$,2):WEND    ' unblank         :
:     IF W$="" THEN          ' if blank line, send null word        :
:        - S0=QH(0) : QH(0)=QLINK(S0) : QDATA$(S0)="" :             :
:        - S2=2 : GOSUB ^APPEND^ : RETURN                           :
:  ^WORDER 2^     ' move a word off working line to queue 2         :
:     GOSUB ^RESERVE^                      ' get a free slot        :
:     S1=INSTR(W$+" "," ")                   ' first blank          :
:     QDATA$(S0)=LEFT$(W$,S1-1) 'peel a word off into slot          :
:     S2=2 : GOSUB ^APPEND^          ' append word to queue 2       :
:     W$=MID$(W$,S1+1)                   ' shift past the word      :
:     WHILE LEFT$(W$,1)=" ":W$=MID$(W$,2):WEND    ' unblank         :
:     RETURN                                                        :
+-------------------------------------------------------------------+
```

Lines are packed to the maximum length specified by the user as COLUMNS.

LINER uses a local string LINER$ to temporarily hold the line being assembled. When a null word in queue 2 signals a blank line, the working string LINER$ is forced out to queue 3. Then a blank line is sent to queue 3.

The WRITER routine writes one line from queue 3 to the output file. As last process in the pipeline, WRITER has the added responsibility of watching for the .EOTEXT. marker and setting the status flag STOPWRITE. BOSS loops until this flag is set, then ends the program.

```
+------------------------------------------------------------------+
: ^LINER^     ' Sub to fill words from q2 into lines in q3         :
:    IF QH(2)=0 THEN RETURN                ' out of words?         :
:    IF QH(0)=0 THEN RETURN                ' out of space?         :
:    S$=QDATA$(QH(2)):S1=2:GOSUB ^DROP^    ' get next word         :
:    IF S$<>"" AND S$<>".EOTEXT." THEN ^LINER 2^                   :
:    IF L$<>"" THEN GOSUB ^LINER 4^ ' force partial line           :
:    L$=S$ : GOSUB ^LINER 4^ : RETURN      ' force word out        :
: ^LINER 2^    ' if word fits add it to line else new line         :
:    IF LEN(L$) + LEN(S$) + 1 <= COLUMNS                           :
:      - THEN L$=L$ + S$ + " "            ' add word to line       :
:      - ELSE GOSUB ^LINER 4^ : L$=S$+" "       ' new line         :
:    RETURN                                                        :
: ^LINER 4^                 ' Sub to send L$ to queue 3            :
:    GOSUB ^RESERVE^ : QDATA$(S0)=L$   ' get, fill a slot          :
:    S2=3 : GOSUB ^APPEND^              ' output it to queue 3      :
:    RETURN                                                        :
:                                                                  :
: ^WRITER^                  ' Sub to write lines to file           :
:    IF QH(3)=0 THEN RETURN               ' out of lines?          :
:    S$=QDATA$(QH(3)):S1=3:GOSUB ^DROP^        ' next line         :
:    IF S$<>".EOTEXT." THEN PRINT #2, S$ ELSE STOPWRITE=1          :
:    RETURN                                                        :
+------------------------------------------------------------------+
```

9.5 The Subroutines

Only a few support routines are needed to manipulate the queues and to allocate the dynamic queue space:

APPEND   Adds a data item to a queue
DROP   Deletes the head of a queue
RESERVE   Reserves a dynamic space node
RELEASE   Releases a dynamic space node

The APPEND routine takes the node S0 and adds it to the queue specified by S2. If the queue is initially empty, it must be set up by initializing its head and tail pointer QH() and QT(). Then the given node S0 is appended to the end of the queue by pointing the old tail link to it and setting its link to zero (since it is now the new tail).

The DROP routine deletes the first item of a queue. (It assumes that there is, in fact, an item in the queue.) All it needs to do, therefore, is to point the head of the queue to the second item in the queue (which becomes the new head). Then it releases the dropped node back to the available pool.

The RESERVE and RELEASE routines are a cooperating pair of dynamic storage management routines, as detailed in Chapter 7. To manage words and lines, we only need one node from the queue space at a time, that is, we can allocate fixed-size blocks of length 1. The queue space is prepared by forming it into a chain (*see* BOSS) and manipulating only the first node of the chain. The RESERVE routine sets S0 to the head node and points the head to the second node, in effect detaching the first node. The RELEASE routine reverses this process; it simply makes the node being released (S0) the new head node of the queue space. (To be more precise, the queue space is set up as a chain stack, as we will see in Chapter 10.)

Even though we reserve 1,000 nodes for the queue space QDATA$() here, in practice you will seldom use more than 100 nodes; they are constantly being recycled by the various routines along the assembly line. This is one of the charms of this design: it takes care of its own resource needs. We give the program a large queue space, and the routines share it among each other like well-behaved children, thus sparing us the headaches of having to figure out how much to allocate to each of them.

```
+--------------------------------------------------------------+
:  ^APPEND^      ' Sub to add data item S0 to end of queue S2  :
:     IF QH(S2)=0          ' if queue is empty, set it up      :
:        - THEN QH(S2)=S0 : QT(S2)=S0                          :
:        - ELSE QLINK(QT(S2))=S0 : QT(S2)=S0                   :
:     QLINK(S0)=0                  ' clear new tail pointer    :
:     RETURN                                                   :
:                                                              :
:  ^DROP^        ' Sub to release the first item of queue s1   :
:     S0=QH(S1) : QH(S1)=QLINK(S0) : GOSUB ^RELEASE^           :
:     RETURN                                                   :
:                                                              :
:  ^RELEASE^        ' Sub to release element S0 to free stack  :
:     QLINK(S0)=QH(0) : QH(0)=S0   'slot S0 is new top slot    :
:     RETURN                                                   :
```

```
:                                                              :
:   ^RESERVE^                   ' Sub to find an available slot S0  :
:      S0=QH(0)  :  QH(0)=QLINK(S0)        ' returns top slot    :
:      RETURN                                                    :
+-------------------------------------------------------------+
```

9.6 Design Review

Let's look at the FILLER program and review our strategy. Why did we select this pipeline design? Why not instead process each source line completely from beginning to end as it is read from the file? The best answer is: Try it! If you try to write the FILLER program as one single processing step, you find yourself quickly in a deeper and deeper logic swamp, looking for space to stash lines that spill, trying to track where the latest line is, and hoping that you won't get some error like "string too long" while trying to fill a line.

The assembly line design is much better. Let's list some of its advantages:

- It breaks the program into several steps. Each step focuses on just one process to be performed on the data stream. This is modular programming, and it is invariably the better design.
- It lets the program take care of its own space needs. When a step runs out of queue space, it waits until there is space. No need for you to spend hours anticipating all the possible situations under which you can run out of space.
- The program is easy to test. If a bug does develop, you will be able to tell by its nature which step or which queue is the most likely problem.
- The program is easy to document. The design is easily grasped even by a casual outsider. Details can be presented in logical units, as we did earlier, for each processing step.
- It is easy to extend the program. You can insert steps and queues anywhere, splitting them and joining them to build a complicated program structure.

9.7 Modifying the Program

The First Law of Programming states that NO PROGRAM IS EVER FINISHED. If the program does not work, it is not finished by definition. If the program works, it will either work poorly or well. If it works poorly, you will want you to correct it; if it works well, you will want to improve it.

Let's assume your boss has just told you to modify the **FILLER** program so that it writes out not a single stream of filled lines but a double stream of columns, side by side, neatly chopped into 8.5- by 11-inch pages, with 50 lines of text between the top and bottom margins. Because an 11-inch page can hold 66 lines, you must output 8 blank lines at the top of each page, 50 double-column text lines, and 8 blank lines as the bottom of each page.

If the paragraph immediately preceding this one is run through the program, the output file would look like this:

```
+----------------------------------------------------------------------+
:                                                                      :
:                                                                      :
:        Let's assume your        between the top and                  :
:     boss has just told you      bottom margins.                      :
:     to modify the FILLER        Because an 11-inch page              :
:     program so that it          can hold 66 lines, you               :
:     writes out not a single     must output 8 blank                  :
:     stream of filled lines      lines at the top of                  :
:     but a double stream of      each page, 50                        :
:     columns, side by side,      double-column text                   :
:     neatly chopped into         lines, and 8 blank                   :
:     8.5- by 11-inch pages,      lines as the bottom of               :
:     with 50 lines of text       each page.                           :
:                                                                      :
:                                                                      :
+----------------------------------------------------------------------+
```

To modify the **FILLER** program to output two columns, we design a routine called **PAGER**, which we substitute for the **WRITER** routine. PAGER accumulates the output lines, properly arranged side by side, until it has a full page. Then it writes out the page and sets up a new one. When it encounters the .EOTEXT. line, it forces out whatever page it has and sets STOPWRITE as before.

For assimilating the columns onto each page, we use a simple array PAGE$() as a temporary storage place. We know that each page will always be 66 lines long, so we can simply lay in the left column first, then append the text to force the right column. (The queue would be an incorrect choice of data structure here, because it does not permit direct access to its member items.)

PAGER uses the variable PC to keep track of which page column (1 or 2) is being filled, and the variable PL to track the next line (9–59) to be set on the page. When PL exceeds 58 we go to the next page column. When PC exceeds 2, we output an entire page of 66 lines and reset the page to null.

```
+--------------------------------------------------------------+
:  ^PAGER^       ' Sub to write text out as 2-column pages   :
:     IF QH(3)=O THEN RETURN              ' out of lines?    :
:     IF PC=O THEN GOSUB ^NEW PAGE^         ' fresh page?    :
:     S$=QDATA$(QH(3)) : S1=3 : GOSUB ^DROP^    ' next line  :
:     IF S$=".EOTEXT." THEN STOPWRITE=1 : GOTO ^PUT PAGE^    :
:     IF PC=1 THEN PAGE$(PL)=LEFT$(S$+SPACE$(40),39) ' set   :
:          - ELSE PAGE$(PL)=PAGE$(PL)+S$   'line into page   :
:     ·PL=PL+1 : IF PL>58 THEN PC=PC+1 : PL=9   ' next line  :
:     IF PC<3 THEN RETURN              ' is line full?       :
:  ^PUT PAGE^     ' Sub to output page and set up a new one  :
:     FOR I=1 TO 66 : PRINT #2, PAGE$(I) : NEXT I            :
:  ^NEW PAGE^               ' Sub to set up a fresh page     :
:     PC=1 : PL=9 : FOR I=1 TO 66 : PAGE$(I)="" : NEXT I     :
:     RETURN                                                 :
+--------------------------------------------------------------+
```

9.8 Uses for the Pipeline

Pipelining is a useful technique for any application that moves data through a number of different processing steps. Even applications with strictly sequential processing can benefit from pipelining because it segments the application into a stream of smaller processes. It modularizes the program into individual processing steps that are decoupled from each other and can be more easily changed and relocated in the processing sequence.

This is one form of "evolutionary programming." It is easy to lay out a complex data flow on paper and then to implement only some of the parts as phase I of the project. You simply provide empty pipes and have a few dummy routines that do nothing but move data from one queue to the next, until you get around to installing phase II.

But pipelining really earns its keep on applications where the data flow through the application is not strictly sequential. When several different data streams (text, figures, and footnotes) enter your program at different points, when each stream requires different processing, when some processes must wait for others (lay out pictures before text), when data streams merge (text and pictures), split (footnotes), double up (two columns per page), or defer to the end (references), that's when pipelining really shines.

Time for a war story. A long time ago, on one of my very first programming assignments, I had to generate a business report consisting of pages and pages of engineering part costs. At the end of the report were the totals for the various columns. Proudly I handed the report to my boss. He glanced at it, turned to me, and said "Very nice, but I'd like the totals at the beginning of the report."

That is the kind of problem where you can use pipelining: storing all the data in some long queue (in this case a temporary sequential file) until you can compute some key item (the totals). Then you can proceed to the next processing step (printing). This type of problem is called "n-pass processing" because you usually have to make n passes to the data to process them completely.

The image to remember here is that of a spiderweb, a system of pipes connected to processing points (Figure 9-5). Compare this with other processing paradigms such as serial processing (each step completely processes all data before the next step begins), timesharing (many processes work independently on independent data), or data base management (independent processes independently access a common data set).

The good uses for pipelining tend to be in the more complex applications. That does not mean they have to be huge projects on the order of the Federal Aviation Administration's air traffic control system. It means that they tend to have a certain special complexity, with time and space dependencies (such as presort, multiple output files), with logical surprises (totals at the begin-

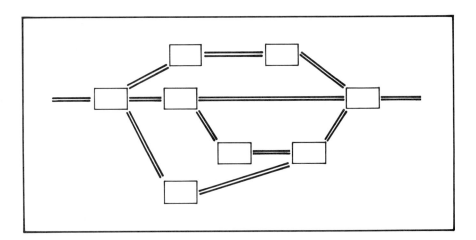

Figure 9-5. Pipelines can be connected to create processing networks.

ning), and with material that is generated and inserted in midstream by the program (diagnostics, page headers, footnotes). Here are some examples where pipelining could be especially useful:

- Consider the Los Angeles freeway system as a network of pipes that transport cars. A model of the system could be built with each exit as a subroutine and the traffic between exits as queues. The BOSS routine would become a giant simulation driver that would give each routine a slice of time in which each car could advance some small distance.

  Other routines could then be added to measure traffic flow, detect stoppages, reroute traffic, and study the effects of planned lane additions, preferential lane assignments, and similar proposals. You would have to use dynamic space management to allocate lane space to vehicles. When the program runs out of dynamic space, it would then simulate what Angelenos refer to as "Gridlock City".

- The Los Angeles freeway system is just one example of a whole class of transport system applications that can be more easily written with pipelining, for example farm irrigation, flood control, railroads, blood circulation, heating and air conditioning, waste recycling, electronic circuit analysis, and so on.

- A related use is for project resource management with PERT (project evaluation and review technique) and CPM (critical path method). These techniques break complex projects into connected tasks and then control the flow of time, resources, and labor for each task in order to meet some overall long-term goal.

- The PREBASIC program was presented in Chapter 2 as a simple two-pass serial process. It could benefit from being redesigned as a pipeline, because then it would be easier to add options that generate and suppress and reformat and insert source code.

- One kind of sort algorithm, called "sort–merge," is based on the fact that it is easier to merge several sorted streams than to sort one stream in place. Pipelining could be used to sort an input stream into several intermediate streams that are later merged into a sorted output stream. Pipelining for this use yields the important benefit that "user hooks" can be built in at various important points. User hooks simply let the user, that is, the program that is calling the sort routine, tap into the stream at various processing points to cull it, to assist in processing, or even to clone it for some secondary use such as sending it to a backup file.

- In this chapter, I only looked at pipelining in memory. It can also be applied to data sets stored on other media. For example, pipelining with RAM disk files should be very effective intermediate use of the fast RAM disk. As a last step, the output file would be piped to a real drive for permanent storage.

9.9 Summary

In Chapter 3, I talked about creating abstract data objects by surrounding data with routines. The pipeline concept is really just a continuation or enhancement of this idea. This time the primitive unit is a routine with a pipe or two going in one end, and one or more pipes coming out the other end. With this building block, we can build just about any structure that can be described.

But the difference this time is that this is not just a data object manipulated by a higher order program. A pipeline is a structure that is executable as a whole. It can be molded to simulate real-world systems more closely, it can be programmed to have specialized behavior patterns. It can also show intelligence because, in a special sense, it is a living data object.

The Stack

10.1 Introducing the Stack

A stack is a data object similar to a vertical pipe or well that is open at the top and sealed at the bottom. Data items enter and leave the stack only at the top. The stack is too narrow for data items to pass each other, so they always leave in the reverse order of their arrival.

The classic example of a stack, after which it was probably named, is a supply of clean dishes on the counter of a cafeteria serving line. The dishes are stored in a vertical well, on a spring-loaded stand that keeps the top dish level with the serving line. When the top dish is removed, the dish below it rises to become the new top dish.

Another example of a stack is the way we dress in layers of clothes. If in the morning a man puts on an undershirt, a shirt, a vest, a jacket, and finally a coat then he must remove them in the evening in reverse order: coat, jacket, vest, shirt, and undershirt. All day long he represents a walking clothes stack. This example illustrates the essential reversing property of the stack (Figure 10-1): data items are removed in exactly the reverse order they are added to the stack.

Accountants use a method of valuing inventory that assumes the last item bought will be the first one sold. They call this accounting method LIFO, meaning Last In First Out, to describe the way each item moves into and out of the inventory.

The stack is an unusual data object and some special terms are used with it. The stack itself is always visualized like the cafeteria dish stack: a vertical shaft, filled with data items. The "top" item is always the one last added to the stack; the "bottom" item is the oldest item on the stack.

Adding to the stack is called "pushing," reminiscent of pushing a dish on top of the dish stack. Removing an item is called

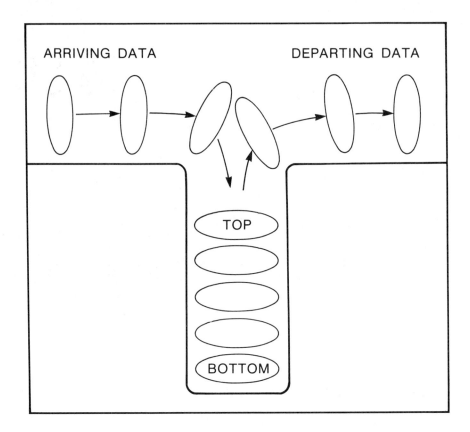

Figure 10-1. A typical stack. The top item in the stack was the last one to arrive and will be the first one to leave.

"popping" because as the top item is removed, the next one pops up to become the new top. A stack without any data items is called "empty." Attempting to pop an item from an empty stack generates a "stack underflow" condition. Stack "overflow" occurs when a stack is full, that is, when the space allocated to hold the stack has been filled.

10.2 Implementing a Stack

BASIC does not have the stack as a built-in data object; we must build our own. As always, this involves a physical data space and some operations on the data in it. We will look at various space objects, and we will need the three fundamental operations SET UP, PUSH, and POP. SET UP defines the data space for the stack and initializes its values to the empty stack. PUSH adds a new top value to the stack, and POP removes the top value from the stack.

The stack can be implemented in a variety of ways. Selection of a method depends on the data volume, the data types to be stacked, the data volatility (how often data items are popped and pushed), the data volume, the operations to be performed, and the available physical space. The stack implementations are much like those of the queue. Actually, the stack is easier to implement than the queue, because it only has one access end.

10.3 Implementing a Stack in a String

In Section 8.3, we implemented the queue in a string. The stack implementation is almost identical except that we add new items at the front instead of at the rear. Assuming that ST$ is a string of 1-byte items and BYTE$ is a single byte of data, we can implement the stack operations in a few statements. We assume a maximum string length of 255 here; for compiled programs, this could be raised to 32767:

```
' SET UP the stack
ST$=""

' PUSH an item to the stack
IF LEN(ST$)=255 THEN ^OVERFLOW^
ST$=BYTE$+ST$

' POP an item off the stack
IF ST$="" THEN ^UNDERFLOW^
BYTE$=LEFT$(ST$,1) : ST$=MID$(ST$,2)
```

One nice extension of string stacks is to define an array of strings, such as DIM ST$(20), and then to use each element of the array as a different stack. This is very effective in text processing and when the stacks are of different sizes as the program progresses. Another technique is to partition the string into larger units than just one character. For example, we can stack integer numbers if we use the MKI$ and CVI functions to convert them to and from string format.

It is also easy to stack string stacks on top of each other by the concatenation operation. This technique is helpful when stacks must be manipulated as a whole rather than just as pure stacks.

10.4 Implementing a Stack in an Array_____

A stack is easily implemented in an array (Figure 10-2). Cell 1 is always the bottom item, and the stack grows toward the higher subscripts. A special variable TOP, called the stack pointer, is used to point to the top element of the stack. When TOP = 0, the stack is empty.

The primitive stack operations are even simpler than they were for the queue. With the queue, we had to worry about the queue slowly creeping toward the bottom of the array, as data items were deleted at the bottom and added at the top. By contrast, all of the stack access activity is at the top of the stack, so the bottom can be permanently anchored.

To push an item, the stack pointer is incremented by 1, and the item is stored in the element to which it points. To pop an item, the top item is copied, and the stack pointer is decremented. As a result, the stack pointer always points to the top item of the stack.

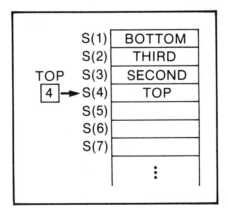

Figure 10-2. A stack implemented in array S(). Element S(4) is the current top item. Even though a particular stack is physically turned upside down, we always refer to the last item added as the top item.

Stack underflow is easily detected: if we agree that the bottom of the stack is anchored at subscript 1, we simply test the stack pointer for 0. Stack overflow, on the other hand, is imminent when the top item is in the largest available element, A(MAXDIM).

```
^SET UP^    ' initialize the empty stack
   DIM A(2000) : MAXDIM=2000
   TOP=0

^PUSH^   ' add ITEM to stack
   IF TOP=MAXDIM THEN ^OVERFLOW^
   TOP=TOP+1 : A(TOP)=ITEM

^POP^    ' remove top item into ITEM
   IF TOP=0 THEN ^UNDERFLOW^
   ITEM=A(TOP) : TOP=TOP-1
```

The stack does not have to start at element 1. Because the elements below the bottom of the stack are never accessed, they can be used effectively to store information about the stack, or as a basket array to keep special values such as options, modes, flags, and other global program information. The stack pointer initialization and underflow testing will have to be adjusted accordingly.

10.5 Implementing a Stack as a Chain

The chain is a linked list of data items and is ideally suited for use as a stack. We only need to track the head node to push and pop items. Assume we use parallel arrays INFO( ) and LINK( ) for the chain, and we use TOP to point to the stack top (Figure 10-3).

Here is the code for managing a chain stack.

```
^SET UP^   ' initialize chain stack
   DIM LINK(2000), INFO(2000)
   TOP=0

^PUSH^    ' add item in element (I) to stack
   LINK(I)=LINK(TOP)
   TOP=I

^POP^    ' remove item from stack
   ITEM=INFO(TOP)
   TOP=LINK(TOP)
```

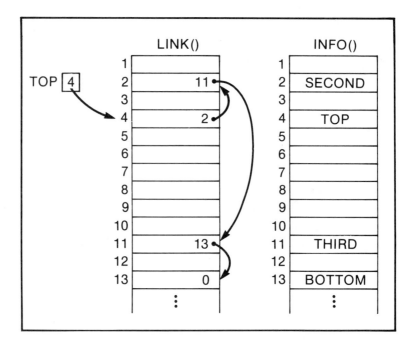

Figure 10-3. A stack installed as a chain in arrays LINK() and INFO().

The TOP variable points to the start of the chain at element 4. LINK(4) indicates that the second item in the chain is in element 2. The chain sequence is shown by the arrows, which are not stored. Element 13 is the last item in the chain and, thus, the bottom item in the stack. LINK(13) contains 0 to indicate that there are no more elements in the chain.

Compared to the array stack, the chain stack has the major advantage that we need not predict or reserve a maximum allocation for the chain stack. If we start a program by creating a single chain stack of all free memory cells, we can share memory among many different stacks by moving cells from stack to stack. Because a chain stack does not require a fixed space allocation, it can overflow only when the entire program runs out of memory. The technique of dynamically sharing space was discussed in Chapter 7.

10.6 Implementing a Stack as a File

A random access file can be treated as an array stored on disk. Thus, we can implement a file stack like an array stack. (The sequential file type is not suitable because it can only be processed as a queue.)

```
+--------------------------------------------------------------+
:  ^SET UP^     ' initialize the empty file stack              :
:     OPEN "R",1,"MYSTACK",128    ' record length 128          :
:     FIELD #1, 128 AS BUFFER1$   ' give buffer a name         :
:     MAXREC=1000           ' max record                       :
:     TOP=0                 ' stack pointer                     :
:                                                               :
:  ^PUSH^       ' write ITEM$ to file stack                     :
:     IF TOP=MAXREC THEN ^OVERFLOW^                             :
:     LSET BUFFER1$=ITEM$   ' move data into buffer            :
:     TOP=TOP+1             ' point to next record              :
:     PUT #1, TOP           ' write buffer to file              :
:                                                               :
:  ^POP^        ' read top record into ITEM$                    :
:     IF TOP=0 THEN ^UNDERFLOW^                                :
:     GET #1, TOP           ' read top record                   :
:     ITEM$=BUFFER1$        ' get data from buffer             :
:     TOP=TOP-1             ' point to new top record           :
+--------------------------------------------------------------+
```

At first glance, using a file as a stack seems terribly inefficient. Stacks tend to be used for short-term, rapid access processing, whereas file access requires relatively slow disk I/O. But if a RAM disk is used for the file stack, it is not hard to envision applications where a file stack would serve very well. For example, in data communications, one often has to accept a mix of messages of different priority levels. If the traffic is heavy and the outgoing channels are clogged, this can be like drinking from a firehose. To solve the problem, one can stack the lower priority messages and focus on the higher priority messages.

One useful technique is to reserve record 1 to store data about the file stack. The file pointer can also be stored there. This lets you save the file information when you close the file. Records in the middle of the file stack can, as discussed earlier, be accessed randomly—a bonus with this implementation. Finally, the whole stack can be deleted with one KILL "MYSTACK" statement.

10.7 Using the Stack

The stack appears rarely in the real world compared to other data objects such as the string and the queue. Inside programs, stacks are extensively used for language translation, for dynamic resource management, to build complicated data structures, to aid in preserving machine state before calling subroutines or functions, and to implement nested control structures as GOSUB-RETURN, FOR-NEXT, and WHILE-WEND loops. The many uses can barely be outlined here in the form of fundamental properties of the stack.

Tracking Items

The simplest use of the stack is as a data object to hold data for a while. Since a stack has only one access end, its access mechanism is exceedingly simple. So, quite apart from its fancier properties, a stack often serves as a collection device to hold items temporarily.

When you are in line at a salad bar, you don't care about the specific sequence of plates on the plate stack. The plates are interchangeable objects: one plate is as good as any other, and the spring-loaded mechanism is there just to hold them. No specific tray sequence needs to be maintained.

You can also use the stack like a shopping cart in a supermarket, to throw items in as you walk down the aisles. You need the stack just long enough to get to the cashier, and the cashier does not care about the order of the items inside the cart. (*See* Section 5.4.)

Sorting and Separating

Two stacks can be used to separate a data set into two classes, like sorting laundry. (That's what "sort" meant before it was adapted to mean arranging into ascending or descending key sequence). To separate a data stream, establish the needed stacks and then proceed to throw items into the proper stack by pushing them on their respective stacks.

Resource Allocation

Use the stack to allocate a limited supply of resources: time, disk space, file slots, buffers, screen areas, cafeteria trays, and so on. To share these among various processes, build a dynamic resource manager that uses a stack to track the resource. Like cafeteria customers, processes that need the resource take it from the stack; those that are finished with it recycle the resource to the stack. For an application, *see* Chapter 7, where a stack is used to track the memory space available for allocation to processes that need the space.

Reversing Order

The most interesting property of the stack is its ability to reverse the order of items in a sequence (Figure 10-4).

The reversing property of stacks is obviously useful when you need to invert a sequence. For example, a file may be sorted in ascending order, but it is to be processed in descending order.

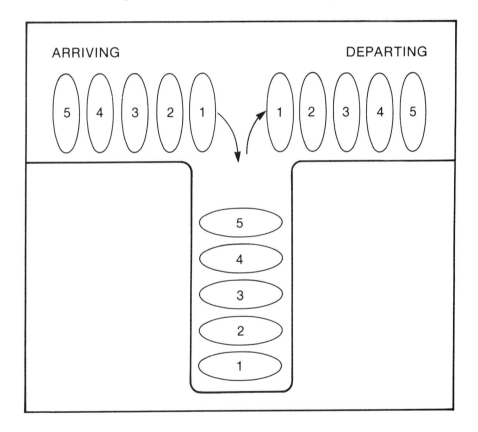

Figure 10-4. The reversing property of a stack.
Because items stored in a stack have to "back out" in LIFO (last in, first out) order, their sequence is exactly reversed as they emerge.

Without a stack, this is not an easy task; with a stack, it is a natural process.

A much more important use of the reversing property arises in the processing of a data stream that contains embedded countermanding commands, such as "BACKSPACE", or "IGNORE LAST LINE", or "NEVER MIND". The program cannot execute commands as it receives them because it may receive a countermanding command at any moment. The program can do nothing with the data stream but store it in a temporary place until the end is reached.

A typical example occurs in printing text strings. When you encounter five "backspace" characters (ASCII code 8), you must delete the previous five characters. This can be mighty difficult if they have already been printed on paper! One way to avoid this embarrassment is to stack all characters until you find the end of the line—then you are sure there will be no surprises. Whenever we encounter this need to "back out" items from a data object, we automatically think of a stack.

Saving Machine State

The concept of "machine state" (or "environment" as it is now called) is a fundamental notion of computer science. It considers every program, from the largest operating system to the smallest subroutine, to be a software mechanism with variables, flags, and functions instead of dials, valves, and levers. As the program runs, it changes some variables, opens some files, closes others, moves file pointers, changes contents of some records, starts some loops, and so on. For example, the BASIC statement CLS clears the screen and, thus, changes the machine state from "cluttered screen with cursor someplace" to "clean screen with cursor at row 1, column 1."

The current status and values of all the variables and settings and file pointers that are important to a program are collectively called its machine state. It represents the essence of a program; if you save a program's machine state, you can restore it days or weeks from now and continue exactly as if nothing has happened. Just like freeze-drying brewed coffee, you can interrupt any running program, save its machine state on a safe disk area, and pull the plug on the computer. Later you can reconstitute the program by loading its machine state back from the disk and continuing execution.

Can this really be done? Certainly. In fact, the concept of machine state and this particular use is what makes timesharing systems work. These systems typically have room inside their machine for maybe 10–20 user programs while they are actually servicing 100–1000 users. They achieve this leverage by rapidly swapping running user programs in and out of the machine in the form of machine states.

Context Switching

Context is simply another name for the machine state of a process, with more emphasis on the logical aspect, its meaning at some point in time. Machine state is a physical concept; context is its logical form. When you use a payroll program to process the payrolls for two different companies, you use the program in two contexts. When you change a pointer from one data object to another, you switch context. In the real world, when you return to a novel you were reading some days ago, you usually recall the context, that is, the setting, the characters, and the storyline of the book. You can do this even though you did not consciously memorize the novel's "machine state."

In general, if process A is interrupted by process B, the machine state of process A must be preserved before process B may proceed. If process B is itself interrupted by process C, process B's state must be saved before process C can proceed. When the latest process to interrupt finally finishes, the context of the prior process is restored, and it resumes execution. The saved contexts are restored one by one until we are back to level 0 where we started. I'm sure you have had one of those days at the office when one thing interrupts another until at the end of the day your desk is literally a "stack" of unfinished interrupted contexts.

The idea of context switching provides the mechanism by which we can accommodate the needs of programs to call each other, to share resources, and to retain their private values in private variable names. Stacks are excellent data objects for context switching because they let you quickly store any number of values in a way that you can reverse, that is, recover and continue later.

Stacks have unlimited depth, they preserve the original sequence of data, and they allow a variable number of items to be saved. A stack can be used to store nested contexts on top of each other and to be unstacked in reverse order. We will explore this in more detail in Chapter 11, where we worry about saving the machine state of the current program before it calls a subroutine.

Parameter Passing

One of the classic examples of context switching occurs in a program when you call a subroutine. A subroutine is really a program nested inside a program, and calling it is really changing context, if only for a moment. To communicate with a subroutine, the calling program must "pass parameters" to it. In many cases the subroutine must return an answer or an echo of some sort. Beginner's programs are small and can get away with using global variable names to pass parameters. But as the programs grow in complexity and as more subroutine levels are added, you need a better way. BASIC does not provide a mechanism for passing parameters locally to a subroutine, so we must invent our own.

The stack is a terrific vehicle for communicating with subroutines in this way. If a common stack is used for parameter passing throughout the program, at all levels, it gives the called routine a well-defined, shared data space for context switching. This parameter passing technique is used throughout the book with the global subroutine stack S( ) and S$( ). It is detailed in the next two chapters.

Recursion

Recursion involves a program calling itself. More precisely, a recursive program saves its own machine state and then calls itself as a subroutine in a slightly different context. Over many calls, the slight difference in context accumulates to cause a large effect; yet we never have to write complicated code that explicitly causes the effect.

Recursion is especially useful for processing data objects that can be subdivided into smaller versions of the same type. The string is an example: it can be broken into two smaller strings. Instead of processing one large complicated string, a program might decide to break it in two, stack the two halves, and then call itself twice to process each half in turn. This method would repeat until the strings had been reduced to a small enough size to process without further reduction. For an interesting application, *see* the binary search routine in Section 6.8 as well as Figure 6-10, where we repeatedly halve a chain until we find a desired insert point.

The stack is indispensable for implementing recursive code while retaining your sanity, since it automatically separates the various machine states as the program repeats a given task at lower and lower levels.

10.8 Stack Notation

There is a special flavor in programming with stacks. You have to learn to visualize them—how they store data and how they return them—and so a good way to acquire a taste for them is to play with them directly. In a moment, we will build two stack-based calculators; but first we need to set the stage with two notations for working with stacks.

The first notation describes the contents of stacks. Stacks are often visualized as vertical objects, but they are usually implemented without any particular physical direction. Moreover, they are documented in writing from left to right. The stack's reversing property adds to the confusion; thus, merely listing a stack's contents such as [CHOPIN MOZART GRIEG BRAHMS] is ambiguous about whether CHOPIN or BRAHMS is the top item. The following convention turns out to be the most natural and the easiest one to remember:

> Items on a stack are listed in the order they were pushed to create the stack.

In this notation, a list of stack items always ends with the top item. Thus, the composer stack [CHOPIN MOZART GRIEG BRAHMS] tells us that item CHOPIN was pushed first, then MOZART, then GRIEG, and finally BRAHMS. Therefore, BRAHMS must be the top item. If the stack contains many items, we usually start the list with an ellipsis (three dots) and list only the top three or four items:

[... NIXON FORD CARTER REAGAN]

Now it is easier to describe a sequence of push and pop operations by using item lists in brackets to show what the stack contains at certain points. We start with an empty stack[ ] and push an item ANT onto it and show the resulting stack as [ANT]. Then we push an item FOX, resulting in [ANT FOX]:

[] push ANT [ANT] push FOX [ANT FOX]

If you remember the simple calculators that used a stack to hold the result, you'll probably remember the sequence required to, say, obtain 3 + 2 − 4:

[] 3 = [3] 2 + [5] 4 − [1]

That is the sequence in which the numbers had to be entered.

The stack contents [n] were always displayed in the calculator's window.

The second notation commonly associated with stacks is called "Polish Notation," after the Polish logician Jan Lukasiewicz (1878–1956). As early as 1924, he proved that—no matter how complex—expressions involving the form A + B can always be rewritten by stripping out the operator and placing it before or after the operands, in the form +AB (prefix notation) or AB+ (postfix notation). Postfix notation is also know as reverse Polish notation (RPN).

In RPN, the operands of an expression appear first, followed by the operation. Instead of writing "A + B / C" we write "A B + C /". If BASIC were written in RPN, we would not write A$ = MID$(B$,2,5) but B$ 2 5 MID$ A$ =.

For our purposes in this chapter, the key properties of RPN expressions are that they require no parentheses and that their operands are available to the program before their operation code is encountered. RPN simplifies processing significantly, because the operands can be pushed on to a stack, and the stack can then be passed to the appropriate routine to perform the operation. This method is how we will build the cheap calculator in the next section.

10.9 A Cheap Stack Calculator

For our first project, we will write a program called 4BANGER to simulate a simple desk calculator. In the trade these cheapies are known as a "four-bangers," because they only have four arithmetic operations: add, subtract, multiply, and divide. Not only that, they use Polish Notation because it is the easiest way to implement one of these things. That means you enter the numbers first, then you enter the operator, entering 123 456 + to add 123 to 456.

Our 4BANGER has the same four operations, plus one to print the result. It also uses the postfix or RPN notation:

Syntax	Code	Operation
12 3 + [15]	+	Add
12 3 − [9]	−	Subtract
12 3 / [4]	/	Divide
12 3 * [36]	*	Multiply
[... 2 1] = [... 2]	=	Print and Pop

4BANGER's central mechanism is a simple number stack. You can enter one or more operations as a single line such as 488 127 − = to subtract 127 from 488 and display the result. The line is broken into "words" at the blanks. If a word is not an operation, for example, 488, it is simply pushed on the stack. If a word is an operation, it is performed at once by using the numbers already on the stack, and the result is pushed back onto the stack.

The detailed steps done to perform "488 127 − =" follow.First, the program encounters the item "488" which—not being an operation—is pushed on the stack. Next, the program encounters the item "127" which is also pushed on top of the stack by the same rule. The stack now contains [488 127]. When the program encounters the minus sign, it recognizes this as an operation code and gives control to the appropriate subroutine. The subroutine pops two numbers off the stack, subtracts them, and pushes the result back onto the stack. Finally, the equal sign is also executed as an operation. Its function is to pop a number off the stack and display it. The program outputs 361 and prompts for the next statement.

Without an = operation the program does not display the result of an operation, it merely leaves it on the stack. This lets you perform chain calculations involving several steps whose intermediate results are of no interest. For example, to compute the sum of three numbers, you can enter

12 34 45 + +

which performs 34 45 + first, leaving [12 79] on the stack. The second + operator then continues the chain calculation; it performs 12 79 + and leaves the answer 91. The 79 left from the previous calculation is used in the second addition as if it had come from the keyboard.

What we have here is the abstract data object in its purest form (*see* Chapter 3). All that follows in this chapter hinges on this idea, so it is worth restating: The stack acts as a physical storage space for the numbers of interest at some given moment; it contains the calculator's entire machine state. The stack is surrounded by operation subroutines that push and pop numbers according to well-defined rules. The subroutines all take their inputs from the stack and leave their results on the stack. The whole thing resembles a giant anthill, with the stack as the queen at the center, fed and protected by scurrying ants.

If an undefined operation is entered, it is treated as a zero and pushed to the stack. If you look closely, you will see an internal operation called PUSH. The user cannot see it, but the program uses it to push undefined operations onto the stack. It is a "primitive" operation, an internal operation out of which others can be composed. We will see more of this in the next section.

Note also that the program uses the usual subroutine stack S$( ) and S( ) to input and process the command lines. This stack has nothing to do with the stack used by 4BANGER to store the user's numbers. But it works, essentially, on the same principle. Thus, inside the inner WHILE-WEND loop, library routine peels the next word and pushes it on top of the S$() stack. After the word is processed, it is dropped with the statement S = S − 1.

```
^4BANGER.PRE^    ' Simulate a simple calculator
    DIM S$(9),S(9)    ' the subroutine stack
    DIM ST#(500)      ' the 4-banger stack
    SP=0              ' and stack pointer
    WHILE 1           ' main command loop
        ' accept a user command line
        LINE INPUT "Next?  "; S$(S)
        ' drop framing blanks and single up
        S(S)=11 : GOSUB ^BLANKS.LIB^
        WHILE S$(S)<>""   ' until line is empty
            ' peel and push word onto S$(S)
            GOSUB ^PEEL1.LIB^
            ' execute the word
            ON 1+INSTR("+-*/=",S$(S))
                - GOSUB ^PUSH^, ^+^, ^-^, ^*^, ^/^, ^=^
            S=S-1      ' pop the word
            WEND
    WEND
        ' the operation subroutines
^PUSH^  SP=SP+1:ST#(SP)=VAL(S$(S)):RETURN
 ^+^    SP=SP-1:ST#(SP)=ST#(SP)+ST#(SP+1):RETURN
 ^-^    SP=SP-1:ST#(SP)=ST#(SP)-ST#(SP+1):RETURN
 ^*^    SP=SP-1:ST#(SP)=ST#(SP)*ST#(SP+1):RETURN
 ^/^    SP=SP-1:ST#(SP)=ST#(SP)/ST#(SP+1):RETURN
 ^=^    PRINT ST#(SP):SP=SP-1:RETURN
```

That is, essentially, the entire code contained in those calculators that used to cost $15 and more. This utterly simple program is capable of some surprisingly complicated calculations. But our first objective is to use it to become more familiar and comfortable with the nature of a stack and with entering operations in the form operands first, operation last.

1. To confirm the reversing property of the stack:

        1 2 3 4 5 = = = = =

2. Some simple operations to verify that the program is working correctly

```
3.456  1.111   +  =
99999  99999   *  =
14400  12000  /  =
```

3. More complicated expressions

```
100  100  +  50  /  =
100  100  50  +  /  =
```

4. Play with formulas. The area of any circle is 3.1416 times the square of its radius. For a circle of radius (say) 27, the area can be calculated this way

```
27  27  *  3.1416  *  =
```
              or
```
27  27  3.1416  *  *  =
```
              or
```
27  3.1416  *  27  *  =
```

For a rude shock, multiply your monthly mortgage payment by the number of years left to pay by 12. It will probably come out to 3 or 4 times what you originally borrowed:

```
750  30  12  *  *  =
```

5. An average of, say, five numbers can be calculated like this:

```
12  35  +  23  +  40  +  81  +  5  /  =
```
              or
```
12  35  23  40  81  +  +  +  +  5  /  =
```

6. Use floating-point numbers and numbers in scientific notation:

```
45.6E35  39D34  -  =
```

The 4BANGER program illustrates the use of a stack as the central data object of a program around which various operations are grouped. It can serve as a simple calculator; but I hope that it has also demonstrated, at a simple level, that stacks are not just another way to mess with an array. Stacks and their reversing and nesting properties offer powerful capabilities to even the most simplistic program. We exploit this aspect of the stack some more in the next section.

10.10 A Better Stack Calculator

Four functions are quite limiting. You will soon want to add other arithmetic functions such as square root, power, and percentage. You will want some special functions to manipulate the stack directly, such as printing the entire stack or duplicating the top item.

So let's expand the 4BANGER program until it contains all of our favorite functions. Let's call this version BANGER to denote its power yet to remind us that it is still a modest little calculator at heart.

Here are the steps to add a new function to BANGER.

1. Define the function's operation and select a symbol for it. For example, let's add a function to compute a percentage and call it "%".
2. Specify the function carefully so that it fits in with the stack concept. The percentage function will divide the second stack number by the top number, multiply the result by 100, and leave it on the stack. Then we can enter 15 60 % = to print 25.
3. Install the new operation symbol in the program, where the program tests the command S$(S) and then calls the operation subroutine. The % symbol is added, so we now test "+−*/=%" and the ∧%∧ routine is added to the end of the GOSUB statement.
4. Write the operation code as a subroutine and append it to the program. In writing this code, take full advantage of the existing routines. For example, the percentage routine simply calls the divide routine first, then pushes 100 and calls the multiply routine.

Here, then, is the BANGER program, a calculator with the following operations:

Syntax	Code	Operation
12 3 + [15]	+	Add
12 3 − [9]	−	Subtract
12 3 / [4]	/	Divide
12 3 * [36]	*	Multiply
3 12 % [25]	%	Percentage
2 3 T [8]	T	To the power
16 R [4]	R	Square root
2 3 S [3 2]	S	Swap top and second items
7 D [7 7]	D	Duplicate top item
[... 2 1] = [... 2]	=	Print and Pop top item

```
+-------------------------------------------------------------------+
: ^BANGER.PRE^    ' A fancier calculator                            :
:    DIM S$(9),S(9)    ' the subroutine stack                       :
:    DIM ST#(500)      ' the banger stack                           :
:    SP=0              ' and stack pointer                          :
:    WHILE 1           ' main command loop                          :
:       ' accept a user command line                                :
:       LINE INPUT "Next?  "; S$(S)                                 :
:       ' drop framing blanks and single up                         :
:       S(S)=11 : GOSUB ^BLANKS.LIB^                                :
:       WHILE S$(S)<>""   ' until line is empty                     :
:          ' peel and push word in caps onto S$(S)                  :
:          GOSUB ^PEEL1.LIB^ : GOSUB ^UPPERC.LIB^                   :
:          ' execute the word                                       :
:          ON 1+INSTR("+-*/=TRSD%",S$(S)) GOSUB ^PUSH^,             :
:             - ^+^,^-^,^*^,^/^,^=^,^T^,^R^,^S^,^D^,^%^             :
:          S=S-1      ' pop the word                                :
:       WEND                                                        :
:    WEND                                                           :
:          ' the operation subroutines                              :
:    ^PUSH^ SP=SP+1:ST#(SP)=VAL(S$(S)):RETURN                       :
:     ^+^     SP=SP-1:ST#(SP)=ST#(SP)+ST#(SP+1):RETURN              :
:     ^-^     SP=SP-1:ST#(SP)=ST#(SP)-ST#(SP+1):RETURN              :
:     ^*^     SP=SP-1:ST#(SP)=ST#(SP)*ST#(SP+1):RETURN              :
:     ^/^     SP=SP-1:ST#(SP)=ST#(SP)/ST#(SP+1):RETURN              :
:     ^=^     PRINT ST#(SP):SP=SP-1:RETURN                          :
:     ^T^     SP=SP-1:ST#(SP)=ST#(SP)^ST#(SP+1):RETURN              :
:     ^R^     ST#(SP)=SQR(ST#(SP)):RETURN                           :
:     ^S^     SWAP ST#(SP),ST#(SP-1):RETURN                         :
:     ^D^     SP=SP+1:ST#(SP)=ST#(SP-1):RETURN                      :
:     ^%^     GOSUB ^/^:S$(S)="100":GOSUB ^PUSH^:GOSUB ^*^         :
:            RETURN                                                 :
+-------------------------------------------------------------------+
```

Look closely at the program, to see how the % operation is implemented. It uses the divide, push, and the multiply operations to do its work. This is one big hint for us: Stack-based operations become simpler and simpler the more operations we add. We can internally use those operations we have already built to construct new ones. We stand on our own shoulders, to put it recursively.

To exercise this program, use the same examples just given for 4BANGER. Now you can also use the new commands to build more complicated lines. In fact, the program can be a handy little calculator to do all kinds of things for you.

For example, given the length of the sides A and B of a right triangle, the length H of its hypotenuse is the square root of the sum of its squares, that is, H = ROOT (A*A + B*B). If the sides are 3 and 4, the hypotenuse is always 5. You could use **BANGER** to compute the hypotenuse with this command line

```
3  3  *  4  4  *  +  R  =
```
or
```
3  D  *  4  D  *  +  R
```
or even
```
3  4  D  *  S  D  *  +  R  =
```

The last one is particularly interesting. It starts out with the sides A and B on the stack and then juggles the numbers on the stack with the D and S operations. It shows that we can just push the two parameters 3 and 4 onto the stack and then perform the operations D * S D * + R = . Since these contain no parameters, we could define it as a new operation. Perhaps you would like to try your hand at adding the H operation to BANGER, in the form of the following subroutine. Don't forget to add the H command to the line that tests for it and calls the subroutine.

```
+----------------------------------------------------------------+
:    ^H^     ' hypotenuse ===    D * S D * + R =.                 :
:            GOSUB ^D^    ' to duplicate top                      :
:            GOSUB ^*^    ' to multiply top by second             :
:            GOSUB ^S^    ' to swap top and second                :
:            GOSUB ^D^    ' to duplicate again                    :
:            GOSUB ^*^    ' to square second side                 :
:            GOSUB ^+^    ' to sum the squares                    :
:            GOSUB ^R^    ' to take the root                      :
:            RETURN                                               :
+----------------------------------------------------------------+
```

Hypotenuses may not be your cup of tea, but the point is that you can evolve BANGER-type programs into your personalized programming language. You can add operations and build others out of old ones to develop any personalized application, be it compound interest, paperhanging, tire wear estimates, real estate, nutrition, engineering, medicine, accounting, law, or jogging.

The Library

Over the years, a programmer accumulates many useful software tools. These tools come in many forms—subroutines, macros, tables, utilities, skeletons, file descriptions, templates, menus, batch procedures, and isolated code fragments. To make effective use of this wealth of work and experience, programmers typically organize and store them in the form of a library.

Properly designed, a software library lets the programmer use past work again and again, without having to reinvent the wheel for every program. A library speeds program development because the tools are readily accessible, well documented, and more reliable than fresh code. Using a library leads naturally to modularized programs that are easy to describe and to extend. In short, a good library is the programmer's best friend.

Presenting the library topic involves three distinct viewpoints or levels. There is the grand concept of a library as a data base specially structured for program development. Then there are the general properties of each member, required to make such a library work. Finally, a sample set of specific subroutines is needed to illustrate the coding techniques and to support some of the programs developed in the book.

These viewpoints are not arbitrary or artificial; they represent three major roles played by every programmer: analysis, specification, and coding. Programmers typically analyze the general requirements of the overall project, develop the detailed specifications for each component, and write the program units for the components.

I have, therefore, arranged the library topic into three chapters. This chapter is concerned with the general concept of and uses for a software library. The next chapter focuses on the typical library subroutine and the properties it must have to fit nicely into the library and cooperate with other library routines. The third chapter, Our Library, presents examples and specific library routines used throughout the book.

11.1 User Requirements

A subroutine library is essentially a collection of subroutines supported by operations to store subroutines, to access, display, index, and print them. One specialized operation is the ability to automatically incorporate selected subroutines as working code into programs under development. In addition, library rules must be established to be followed by the library routines, so that they can be used easily in any application without interfering with the program logic.

Every programming project starts with some form of user requirement statement, whether developed into a formal document or just thought of as a vague objective. The formal theory is that users present "user requirements" to programmers who then design "program specifications" which they use to write the program "code." In practice, programmers often develop the requirements document themselves after interviewing the users and studying their current procedures and policies. In the case of our library, we will ourselves be the users, so let's write down the main features we require:

- We want to set up and maintain a collection of subroutines as a library in machine-readable form. The routines must be stored on disk as standard text files, so that we can use standard text editor and utility programs to maintain the library.
- We want the PREBASIC program to automatically load subroutines as they are referenced in the main program. Therefore, each routine must be written in PREBASIC and stored as an individual file that can be selectively accessed and incorporated into a program.
- For maximum flexibility, any routine must be able to call any other routine, pass data *to* it, and receive data *from* it. This includes the ability for a library routine to call another library routine and even to call itself recursively.
- To avoid interfering with the main program code (and with each other), subroutines cannot use arbitrary names for variables or line labels. There must be a simple yet specific naming scheme, and exceptions must be clearly documented.
- Since a subroutine will be a part of a large application that requires control of the computer, a subroutine must handle its own errors and must return control to its caller unless otherwise documented.

- A subroutine must not change the contents of any hardware or software variables except as documented. No undocumented side effects are allowed. A subroutine must always leave the machine in a predictable state.

Note that each requirement of this wish list includes a reason for the requirement. It is usually easier to understand and implement a rule if you know the reason for it. In designing a program, it is often simpler to implement a desired feature in some way other than that specified. By stating the reason for the requirement, it is easier to decide how much the rules can be bent, and what the important consequences are. It is also helpful to distinguish the global (library) from the local (subroutine) level.

11.2 Storing and Accessing

We can use the standard DOS directory and file scheme to store our library. Our library subroutines will be stored on disk as standard sequential text files, without any special file formats or line delimiters. Library files will be written and updated with any text editor that handles standard text files. To distinguish library files, we decide to use the file name extent ".LIB". This will help us identify library routines in source programs, but it is not essential to the scheme.

In the chapter on PREBASIC, we developed a source language preprocessor program that converts the un-numbered, symbolic-label source code used throughout this book into standard numbered BASIC. PREBASIC includes a feature for automatic inclusion of library routines from a library disk. When PREBASIC cannot find a label, it searches the library disk for a matching file name and appends that file to the source code being processed. To cause a subroutine to be loaded, all you have to do is mention the name as a label anywhere in your code. For example, to convert a string to uppercase letters:

```
+---------------------------------------------------------------+
:      S$(S) = "string to be capitalized"                       :
:      GOSUB ^UPPERC.LIB^                                        :
+---------------------------------------------------------------+
```

The GOSUB ^UPPERC.LIB^ statement causes PREBASIC to load the file UPPERC.LIB from the library disk, append it to the source program, and record its label name in the label table.

Subsequent GOSUB ^UPPERC.LIB^ statements will find the label in the table and use it as if it had been part of the main program from the beginning. Hence, duplicate loading of routines is no problem.

If a library routine itself references another missing routine, the loading process will be repeated to load the secondary reference. In this manner, you can automatically load an entire hierarchy of programs with just one simple label reference. This can be a very useful program development tool, as we will discuss later in this chapter.

The effect of this design is that you can freely reference library routines in your source programs without having to track their names or worry about including them. That is all taken care of by PREBASIC, and you can focus on the task at hand: writing good source code for the main application.

11.3 Subroutine Documentation _____

Much has been said and written about the need for good program documentation. Much of it criticizes programmers for not documenting. Much of it misses the following points, in my opinion.

First, when you think about it, a source program *is* the primary documentation. After all, a source program is not a "program" at all, since the computer never executes it. Strictly speaking, a source program (including both code and comments) is exactly what lay people mean by documentation: a description of what the computer will do at execution time. It is the primary document for the program. It is not unreasonable to argue that, having written and debugged the program, the programmer's job is finished.

Second, documenting is a different activity than **programming**. A surgeon does not write a textbook about every operation. A composer does not write a reference manual on how a symphony was constructed or on how it should be played. Why should programmers be expected to write outlines, summaries, tutorials, walkthroughs, flowcharts, data diagrams, reference manuals, user manuals, cross references, indexes, operator manuals, advertising copy, sales brochures, and so on? Documentation is the job of technical writers, not of programmers.

Third, and as a consequence of the first two points, programmers hate to document. Having already documented the program as source code and comments, all other documentation is repetition. Programmers resent being asked to do something that is not their job. They feel that if managers want programs to be more extensively documented, they should establish a technical documentation department.

Fourth, one of the classic reasons programmers avoid comments in source code is that comments often cost space and time during execution. Programmers intuitively avoid anything that makes programs slow or bulky. If language designers want programmers to comment, don't penalize programs for being commented.

Having said that, where does it leave us and our library? Since the source program is supposed to be the primary program document, the place to document a program is in the program itself. If you generate documents separate from the program code, the two documents will soon get separated and will soon get out of sync as you modify one or the other separately. You learn quickly to mistrust separate documentation, even if you can find it.

Every subroutine should include its own documentation in the form of source comments. Then you can have a complete hardcopy of the library in a binder by your side when you write new code. Nothing less works. The documentation *must* be right there, or you will not use it. You will guess, and you will guess wrong.

With PREBASIC, comments don't cost us anything at execution time. PREBASIC has an option that deletes all comments before generating the BASIC code, you can include pages of documentation in your source code without the slightest penalty at execution time.

11.4 Handling Global Variable Names

One of the side effects of constructing a program out of independent routines is the possibility that they may use the same name for different variables. The extent of this problem depends on the "scope" of variable names in the language being used. Is a name known only within the procedure or subroutine where it is declared (that is, locally) or is it known throughout the program (that is, globally)?

Since no block or procedure boundaries are found inside a

BASIC program, BASIC has only global names. Every variable name is known everywhere inside the program, any subroutine can change the contents of any variable. BASIC is definitely NOT the language of choice if you have to combine code from uncooperative, hostile, competitive, or ignorant programmers!

The lack of local names poses a problem for us if we want to modularize a program or to use a subroutine library. We want to give subroutines a little privacy, so they can do their work without interfering with our variables. On the other hand, we need to communicate with subroutines, to pass parameters to them and to receive results. How can we ever hope to write a generalized subroutine, one that will work far into the future, when we don't know what variable names to use?

How can we solve the problem of global variable names in BASIC? The solution is to manipulate data values, not data names. Remember the old joke:

Man to Doctor: "It hurts when I do this."
Doctor to Man: "Don't do this."

If global variables hurt, don't use them. Use one common variable name that is used by every subroutine. How can you pass more than one value if you only have one variable name? Use an array. How can you avoid values interfering with each other inside the array when subroutines themselves call other subroutines to several levels? Use the array as a stack.

To call a subroutine with a set of data values, push the values on top of the stack and call the routine. The routine knows how many values to expect and peels them off the stack. If the routine needs some temporary local variables for its work, it pushes and pops them on and off the stack. If the subroutine itself wants to call a subroutine, it repeats the process, pushing its own parameters on top of the stack before it calls. Given a large enough stack, this mechanism works to any desired level of subroutine nesting as well as for routines that call themselves recursively.

The net result is that routines have all the space they need for their values, without using more than a single variable name: the name of the stack. The idea of passing parameters via a stack is developed in more detail in Chapters 10 and 12.

11.5 The Subroutine Stack

To implement the idea of a subroutine stack, we reserve some specific variable names. All begin with the letter "S":

Global Names Used by All Subroutines

S	S$	S%	S!	S#
S()	S$()	S%()	S!()	S#()
S0-S9	S0$-S9$	S0%-S9%	S0!-S9!	S0#-S9#

We agree in every program to dimension the integer array S( ) and use the integer variable S as pointer to the current top of the stack. (We decide not to use S%( ) and S% simply because the percent symbol adds keystrokes and confusion. To compensate, we agree to always preface all our programs with the statement DEFINT S, which automatically treats all variable names S as S%.)

We also agree to dimension a string stack S$( ), because—as we will see—the string is a powerful tool for formatting and passing parameters. The S$( ) array will be parallel to S( ), so that we only need one stack pointer for both. This gives us a single stack with one stack pointer S and yet lets us pass both integer and string variables. (We reserve the right to dimension S!( ) and S#( ) as additional parallel stack arrays, for those applications that manipulate floating-point numbers.)

In addition to these arrays, we reserve a specific set of names to be used as individual variables. Individual variables are convenient to have around and are necessary in some cases. For example, many BASIC dialects do not let you use an array element as a FOR-NEXT loop control variable; you need a plain integer variable for that. As another example, it is much faster and cleaner to reserve and release dynamic storage with a global integer variable. String function calls are simpler if you can use S$ and S1 instead of S$(S+5), and so on. Finally, array references such as S(3) require computations behind the scenes. In high-iteration loops, execution time can be saved by referencing individual variables rather than array elements.

Therefore, we agree to reserve the individual variable names S$, S!, and S# as well as S0-S9, S0$-S9$, S0!-S9!, and S0#-S9#. These variables are officially declared to be "fair game." They can be changed by any subroutine without notice. As a result, they are only useful in code where there is no intervening subroutine call. If you call a subroutine, you must expect these special variables to be destroyed, either by the subroutine itself or by subroutines it calls in turn.

On the other hand, the subroutine stack is completely controlled and predictable. Because a subroutine is only authorized to pop its own set of values off the stack, the rest of the stack is perfectly safe, regardless of how many call levels are already stacked on it. Moreover, when it returns, every subroutine must leave the stack pointer S set to the top of the stack as expected by the caller. (This must be documented for each subroutine). If these rules are followed, the stack can be used to save data across subroutine calls to any nesting level.

11.6 The Machine State Problem

Chapter 10 introduced the concept of machine state and how to switch context by using a stack. These ideas find significant application in designing a library. If we plan to modularize our programs, we must be extremely careful to handle the machine state for each module correctly. When program A passes control to program B, program B expects a certain machine state. When program B returns control to program A, program A equally expects a certain machine state.

The fact is that—with regard to machine state—calling a subroutine is the same as returning from a subroutine. Beginning programmers quickly learn that things must be set up carefully before calling a subroutine. But they often do not think just as carefully about setting things up before executing a RETURN statement. I suspect that this is caused partly by the very misleading word "subroutine". The prefix "sub" implies that the subroutine has a lower status than the calling routine, and that, therefore, its returning control is not nearly as "important" as the original call. After all, how much importance can some "lowly" square root subroutine have compared to the "mighty" program that controls the Space Shuttle?

The fact is that, after program A passes control to program B, program A is quite helpless until program B passes control back with the correct machine state. The "lowly" square root subroutine can bring down the Space Shuttle by returning an incorrect value, by popping more values off a stack than it is authorized, by pushing extraneous values onto a stack, by entering an infinite loop, by calling another routine that fails to return, by displaying a false error message on some control screen, and so on.

This problem is not limited to calling subroutines. Much has been written about the "dangerous" GOTO statement. Entire languages have been designed to eliminate it. But the GOTO statement cannot be the problem. (If it were, few programs would work correctly, since assembly language programs are full of Jump and Branch statements).

True, beginners tend to abuse the GOTO, but they also abuse arrays and files and loops and even innocent PRINT statements! The problem is that beginning programmers are rarely taught this business of machine states. The GOTO statement is tricky, precisely because—as innocent as it looks—it can transfer control to another part of the program without necessarily preparing the machine state first. We know better than to call a subroutine without setting up its parameters; we tend not to think about setting up the machine state before using the GOTO.

In summary, many nasty program bugs are caused by setting up the wrong machine state for a loop or a subroutine, by inadvertently destroying the correct machine state, or by forgetting to set up the correct machine state before continuing after a loop or returning from a routine.

If you want to design better programs with fewer difficult bugs, you might adopt the view of programs as a set of modules (of equal status) that share machine states in predictable ways. At execution time, program modules are like a group of aerial acrobats: For a trick to work, every trapeze must be at the right place at the right time. The key to staying alive in the three-ring circus of computing lies in how machine states are juggled between modules.

11.7 Handling Specific Machine States⎯⎯

To design a successful subroutine library, we must pay careful attention to the policies for switching context, that is, for setting up and passing machine state to other modules and back. If we decide something is a global state, then we mean that it must be preserved across a subroutine call; it must be restored exactly before returning control to a caller. On the other hand, local machine state can be changed by anyone locally, so nobody expects it to be preserved.

Once you decide to list them, it is amazing how many different states must be considered. Here is a list of the more common ones to be considered; some are detailed later in this chapter and the next one.

- We explored the topic of global variable names in this chapter. The general rule we developed is that variable names may not be referenced inside subroutines except for the special name series starting with "S". There are some circumstances where subroutines reference other global variables, such as in Error and Function Key Handling. Such special exceptions are always documented with the subroutine; the normal way to communicate data values is via the subroutine stacks S( ) and S$( ).

- FOR-NEXT loops must be formally exited under all circumstances. If a subroutine leaves a loop prematurely, it leaves a mechanism behind that consumes a little memory. No harm is done over a few calls, and the bug lies dormant. But after many calls, it can cause memory overflow and strange aborts. On the other hand, it is perfectly proper to abandon a WHILE-WEND loop, because it was designed not to leave a mechanism behind. (*See* Chapter 1 for details.)

- The best way to handle files is generally to open and close them outside the subroutine. A subroutine that reads or writes a file should only know the channel it is using and the data to be transmitted, because that way it is more independent of file names and opening modes.

- The contents of the screen are a global machine state. In general, a subroutine should *not* print anything on the screen or move the cursor unless this is its documented function. No matter how well intended, courtesy messages displayed by subroutines can raise havoc with a carefully planned screen layout.

- The same goes for resetting the color or the cursor specifications. These are typically considered part of the global machine state, to be kept intact unless the subroutine is authorized to change them.

- The current segment selected by the DEF SEG statement is considered to be a local machine state and can be changed by any subroutine. In general, therefore, programs that require a segment setting must set it up just prior to peeking or poking into memory.

- The pointer into the internal DATA file is a local machine state. It can be changed by any subroutine by using the RESTORE statement to point into some local DATA set.

- Errors must be handled both globally and locally, depending on the context. This is described in a later section.

- Special global and local machine state handling is required to process interrupts from peripheral devices.

11.8 Handling Errors

BASIC provides an excellent mechanism for trapping and processing errors and exception conditions. Essentially, errors are treated as interrupts and processed as such. Each error type has a specific error number. The error trap is set up with the ON ERROR GOTO statement, which specifies an error-handler label.

When an error occurs (or is deliberately caused with the ERROR statement), BASIC interrupts the program and transfers control to the error-processing code, together with the system variables ERR and ERL which identify the error and the line where it occurred. When the error handler is done, it can return to the interruption point with the RESUME statement. (*See* Chapter 1 for more details.)

Errors must be handled with a careful mix of global and local processing. To implement a library, we establish these additional rules:

1. All main programs must use the label ^GLOBAL ERROR HANDLER^ to process errors that are not handled locally.
2. A library subroutine can change the error handler to a local name with the ON ERROR GOTO statement, as long as the handler is reset to ^GLOBAL ERROR HANDLER^ before returning.
3. Inside error handlers, only variable names starting with "ERRR" (note the 3 Rs), such as ERRRLINE and ERRRMESS$, may be used. These names are reserved for error handlers, to ensure that no program variable is inadvertently modified during an interrupt.

Here is an example that handles the eternal problem of the printer not being ready or being out of paper. The main program sets up the error handler, then goes about its business. Whenever it attempts to print (but the printer is not ready), control passes to the error handler, which—in this example—beeps and allows the user to prepare the printer. Then it continues. Note its use of variable ERRRMESS$ as a dummy to catch the user's ready signal. Since we reserve this name for use in the error handler, it is guaranteed not to interfere with the main program.

```
+----------------------------------------------------------------------+
:       ON ERROR GOTO ^GLOBAL ERROR HANDLER^                           :
:       ....                                                           :
:       ....           main program                                   :
:       ....                                                           :
:       END                                                           :
:                                                                      :
: ^GLOBAL ERROR HANDLER^                                               :
:       IF ERR = 27 THEN                                               :
:           - BEEP :                                                   :
:           - PRINT "Hit RETURN When Printer Is Ready "; :             :
:           - INPUT ERRRMESS$ :                                        :
:           - RESUME                                                   :
:       IF ERR = ...         ' handle other errors                    :
:                                                                      :
:       PRINT "Error"; ERR; "Has Occurred At Line"; ERL               :
:       STOP                                                           :
+----------------------------------------------------------------------+
```

In addition to the involuntary error-trapping mechanism, BASIC also provides the ERROR statement, which simulates the occurrence of an error at any time. Using this statement, you can define your own errors and you can deliberately invoke the error-trapping mechanism. This ability is quite useful for testing the mechanism as well as for building your own set of errors and handling them globally.

11.9 Using the Library

Designing and implementing a software library involves quite a few considerations and rules and regulations. All of this represents work that you, the programmer, must do. What is your payoff? Is it worth your time and effort?

The answer depends on your individual circumstances. If you expect to write one or two short programs per year, you won't benefit much from setting up a fancy library. The library included in this book should be more than enough to support your needs.

If you expect to write five new programs per year over the next five years, you can save as much as 20% of effort. About one-third of the code of those 25 programs will be almost exactly repeated: same screens, same keyboard input, same error handling, same open/read/close file, same "Hit Return When The Printer Is Ready" messages. Another one-third will be close variations on a basic coding task: Sorting, Searching, Queue Managing, Parameter Stacking, File Definitions, Record Layouts, Menus, and so on.

In other words, out of those 25 programs, 8 will be pure duplication and 8 more will be only half new. In effect, you will only be writing 13 new programs. Looking at it pessimistically, 50% of your time will be wasted over the next five years! Under those circumstances it would clearly pay you to set up a library, for four reasons:

1. Even if it takes you six months to set up the library, it will save you 2.5 years of work—a return on investment of 400%. We're not talking about saving some company money or computer time or disk storage; we're talking about saving 50% of your working life!
2. You will end up with a library that will support you indefinitely at little additional cost, continuing to save half your time and making you highly competitive.
3. The library will be yours. It will contain the routines you need, written in your style, documented to your specifications, and tested to your standards. You will own the library, and you won't have to pay royalties for using it.
4. The library will be transportable. Written in BASIC, the classic subroutines of data processing will be useful indefinitely. You will be able to move the library to new computers and to new languages.

Let's see, then, to what uses we can put the idea of a subroutine library. It is amazing how far the concept of a "subroutine" can be stretched to include tables and text and so forth:

Classic Subroutines

Library routines are excellent vehicles for building a collection of tasks common to many programs. Once a subroutine has been carefully designed, tested, and documented, it becomes a permanent tool that can be used again and again. You invest extra time in a careful design and benefit by saving time later.

Example: The routine UPPERC.LIB converts a string to uppercase letters. This task is required many times in most programs.

Skeleton Routines

Quite a few uses can be found for library routines that are mere skeletons or templates to be filled in. Any code fragment that occurs frequently but will be inserted in place rather than called as a subroutine qualifies. Such routines are placed in the library to assist you in developing new code.

Examples: SKELETON.LIB is a file that is the framework to help you start a new program.

VFILE.LIB is a skeleton routine to establish a variable-length random access file.

Data Tables

Instead of performing a specific task, a subroutine can be used more as a table look-up function. This is especially helpful if different tables are required for different applications: to switch tables, you simply switch to a different library.

Examples: ERRMESS.LIB looks up an IBMPC error code and returns a user-oriented message string.

VIDEO.LIB returns the proper screen address (mono or color) for the installed equipment that is currently active.

Use to Document

Library files need not be executable subroutines. It is quite useful to have some text routines that help to document programs. These are often called "boilerplate" files.

Example: A text file that gives your name, your logo, and your copyright notice—all nicely framed—can be stored as a "routine" that you incorporate into every program.

Customizing Programs

Programs can be modularized at very high functional levels, where the word "subprogram" would be more correct. Several programmers can then work independently on a project, each writing a different subprogram with its own library. These are then combined to form the application program.

For example, to write a payroll program for a national corporation, you might develop one library for each state, to handle the different state tax rules. To generate a payroll program for Delaware, you would then use the Delaware Library to compile the program.

Another example might be to write a routine that contains nothing but GOSUB statements to every library routine. This could serve as a library index. By compiling that routine as a main program, you can quickly detect missing routines in the form of missing label messages. This is useful if you are shipping tailored production libraries to a customer and don't want to omit any needed subroutines.

Trapping Control

One of the great uses of a subroutine is as a trap or filter to force program control through a given point. If a call to subroutine MONITOR is inserted into programs at judicious places, program progress can be observed (and interrupted if necessary) inside the MONITOR routine. When such monitoring is not required, a no-operation routine is substituted for the monitor routine.

This provides a convenient access point to a program at interesting times in its execution. It can be used to collect program time and variable usage statistics with the aim of improving the program on the basis of execution-time performance. Finally, it can be used as a probe to debug the program in production.

Evolutionary Programming

The art of programming is the art of reducing the uncertainties of the real world to the precise forms required by the computer. The programmer seldom has enough time or money or information to do a complete and proper job. Resources are always "coming up soon," equipment is always "on order," and users will "let you know soon" about final specifications. You have to defer decisions while yet making progress on the project. You learn to hedge, to keep options open, to delay decisions, and to avoid commitment to the last possible moment.

A software library can aid this purpose. Basically, you start a new project with the skeleton program discussed earlier and copy whatever fits from other libraries. You fill in the missing pieces with quick and dirty subroutines that you put into the project library. Within a few days, you have at least a faltering prototype program running. From then on, programming consists of selectively improving those quick and dirty routines that need it the most and for which the needed resources have arrived.

This is "evolutionary programming." Your program gets a quick start and then grows in the direction of greatest need, quite often in totally different directions than you or the user anticipated. You always have something running; and it is much easier to debug a program incrementally, as you add or change a specific area.

Personal Productivity

A library gives you an organized vehicle for storing useful source code, be it in subroutine or function or table or overlay form, in PREBASIC or BASIC or FORTRAN or Assembly Language. If you see a good code fragment in a book or magazine, you can store it in a way that will be accessible later.

It can include routines to help you over those special areas where you lack expertise or where you are uncomfortable. For example, I personally don't care to memorize the IBM PC's convoluted color-coding scheme. So, someday I will sit down, establish a code of my own, and write it up as a subroutine that translates my color code to IBM's. Then I won't have to scramble around anymore, trying to remember the color code for under-lining with reverse video or for magenta on yellow background.

And you will have different libraries. No doubt you will want to play around with some "far out" ideas, such as subroutines that are generated by programs and stored into the library, or subroutines that are dynamically selected from the library when the program is running and has determined the data volume to be processed. You may get into "hybrid programming," where you selectively modify key routines by rewriting them in faster machine language. On the other hand, you may delve into the wonderful worlds of graphics, or encryption, or sound, or chess...

Use the Stack Mechanism

When you are in the midst of your creative programming throes, and you need a variable name or two, it is really handy to have available a stack such as S( ) that is guaranteed safe to store the variables or to pass them to a subroutine.

Inventing new variable names, especially for temporary trash values, is distracting and dangerous. Sooner or later, you get into the habit of naming everything T or TEMP, and then you get variable name conflicts that are hard to trace.

Once you adapt to using a stack to pass variables, you may find it so convenient that you will use it in all programs whether or not they reference the library. After all, what we have done here is, simply, invent local variables for BASIC. Why not use them?

I'm sure I have made my point by now. A library preserves your past creations, makes them available for present work, and provides a framework for collecting your future efforts. Properly cared for, it will support you throughout your career.

The Library Subroutine

12

The subroutine is one of the oldest and most versatile software tools; its uses range over the whole spectrum of programming. Subroutines serve to modularize complex programs, to compute functions, to save space, to interface between languages, and as a table look-up. The species includes such marvelous creatures as co-routines, tasks, user hooks, stubs, dummies, spacers, overlays, traps, passkeys, reentrant routines, routines that call themselves, routines that generate other routines, and even routines that call their caller back. There are enough types and uses to fill another book.

This chapter focuses on just one of these types: the subroutine used as a canned code for inclusion in a variety of programs. The last chapter developed the design for a subroutine library; this chapter focuses on designing its components—the typical library subroutine.

In this chapter, we tame the subroutine to perform common chores needed to support our application programs. We restrict its freedoms with some rules so that it will mesh with the other routines and with the main programs that call them.

12.1 Designing the Routine

A subroutine is really a miniature program, and the steps involved in designing one are similar to the steps involved in designing a program. But there are significant differences. For the normal program, you develop User Requirements in consultation with the end user; for a library subroutine, not only are you the end user, the requirements are quite open ended. For the normal program, the design specifications derive from the User Requirements; for the subroutine, you still have a range of designs to choose from. After all, you can define and design your own subroutine as conservatively or as fancy as you please.

Designing a library subroutine requires some delicate balancing between too much generalization and too much specificity. An overdesigned subroutine will contain unrelated functions or too much source code. It will be so complex that you won't want to study its documentation every time you use it. You will have to load the whole thing just to perform some little function, and it will contain so much code that it will have some nasty bugs in it.

On the other hand, the underdesigned routine will be incomplete. It will never quite satisfy your needs of the moment. It will work very well because it does nothing significant. You will end up with a two-line subroutine that clutters the library and is rarely used.

You will soon find that Murphy's Law operates here both ways: If you include n options in a subroutine, you will someday regret not having included option $n+1$. If you include option $n+1$, your program will someday exceed the available memory, and you will regret including it.

Obviously this is a fundamental dilemma for which only general advice can be given. What do programmers do when they hit such an ambivalent decision point? They use the ancient design technique called KISS: Keep it simple, stupid. Since Murphy says you will regret your decision in either case, you may as well save your energy. When in doubt, underdesign!

The typical design starts with some specific need. Over the last few weeks, you may have become increasingly irritated by having to constantly open a file for input and close it just to verify that it exists on the disk. You decide to design a library subroutine that will test for the presence of a file on a drive.

Now comes the design decision: What else should you include in this routine? Obviously, you would not include a random number generator or a federal tax table—these are unrelated and don't belong here. But you may well consider what other file-related functions have irritated you in the past, for example, testing a string to see if it is a valid file name, opening a file unless it is already open, killing a file without an error if it is already dead.

These file functions are all reasonably related, and you might jot them down as a tentative set to go into one routine. Later, as you design the routine in more detail, you may decide that some of them are really quite different from the others. At that time you can drop these, or redefine them as a second subroutine. The advantage of considering all related functions in one design session is that your brain will be focused on the subject in detail, and you will not have to relearn the details in some future session. You steep yourself in one topic for a weekend or two, and then you never have to think about it again.

As an aside, note that the set of functions to be included changes as you progress with designing and writing the routine. This is one of the facts of life of advanced programming: Design is an iterative activity, and the act of designing often impacts the design itself. Whenever I read in a textbook that first you design the program and second you code it, I know that the author may have written many books but has not written many programs. The fact is that programmers often only know approximately what a program will do and how it will look at the end. Programs evolve as they are used, and as the programmer and the user learn what is feasible, what is slow, and what is expensive. All the more reason to adhere to the KISS principle.

12.2 The Physical Form

Subroutines come in all sizes and formats. The subroutines in this book have the following format. In fact, this is an actual routine from our library. It is a "template" routine, a skeleton used to generate new routines in standard library formats. To write a new routine, you can start with a copy of this one to guide you. (Note also the larger SKELETON.PRO, which is an outline for an entire program.)

```
+----------------------------------------------------------------+
:   ^SKELETON.LIB^     ' Sub to xxxxx       date                 :
:       ' Enter with  S(S) =  xxx                                 :
:       '                                                         :
:       ' Return with S(S) =  xxx                                 :
:       '             S$(S) = xxx                                 :
:       ' Note:   xxx                                             :
:                                                                 :
:       code                                                      :
:       code                                                      :
:       RETURN                                                    :
+----------------------------------------------------------------+
```

The salient features of the format are

1. The documentation is part of the routine.
2. There is a date to identify the version.
3. It ends with a RETURN statement.

Placing at least one RETURN statement at the physical end of the routine turns out to be an excellent device for highlighting the end of routines in later BASIC source programs. After the comments have been deleted, and the labels have been replaced by line numbers, you can find your way around the naked source code by scanning for these RETURN statements.

Here is another sample routine from our library. This routine converts letters of a text string given in S$(S) to uppercase:

```
+----------------------------------------------------------------+
:  ^UPPERC.LIB^     ' Sub to convert to capitals      2-10-85   :
:     ' Enter  with S$(S)=string to be processed                :
:     ' Return with S$(S)=string with letters capitalized       :
:                                                               :
:     S1=LEN(S$(S))                                             :
:     WHILE S1                                                  :
:       S2=ASC(MID$(S$(S),S1,1))                                :
:       IF S2>96 AND S2<123 THEN MID$(S$(S),S1,1)=CHR$(S2-32):
:       S1=S1-1                                                 :
:       WEND                                                    :
:     RETURN                                                    :
+----------------------------------------------------------------+
```

A rough guide to the physical size of a subroutine is that it should not exceed 100 lines of source code, regardless of the language it is written in. This rule of thumb derives from the fact that library routines are typically printed on 8.5- by 11-inch sheets and are saved in some three-ring binder. When you are looking for one of your favorite routines, you flip through this binder. At this time, it is convenient to have the entire source code on one or two pages. You can review it as one unit.

But this rule is not rigid, and it is often violated in the interest of grouping useful functions into a routine or providing good documentation. For more solid guidelines on what a reasonable library routine design is, take a look at the routines supplied with this book. Most of them fit on one-half of a page, including their documentation. A few run to two and even three pages.

12.3 The Calling Sequence

Before you call a subroutine, some statements have to be executed to set up the machine state for the routine, to arrange the data into the order expected by the routine. This preparation and the ordered parameters themselves are collectively named the "calling sequence." It is much like the countdown used for space launches: an opportunity to get everything ready for the launch. The calling sequence is different for every subroutine and depends on the context in which it is written. Let's look now at implementing this in source code.

The subroutine stack is our most powerful tool to pass data to and from the subroutine. As discussed in Chapter 10, this data object can only be accessed at the top, by "pushing" new items on top and "popping" existing items off the top. In Chapter 11, we agreed to use the arrays S( ) and S$( ) as our subroutine stack, with the variable S pointing to its top.

A typical calling sequence consists of pushing the data to be passed on the subroutine stack, passing control to the routine, and—after it returns control—processing the stack as left by the routine. Let's now work through a simple example.

Assume that we are at a point in the program where we want to ask the user whether or not to clear the screen. We know that there is a routine in our library that handles the task of asking the question and verifying that the user's reply is YES or NO. We begin by looking at the library listing to see what machine state the routine requires:

```
+------------------------------------------------------------------+
:   ^YESNO2.LIB^ ' Sub to prompt for Y or N answer   2-10-85 :
:      ' Enter  with S$(S) = the prompt message             :
:      ' Return with S$(S) = "Y" if user replied positive   :
:      '                   = "N" if user replied negative    :
:                                                            :
:      PRINT S$(S);                                          :
:      PRINT "  (Y N) ? "; : LINE INPUT S$(S)                :
:      GOSUB ^UPPERC.LIB^                                    :
:      IF S$(S)<>"Y" AND S$(S)<>"N" THEN BEEP:GOTO ^-2^     :
:      RETURN                                                :
+------------------------------------------------------------------+
```

We see that the routine expects the prompt string on top of the string stack, and that it returns with the user's reply on top of the string stack.

Now we can write the calling sequence to call YESNO2.LIB. We begin by adding 1 to the stack pointer S. This gives us a free top element where we store the question to be asked. Then we give the subroutine control. When the routine returns control, we know that the user's answer is on top of the stack, and we take action depending on the answer. Finally we reduce the stack pointer by 1, so as to reset the machine state exactly to what it was before the calling sequence:

```
+------------------------------------------------------------------+
:       ' Calling Sequence for YESNO2 routine               :
:       S=S+1               ' acquire a stack element        :
:       S$(S)="Ok to Erase" ' prepare the question           :
:       GOSUB ^YESNO2.LIB^  ' ask question and get reply      :
:       IF S$(S)="Y" THEN CLS ' take action based on reply   :
:       S=S-1               ' release the stack element       :
:       ' End of Calling Sequence                            :
+------------------------------------------------------------------+
```

Now we are starting to benefit from all of the groundwork we have done with our library. First of all, PREBASIC automatically loads the source code for YESNO2.LIB from the library disk. Since YESNO2.LIB itself calls UPPERC.LIB, that will also be loaded if necessary. We do not have to worry about loading library routines at all.

Next, we need not worry that one subroutine will interfere with another. Because we agreed to use S$( ) to pass parameters to and from subroutines, the subroutines do not use any of our data names at the higher level. Because we use the stack data structure, every routine can use the stack for its own local values.

Finally, note that the calling sequence includes statements *after* the call, not just before, just as there are lengthy debriefings after our astronauts return from a mission. A common programming error is to initialize a subroutine call perfectly, but to forget to reset the machine state after the return. In our example, if you fail to decrement the stack pointer after the call, and you execute this code many times, the stack pointer will be incremented many times, and the stack will ultimately overflow its array and cause an error. To keep a stack happy, you must sooner or later pop whatever you push.

12.4 Parameter Formats

There are many ways to format and pass parameters to a subroutine; much depends on the number of parameters involved and their data types. The method used must be documented clearly inside the subroutine. Here are a few typical techniques for designing the parameter scheme for a subroutine:

- Simply pile parameters on top of each other into the string stack. The top item is parameter 1, the second item is parameter 2, and so on to the nth parameter, which is passed as element S$(S-n+1) (Figure 12-1). When the routine gets control, it can access each parameter selectively as needed. After control is returned, the caller reduces the stack pointer S appropriately to reset it to conditions as they were before the call.

    Incidentally, this is the way all programming languages implement subroutine calls and function references internally. The difference between other languages and BASIC is that in BASIC we do it ourselves. BASIC forces us to learn

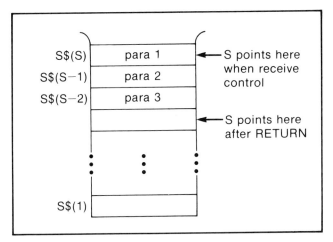

Figure 12-1. A parameter stack as it might be received by a routine several levels below the main program.

how these things are done and, I believe, we become better programmers.

* Use parallel subroutine stacks to pass parameters with different data types. Instead of forcibly converting all parameters to string type for the S$( ) stack, simply pass integer parameters in the S( ) stack, and pass floating parameters in the S!( ) stack (Figure 12-2).

* Pack all the parameters, separated by commas, into one string and pass that string in S$(S). Programmers who have worked

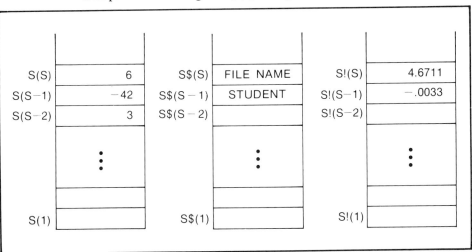

Figure 12-2. Several parallel stacks can be used to pass several data types to a subroutine.

in other languages such as FORTRAN or C or PL/1 appreciate the simplicity of specifying several parameters as a simple list such as "10,30,FILENAME,357". Note that routine UNPACK.LIB is available to help the subroutine unpack the passed parameters into individual variables.

- Pass the parameters as values above the stack top (Figure 12-3). With this technique, you store parameter 1 into S$(S+1), parameter 2 into S$(S+2), and so on. Then you pass the count of parameters in S(S). The called routine can process the parameters where they are and can return control without having to adjust the stack.

12.5 Function Codes and Flags

In general, a subroutine performs a single function, such as operating on some data object. But a function often has options or variations from which the user wants to select one. For example, a routine whose function is to delete blanks may have the options to single up all blanks, or to delete only leading blanks, or to delete only trailing blanks.

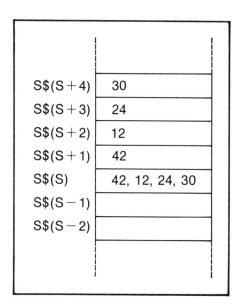

Figure 12-3. The UNPACK.LIB routine takes a packed parameter string such as "10,30,FILENAME,357" and unpacks it into S$(S+1) through S$(S+4). It is typically used by library routines themselves to prepare a parameter string for processing.

To select the function to be performed on a given call, we pass a function selector as (usually) the first parameter. Function selectors come in two flavors: the function code and the function flag.

A function code is simply an integer that selects one function from a set offered by a routine. It is used when only one of the functions will be requested at a time. For example, the subroutine VFILE.LIB (developed in section 7.8) manages file space dynamically. It uses a function code to select one of four possible operations:

    1 = Open a new file.
    2 = Open an existing file.
    3 = Reserve a block.
    4 = Release a block.

It makes sense to design this routine as one routine rather than as four, because the functions belong to the same activity, they manipulate the same variables, and a typical call will only request one of the functions. Therefore, we use a function code to select the operation.

But there are times when we want a routine to perform several of its functions at once. We need to tell the routine which combination of functions we want for a given call. This calls for the use of a bit string in which the bits corresponding to the desired functions are set by the caller. In BASIC, the simplest bit string is the 16-bit integer. Let's see how we can use the integer to build a function mask or "function flags," as I call it.

Let's look in detail at the BLANKS.LIB routine. It cleans up the blanks in a given string, a need that arises in many situations. Again, there are four functions related to blank processing. But this time—in anticipation of using function flags instead of a function code—we number them as a power of 2:

    1 = Delete leading blanks.
    2 = Delete trailing blanks.
    4 = Delete all blanks.
    8 = Reduce all blank sequences to one blank.

Due to the workings of binary arithmetic, we can now specify any combination of these functions simply by arithmetically adding their respective numbers to obtain the function flags integer. If we want to delete both leading and trailing blanks, we see that these are numbered 1 and 2, so we pass function flags 3 to the routine. To single up on all blanks and drop trailing blanks as well, we pass function flags 2 + 8 = 10 to the routine.

Function flags set up in this way can never be ambiguous, because each flag is actually a bit position in binary. In binary, our function flags 1, 2, 4, and 8 are written as 0001, 0010, 0100, and 1000. To single up on all blanks and drop trailing blanks as well, we pass function flag 0010 + 1000 = 1010 in binary. All we have done is reserve one bit position for each different function. Now we can use the logical operators OR and AND to set and test the bit positions selectively.

Here, then, is the source code for the BLANKS.LIB routine. It tests the function code repeatedly and performs the desired operation. Note how we use the AND operator to look at very specific bits of the function code.

```
+-------------------------------------------------------------------------+
:  ^BLANKS.LIB^    ’  General Blanks Handler      12-10-84   :
:     ’ Enter with S$(S)  the string to be processed         :
:     ’            S(S)   the function flags:                :
:     ’                   1 = drop leading blanks            :
:     ’                   2 = drop trailing blanks           :
:     ’                   4 = drop all blanks                :
:     ’                   8 = single up on all blanks        :
:     ’ Return with S$(S) selectively deblanked             :
:                                                            :
:     IF (S(S) AND 8)<>8 THEN ^+3^                           :
:     S1=INSTR(S$(S)," ")  : IF S1=0 THEN ^+2^               :
:     S$(S)=LEFT$(S$(S),S1)+MID$(S$(S),S1+2) : GOTO ^-1^     :
:     IF (S(S) AND 5)=0 THEN ^+2^                            :
:     WHILE LEFT$(S$(S),1)=" ":S$(S)=MID$(S$(S),2):WEND      :
:     IF S(S) AND 6 THEN WHILE RIGHT$(S$(S),1)=" " :         :
:       - S$(S)=LEFT$(S$(S),LEN(S$(S))-1) : WEND             :
:     IF (S(S) AND 4)=0 THEN RETURN                          :
:     S1=INSTR(S$(S)," ") : IF S1=0 THEN RETURN              :
:     S$(S)=LEFT$(S$(S),S1-1)+MID$(S$(S),S1+1) :GOTO ^-1^    :
+-------------------------------------------------------------------------+
```

12.6 Handling Line Labels

The whole idea of a common subroutine library depends on the ability to write source code without numbered lines. PREBASIC gives us this ability, and the library mechanism works quite well, with a couple of cautions in order.

Since PREBASIC incorporates library subroutine code at the end of the main program, as if we had written the code ourselves, we cannot use arbitrary label symbols like ^LOOP^ or ^START^ in our library routines, because they might duplicate names in other routines or in the main program. This problem is not major, and there are at least three solutions:

1. Use extensions of the subroutine name to generate internal labels. In PREBASIC, label names can be up to 250 bytes

long, so use modified names to distinguish them. If a subroutine is named SERVICE.LIB, then use such labels as ∧SERVICE LIB 1∧ or ∧SERVICE LIP LOOP∧. This naming convention ties the label to the routine, lets you give meaningful names to subroutine labels, and causes no interference with main programs as long as they stay away from labels that look like library routine names.

2. Then there is the relative label. If you want to pass control three lines forward, why invent a whole new label? PREBASIC lets you reference *n* lines forward or backward relative to the current line in the form GOTO∧+3∧ or GOTO ∧−5∧. To reference the same line, use ∧+0∧ or ∧−0∧. For example, to change all asterisks in S$ to blanks, use a GOTO loop like this:

S1=INSTR(S$,"*"):IF S1 THEN MID$(S$,S1,1)=' ':GOTO ∧+0∧

Relative lables reduce label clutter in subroutines, and they don't cause reading problems since subroutines are seldom read once they are debugged and installed in the library. (*See* the PREBASIC chapter for some cautions.)

3. Finally, you might get ambitious enough some weekend to modify the **PREBASIC** program so that it resolves subroutine label references before it appends the subroutine to the main program.

To illustrate the use of techniques 1 and 2, here are two versions of the YESNO2 routine we saw earlier. First, a reprint of the routine, showing the use of a relative label ∧−2∧:

```
+--------------------------------------------------------------------+
:  ^YESNO2.LIB^  ' Sub to prompt for Y or N answer   2-10-85  :
:         ' Enter  with S$(S) = the prompt message           :
:         ' Return with S$(S) = "Y" if user replied positive :
:         '                   = "N" if user replied negative :
:         '                                                  :
:                                                            :
:    PRINT S$(S);                                            :
:    PRINT "  (Y N) ? "; : LINE INPUT S$(S)                  :
:    GOSUB ^UPPERC.LIB^                                       :
:    IF S$(S)<>"Y" AND S$(S)<>"N" THEN BEEP:GOTO ^-2^        :
:    RETURN                                                  :
+--------------------------------------------------------------------+
```

Note the use of the local label ∧−2∧ in this routine. To PREBASIC, this code means "2 lines before this one" and is replaced by PREBASIC with the appropriate line number. Here is the same routine, modified to use a global label. (The BEEP has been omitted for space reasons):

```
+------------------------------------------------------------------+
: ^YESNO2.LIB^ ' Sub to prompt for Y or N answer   2-10-85   :
:      ' Enter  with S$(S) = the prompt message              :
:      ' Return with S$(S) = "Y" if user replied positive    :
:      '                   = "N" if user replied negative     :
:                                                             :
:      PRINT S$(S);                                           :
: ^YESNO2 LIB 1^                                              :
:      PRINT "  (Y N) ? "; : LINE INPUT S$(S)                 :
:      GOSUB ^UPPERC.LIB^                                     :
:      IF S$(S)<>"Y" AND S$(S)<>"N" THEN ^YESNO2 LIB 1^       :
:      RETURN                                                 :
+------------------------------------------------------------------+
```

12.7 Handling the Stack

In Chapter 11, I established the subroutine stack as a global data structure to be used for communication among subroutines. Now we are ready to pay more detailed attention to the stack from the viewpoint of the individual subroutine, that is, as a "local stack" of "local variables."

We recall that a stack is really a layer cake of values. Each layer is a set of parameters for some subroutine. Seen as a whole, the stack represents the "calling path"—the sequence of subroutine calls made from the main program to the current subroutine (Figure 12-4). The top parameter set belongs to the currently running routine, the next set belongs to the parent (that is, the caller) of the current routine, and so on down to the bottom set.

I have purposely used the word "belongs" here to indicate as forcefully as possible that a set of parameters is exclusively tied to a given subroutine. Subroutines are independent, selfish, and antisocial creatures. They only care about their own parameter set and want to know nothing about any other parameters. This deliberate isolation of subroutines and their parameters from the rest of the world is what makes the whole concept of modular programming work. To make it work, we must understand the stack and what we can and cannot do to it locally.

To begin, it is worth repeating that only the top parameter set belongs to the subroutine that currently has control of the computer. Anything stored on the stack below the current set is of no concern to the current routine; it must be preserved and returned exactly as received.

How do we know just what is the current parameter set? Since parameter sets come in different shapes and sizes, how do we identify our current set? The answer is: by documentation. The subroutine documentation tells you exactly what is expected on

p1
p2
p3
p1
p2
p1
p2
p3
p4
p5
p1
p1
p2
p3

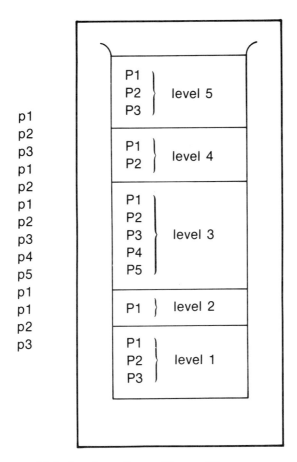

Figure 12-4. A subroutine calling path.

the stack upon entry to the routine and what is expected upon return from the routine. Let's look at a typical library routine:

```
+--------------------------------------------------------------+
: ^OCCURS.LIB^   ' Count occurrences of one string   12-5-84 :
:    ' Enter  with S$(S) the occurring string                  :
:    '               S$(S-1) the containing string             :
:    ' Return with S(S) the number of occurrences              :
:    ' Pops 1 stack level                                      :
:                                                              :
:    S$=S$(S) : S=S-1 : S(S)=0 : S1=INSTR(S$(S),S$)            :
:    WHILE S1                                                  :
:       S(S)=S(S)+1 : S1=INSTR(S1+LEN(S$),S$(S),S$) : WEND     :
:    RETURN                                                    :
+--------------------------------------------------------------+
```

Upon entry, two parameters are defined, namely the contained string and the containing string. This is the parameter set given to the routine. Upon return, only one parameter is defined: the containing string. In other words, the large global stack has decreased by one element. You can see this in the subroutine, where the statement S = S − 1 lowers the stack pointer.

The subroutine OCCURS.LIB does not care at all what the absolute value of the stack pointer S is. It merely takes the top two values from the stack, performs its function, and puts one value back on the stack. The routine assumes nothing about what is stored below its parameters or how high the stack is.

The second major point of this section is: The same rule of minding your own business applies to the routine that calls OCCURS.LIB. If you look at the routine code, you can see that the occurring string is still stored at S\$(S+1) after the routine returns control. Even though officially the subroutine returns one parameter, we really know some "inside info" about the stack because we have looked inside the subroutine code.

But the calling routine should never use this knowledge because the library routine code may be changed in the future. It will still work logically as documented, but it may no longer leave the physical stack as before. If the calling routine relies on the physical stack format, it will not work correctly after the library is changed.

Remember that the whole idea of modularization is that routines are independent of each other and can be independently changed. The only thing that cannot be changed is the officially documented interface, the entry parameter set, and the returned parameter set. If you rely on undocumented side effects, you will find your running programs suddenly bombing out for mysterious reasons. Don't do it.

12.8 Handling Control Flow

There are no ceremonies in BASIC associated with passing control to a subroutine. The subroutine simply receives control, does its work, and returns control. Inside the routine, there are no restrictions on how control is passed around. The routine may use any statements such as GOSUB, GOTO, IF-THEN-ELSE, FOR-NEXT, and WHILE-WEND. The choice of control-coding techniques is up to the programmer. Some like to write one statement per line; others like to group statements logically. Some like to include internal subroutines; others modularize everything they can.

Now for some useful rules. For starters: ALWAYS RETURN CONTROL TO YOUR CALLER. The concept of modular programming depends on this rule. A subroutine may only fail to return control if that is a part of its documented function, such as with routines used for diagnostics or fault isolation. Or you may temporarily insert a STOP statement into a routine to freeze the machine and observe its machine state in detail. The last method is particularly useful in BASIC with its ability to inspect and modify variables during such interruptions.

But as a general rule, a subroutine treats control like a hot potato: gingerly juggling it and returning it as fast as possible. As long as the subroutine is executing, it controls the computer, the program, and the data. For modularity to work, it is obviously important to treat program control with respect.

But, promising to always return control is easier said than done. An unexpected condition or an outright error can leave the subroutine caught in a bind: If it returns control prematurely, without having performed its function, it violates the rule of completing the task as documented. If it prints an error message and stops, it violates the rule against stopping. If it cannot take logical action to fix the error, what can it do?

The solution is to design the routine with an "echo" parameter that reports normal and abnormal conditions. In other words, part of the task definition of every subroutine is to report unexpected errors to their caller.

12.9 Handling the RESTORE-DATA Feature

Library subroutines are sometimes used to store data in tables. Calling the subroutine gives access to the data. This idea is particularly easy to implement in BASIC because of the DATA statement.

In IBM PC BASIC, the RESTORE statement can specify a line number that selects the starting point for reading data from the table. This gives us an excellent tool for accessing the global DATA file at any desired point, making it a random file! For example, here is one of our library routines used to convert a PC BASIC error code to a user-oriented message:

```
+-----------------------------------------------------------------+
:   ^ERRMESS.LIB^   ' Convert error code to message 1-29-85   :
:      ' NOTE: To preserve machine state, this routine         :
:      ' uses global variable names   ERRRx                    :
:      ' Enter  with ERRRN = BASIC error number (from ERR)      :
:      ' Return with ERRR$ = the error message or ""            :
:                                                               :
:      RESTORE ^+1^                                             :
:      DATA  6, "Overflow"                                      :
```

```
:     DATA   7,  "Out Of Memory"                           :
:     DATA   9,  "Bad Subscript"                            :
:     DATA  14,  "Out Of String Space"                      :
:     DATA  15,  "String Too Long"                          :
:     DATA  16,  "Bad String Expression"                    :
:     DATA  24,  "Device Timeout"                           :
:     DATA  27,  "Printer Not Ready"                        :
:     DATA  52,  "Bad File Name or Channel"                 :
:     DATA  53,  "File Not Found"                           :
:     DATA  54,  "Bad File Mode"                            :
:     DATA  55,  "File Is Already Open"                     :
:     DATA  61,  "Disk Is Full"                             :
:     DATA  64,  "Bad Filename"                             :
:     DATA  67,  "Too Many Files"                           :
:     DATA  68,  "No Such Device"                           :
:     DATA  70,  "Write-Protected Disk"                     :
:     DATA  71,  "Drive Not Ready"                          :
:     DATA  72,  "Diskette Fault"                           :
:     DATA   0,  ""                                         :
:     READ ERRR1,ERRR$                                      :
:     WHILE ERRR1>0 AND ERRR1<>ERRRN                        :
:        READ ERRR1,ERRR$ : WEND                            :
:     RETURN                                                :
+--------------------------------------------------------------+
```

If you use the DATA feature extensively, I recommend the technique used in this routine: Just before reading the internal DATA file, use the RESTORE command with an appropriate label to identify the data you want. Not only does this guarantee that you are reading the correct data set, it lets you store the data set near the code that uses it, instead of somewhere else in the program.

Many textbooks on structured programming urge you to put all DATA statements together at the beginning (or end) of the program. That is good advice for those BASIC dialects that do not allow the RESTORE statement to select a particular DATA line. Those dialects only let you reset the DATA file pointer to the beginning. In that case, you cannot use DATA statements inside library subroutines, or at best it requires the DATA themselves to contain segment identifiers.

In IBM PC BASIC, the RESTORE statement lets you select the subset of DATA you want, so the data should be included in the routine that uses them.

12.10 Writing Library Subroutines

Some special considerations are involved in developing library subroutines. Designing them is different from designing a well-specified program: You must decide which features will be needed and how to group them into different routines. Library routines are usually highly generalized routines that must provide a range of useful options and features; yet they must stay reasonably small so that a specific feature can be loaded without having to load a lot of "bundled" features.

Coding is different, too. You are writing generalized code for an unknown audience, and you have to be doubly careful to follow the rules. You must avoid naming conflicts, you must write reasonably fast code without consuming excessive space, you must handle abnormal conditions and errors, and you must document all of this inside the routine so future users can understand its features and limitations.

Routines must be thoroughly debugged, especially with respect to subtle side effects such as variables being changed by routines called by the routine, not resetting the error-trap label to the global name, and consuming memory by prematurely leaving FOR-NEXT loops. The stack must be left correctly upon all exits. If errors can occur, they must be trapped and reported as an output parameter. Finally, the routine must be dated and entered on the various library disks and directories.

In short, writing a subroutine library requires the programming skills and tricks developed throughout this book. In the next chapter, we show how these techniques are applied in our subroutine library.

12.11 Summary

We have done a lot of work in this chapter, and it is time to bring the whole thing into focus. Here, then, are the "Rules of Etiquette" that we have developed for library subroutines. Please note that these are the default rules. Any routine can violate these rules as necessary, as long as this is documented with the routine.

- A subroutine can expect the machine state as promised in the documentation. It should not double-check this because otherwise every routine wastes much time and code checking something that has to be correct anyway. It should perform its task, reset the machine state as promised in the document-ation, and return control.
- A subroutine must return control to its caller under all circumstances. Stopping or exiting to the system is specific-ally prohibited. The use of echo parameters to flag abnormal outcomes is recommended.

- Routines use the parallel arrays S( ), S$( ), S!( ) and S#( ) as stacks to transmit and receive parameters. The stack pointer is S. A subroutine is free to use all of the space above the stack pointer for temporary values. Therefore, a calling routine must not expect the stack above the pointer to be saved.
- A routine is free to use the variable names S0-S9, S$-S9$, and so on, but may not use or change the contents of any other name. Because this rule applies also to subroutines called by subroutines, these variable names can only be safely used when there is no intervening call to a subroutine.
- To avoid label duplication, a subroutine may only use label names that are an extension of its own name. Relative line references are, therefore, encouraged.
- A subroutine may locally change the error trap, but must reset it to ^GLOBAL ERROR HANDLER^ before returning.
- A subroutine may arbitrarily change the DATA file pointer (RESTORE) and the code segment register (DEF SEG) and leave them changed.
- A subroutine should not change the settings of function key or other interrupt traps.
- A subroutine should not clear the screen, print any text, or move the screen cursor.
- A subroutine should generally not open or close any files.
- As a general rule, any unusual changes in machine state should be documented with the subroutine to such an extent that a future user of the routine gets fair warning.

Our Library

This chapter presents the source code of the library subroutines we have used in this book as well as some of the longer example programs from the chapters. Only a few of the routines are described in detail here since most of the routines contain sufficient comments or have been described elsewhere (see the Index).

This library is by no means complete or uniform. It is at best a beginning collection of useful routines that generally follow a uniform policy for variable naming and parameter passing and observe the rules discussed in Chapters 11 and 12.

Available Diskette
The source code listed in this chapter is also available on a diskette for $25.00

Write to:
Brady Communications Company, Inc.
Simon&Schuster Building
1230 Avenue of the Americas
New York, NY 10020

13.1 Contents

BANGER	Multifunction calculator
BASPRE	Convert **BASIC** to **PREBASIC**
BLANKS	Delete or reduce blanks
BUGLER	Generate bugle calls
CLICHE	Print fractured proverbs
CULL	Delete alien bytes from a string
DATIME	Compute date and time string
DSMSIMUL	Simulate dynamic space management
ERRMESS	Compute standard error messages
FILLER	Process words through pipeline
HXLATE	Translate ASCII to Hex ASCII
LJUST	Drop leading blanks
LOWERC	Convert string to lowercase
MENU2	Input a word from a menu
NOBLANKS	Drop all blanks
OCCURS	Count string occurrences
PEEL	Peel a field from string
PEEL1	Peel a blank-delimited field
PEEL2	Peel a comma-delimited field
PEEL3	Peel a self-delimited field
PREBASIC	Convert **PREBASIC** to **BASIC** code
RANK	Find a word in a list
RESERVE	Allocate a variable DSM block
RJUST	Drop trailing blanks
SKELETON.LIB	Framework for library routine
SKELETON.PRE	Framework for program
SORT	Chain sort with binary search
STRING	Compute a string constant
TELLER	Multitasking simulator
UNPACK	Unpack a comma list
UPPERC	Convert a string to uppercase
VFILE	Manage a DSM file
VIDEO	Find start of video RAM
YESNO	Answer a yes/no question at keyboard
YESNO2	Answer a yes/no question at keyboard

13.2 4BANGER

This is the simple calculator program developed in Chapter 10. It simulates a cheap calculator with four elementary arithmetic operations.

```
+-------------------------------------------------------------------+
:  ^4BANGER.PRE^    ' Simulate a simple calculator                  :
:      DIM S$(9),S(9)    ' the subroutine stack                     :
:      DIM ST#(500)      ' the 4-banger stack                       :
:      SP=0              ' and stack pointer                        :
:      WHILE 1           ' main command loop                        :
:          ' accept a user command line                             :
:          LINE INPUT "Next?  "; S$(S)                              :
:          ' drop framing blanks and single up                      :
:          S(S)=11 : GOSUB ^BLANKS.LIB^                             :
:          WHILE S$(S)<>""   ' until line is empty                  :
:              ' peel and push word onto S$(S)                      :
:              GOSUB ^PEEL1.LIB^                                    :
:              ' execute the word                                   :
:              ON 1+INSTR("+-*/=",S$(S))                            :
:                  - GOSUB ^PUSH^, ^+^, ^-^, ^*^, ^/^, ^=^          :
:              S=S-1      ' pop the word                            :
:          WEND                                                     :
:      WEND                                                         :
:          ' the operation subroutines                             :
:  ^PUSH^  SP=SP+1:ST#(SP)=VAL(S$(S)):RETURN                        :
:  ^+^     SP=SP-1:ST#(SP)=ST#(SP)+ST#(SP+1):RETURN                 :
:  ^-^     SP=SP-1:ST#(SP)=ST#(SP)-ST#(SP+1):RETURN                 :
:  ^*^     SP=SP-1:ST#(SP)=ST#(SP)*ST#(SP+1):RETURN                 :
:  ^/^     SP=SP-1:ST#(SP)=ST#(SP)/ST#(SP+1):RETURN                 :
:  ^=^     PRINT ST#(SP):SP=SP-1:RETURN                             :
+-------------------------------------------------------------------+
```

13.3 ALIEN

This routine is from Chapter 4. Here it has been rewritten as a standard library routine.

```
+-------------------------------------------------------------------+
:  ^ALIEN.LIB^                                                      :
:    ' Verify that string comes from alphabet      2-11-85          :
:    ' Enter with  S$(S)   the data string                          :
:    '             S$(S-1) the alphabet string                      :
:    ' Return with S(S) = n if the nth byte is an alien             :
:    '             S$(S) and S$(S-1) are undisturbed                :
:                                                                   :
:    FOR S1=1 TO LEN(S$(S))                                         :
:        S(S)=INSTR(S$(S-1),MID$(S$(S),S1,1))                       :
:        IF S(S) THEN S1=LEN(S$(S))   ' abort loop                  :
:        NEXT S1                                                    :
:    RETURN                                                         :
+-------------------------------------------------------------------+
```

13.4 ASTRADD

This routine is an example of using strings for extended high-precision arithmetic. It performs addition on numbers with up to 255 digits.

```
: ^ASTRADD.LIB^   ' ASCII Digit String Addition  9-11-83  :
:    ' Enter  with S$(S) and S$(S-1) ASCII digit strings   :
:    ' Return with S$(S) = the sum of the given strings     :
:    '            S1=1 if overflowed 255 bytes; else =0     :
:    ' On overflow, returns S1=1 and the 255-byte sum       :
:    ' Pops 1 stack level                                   :
:    ' S1 is carry; S2 is current result byte               :
:    ' S3 is current addend byte; S4 is sum of codes        :
:                                                           :
:    S=S-1 : S1=0 : S2=LEN(S$(S)) : S3=LEN(S$(S+1))         :
:    IF S2 < S3 THEN SWAP S$(S),S$(S+1) : SWAP S2,S3        :
:    WHILE S3                                               :
:      S4=ASC(MID$(S$(S),S2,1))+ASC(MID$(S$(S+1),S3,1))+S1  :
:      IF S4 < 106 THEN S1=0 ELSE S1=1 : S4=S4-10           :
:      MID$(S$(S),S2,1) = CHR$(S4-48)                       :
:      S2=S2-1 : S3=S3-1                                    :
:      WEND                                                 :
:    WHILE S1=1 AND S2>1                                    :
:      S4=ASC(MID$(S$(S),S2,1)) + 1                         :
:      IF S4 < 58 THEN S1=0 ELSE S4=S4-10                   :
:      MID$(S$(S),S2,1) = CHR$(S4)                          :
:      S2=S2-1                                              :
:      WEND                                                 :
:    IF S1=1 AND LEN(S$(S))<255 THEN S$(S)="1"+S$(S):S1=0   :
:    RETURN                                                 :
```

13.5 AXLATE

This routine is one of a set of routines that translate strings containing arbitrary binary codes into Hex ASCII for transmission as pure ASCII display codes. (*See* Chapter 4.) This routine expects pure Hex ASCII and translates it back to an arbitrary binary string. Here it has been recast as a standard library subroutine. The reverse translation routine is HXLATE.LIB.

```
: ^AXLATE.LIB^                                             :
:    ' Sub to compress HEX ASCII to ASCII   2-11-85         :
:    ' Enter with  S$(S) = Hex ASCII string                 :
:    ' Return with S$(S) = Compressed string                :
```

```
:
:        S$="123456789ABCDEF"      ' indexed translator      :
:        FOR S1 = 1 TO LEN(S$(S))                            :
:            S1$ = MID$(S$(S),1,1)  '  left nybble           :
:            S2$ = MID$(S$(S),2,1)  ' right nybble           :
:            S2 = 16*INSTR(S$,S1$) + INSTR(S$,S2$)           :
:            S$(S)=MID$(S$(S),3) + CHR$(S2)                  :
:            NEXT                                            :
:        RETURN                                              :
+------------------------------------------------------------+
```

13.6 BANGER

This is the fancy calculator program developed in Chapter 10. It represents the framework for building your own stack-based application language.

```
+------------------------------------------------------------+
: ^BANGER.PRE^    ' A fancier calculator                     :
:    DIM S$(9),S(9)     ' the subroutine stack               :
:    DIM ST#(500)       ' the banger stack                   :
:    SP=0               ' and stack pointer                  :
:    WHILE 1            ' main command loop                  :
:      ' accept a user command line                          :
:      LINE INPUT "Next?  "; S$(S)                           :
:      ' drop framing blanks and single up                   :
:    . S(S)=11 : GOSUB ^BLANKS.LIB^                          :
:      WHILE S$(S)<>""   ' until line is empty                :
:          ' peel and push word in caps onto S$(S)           :
:          GOSUB ^PEEL1.LIB^ : GOSUB ^UPPERC.LIB^            :
:          ' execute the word                                :
:          ON 1+INSTR("+-*/=TRSD%",S$(S)) GOSUB ^PUSH^,      :
:          - ^+^,^-^,^*^,^/^,^=^,^T^,^R^,^S^,^D^,^%^          :
:          S=S-1      ' pop the word                         :
:          WEND                                              :
:      WEND                                                  :
:          ' the operation subroutines                       :
: ^PUSH^  SP=SP+1:ST#(SP)=VAL(S$(S)):RETURN                  :
:   ^+^    SP=SP-1:ST#(SP)=ST#(SP)+ST#(SP+1):RETURN          :
:   ^-^    SP=SP-1:ST#(SP)=ST#(SP)-ST#(SP+1):RETURN          :
:   ^*^    SP=SP-1:ST#(SP)=ST#(SP)*ST#(SP+1):RETURN          :
:   ^/^    SP=SP-1:ST#(SP)=ST#(SP)/ST#(SP+1):RETURN          :
:   ^=^    PRINT ST#(SP):SP=SP-1:RETURN                      :
:   ^T^    SP=SP-1:ST#(SP)=ST#(SP)^ST#(SP+1):RETURN          :
:   ^R^    ST#(SP)=SQR(ST#(SP)):RETURN                       :
:   ^S^    SWAP ST#(SP),ST#(SP-1):RETURN                     :
:   ^D^    SP=SP+1:ST#(SP)=ST#(SP-1):RETURN                  :
:   ^%^    GOSUB ^/^:S$(S)="100":GOSUB ^PUSH^:GOSUB ^*^      :
:          RETURN                                            :
+------------------------------------------------------------+
```

13.7 BASPRE

This is a utility program to convert standard **BASIC** programs to
PREBASIC form. It converts those line numbers that are referenced in other statements into **PREBASIC** labels, such as ^120^.
This lets you cross reference the generated **PREBASIC** program
back to the given **BASIC** program.

As an added attraction, **BASPRE** lists all references to a line
label as a comment with that label line. This can be helpful to
unspaghetti some existing programs with convoluted line number
references.

```
+----------------------------------------------------------------+
: ^BASPRE^    ' Convert BASIC to PREBASIC    2-11-85           :
:   CLS : DEFINT A-Z : HAT$="^"                                :
:   DIM LABEL$(5000),CFLABEL$(5000)                            :
:   PRINT "This program converts BASIC to PREBASIC"            :
:   PRINT "Place scratch disk in drive A ";                    :
:   PRINT "       source  disk in drive B"                     :
:   INPUT "Press RETURN When Ready "; I                        :
:   INPUT "Enter source (BASIC) file name  "; SOURCEFILE$      :
:   INPUT "Enter target (PREBASIC) file name ";TARGET$         :
:   PRINT ""                                                   :
:                                                              :
:   PRINT "Pass 1"                                             :
:   OPEN "I",1,SOURCEFILE$ : OPEN "O",2,"A:TEMP"               :
:   WHILE NOT EOF(1)                                           :
:     LINE INPUT #1, INLINE$                                   :
:     ' strip lead blanks                                      :
:     WHILE LEFT$(INLINE$,1)=" "                               :
:       INLINE$=MID$(INLINE$,2):WEND                           :
:     ' get its line number for cf                             :
:     I=INSTR(INLINE$+" "," "):CFLABEL$=LEFT$(INLINE$,I-1)     :
:     ' upper case the line to speed search                    :
:     XLINE$=INLINE$ : S1=LEN(INLINE$)                         :
:     WHILE S1>0 : S2=ASC(MID$(XLINE$,S1,1))                   :
:       IF S2>96 AND S2<123                                    :
:          - THEN MID$(XLINE$,S1,1)=CHR$(S2-32)                :
:       S1=S1-1 :   WEND                                       :
:     ' search for keywords that use labels and replace        :
:     RESTORE  ^+1^                                            :
:     DATA "GOTO ", "GOSUB ", "THEN "                          :
:   · DATA "ELSE ", "RESTORE ", "RESUME "                      :
:     FOR KEYY=1 TO 6                                          :
:         READ KEYY$                                           :
:         IF INSTR(XLINE$,KEYY$)>0 THEN GOSUB ^LABELS^         :
:         NEXT KEYY                                            :
:     PRINT #2, INLINE$                                        :
:     PRINT INLINE$                                            :
:     WEND                                                     :
```

```
   CLOSE

   PRINT "Pass 2"
   OPEN "I",2,"A:TEMP" : OPEN "O",3,TARGETFILE$
   WHILE NOT EOF(2)
     LINE INPUT #2, INLINE$
     I=INSTR(INLINE$+" "," ")
     D$=LEFT$(INLINE$,I-1)
     INLINE$=MID$(INLINE$,I+1)
     WHILE LEFT$(INLINE$,1)=" "
         INLINE$=MID$(INLINE$,2):WEND

     ' if line number is in label table, force a label
     ' and all come-from labels
     FOUND=0
     FOR J=1 TO LABMAX
         IF LABEL$(J)<>D$ THEN ^NEXTJ^
         IF FOUND=0 THEN LOUT$=HAT$+D$+HAT$:FOUND=1
         IF FOUND=15 THEN
             - PRINT #3,"" : PRINT #3,LOUT$ :
             - LOUT$="          " :
             - FOUND=1
         IF FOUND>1 THEN
             - LOUT$=LOUT$+",  "+CFLABEL$(J):FOUND=FOUND+1
         IF FOUND=1 THEN
             - LOUT$=LOUT$+"   '   <--  "+CFLABEL$(J):
             - FOUND=2
^NEXT J^    NEXT J
     IF FOUND>0 THEN PRINT #3,"":PRINT #3,LOUT$
     PRINT #3,"    "+INLINE$
     WEND
   CLOSE
   PRINT "Normal End"
   END

^LABELS^    ' sub to mark line number following keyword
   BYTE=1 : K=LEN(KEYY$)
   WHILE 1
     S$(S)=INLINE$:GOSUB ^UPPERC.LIB^:CAPLINE$=S$(S)
     BYTE=INSTR(BYTE,CAPLINE$,KEYY$)
     IF BYTE=0 THEN RETURN
     ' l1$=line thru key and l2$=line after key
     L1$=LEFT$(INLINE$,BYTE+K-1)
     L2$=MID$(INLINE$,BYTE+K)
     BYTE=BYTE+K    ' shift byte to next search point

^PEEL^    ' peel label(s) off l2 onto l1
     ' drop blanks after keyword
     WHILE LEFT$(L2$,1)=" " : L2$=MID$(L2$,2) : WEND
     ' if byte 1 is not a digit then just rejoin the line
     X$=LEFT$(L2$,1)
     IF INSTR("0123456789",X$)=0 THEN ^APPEND^
```

```
:        ' accumulate digits to d$
:        D$=""
:        D$=D$+X$ : L2$=MID$(L2$,2) : X$=LEFT$(L2$,1)
:        IF X$<>"" AND INSTR("0123456789",X$)>0 THEN ^-1^
:        IF D$=HAT$+"0"+HAT$ THEN D$=" 0"
:        ' add hatted 11 number to line
:        L1$=L1$+HAT$+D$+HAT$+" "
:        ' record the label and where referenced
:        LABMAX=LABMAX+1
:        LABEL$(LABMAX)=D$
:        CFLABEL$(LABMAX)=CFLABEL$
:        ' see if there is a comma after the label
:        WHILE LEFT$(L2$,1)=" " : L2$=MID$(L2$,2) : WEND
:        X$=LEFT$(L2$,1) : IF X$<>"," THEN ^APPEND^
:        ' we have another label in a comma-list
:        L1$=L1$+"," : L2$=MID$(L2$,2)
:        GOTO ^PEEL^
: ^APPEND^  ' append a come-from label to label line
:        INLINE$=L1$ + L2$
:        WEND
+----------------------------------------------------------------+
```

13.8 BLANKS

The need to delete blanks from a string arises in many situations. As it turns out, there are four different functions: to delete leading blanks, embedded blanks, and trailing blanks, and to single up all blanks. This calls for a function flag.

We define the function flag so that 1 = drop leading blanks, 2 = drop embedded blanks, 4 = drop trailing blanks, and so on. To drop both leading and embedded blanks, we request function 3, which means 1 + 2. To delete all blanks, we request function 7 = 1 + 2 + 4.

```
+----------------------------------------------------------------+
: ^BLANKS.LIB^    ' General Blanks Handler      12-10-84   :
:     ' Enter with S$(S) the string to be processed       :
:     '            S(S)  the function flags:               :
:     '                  1 = drop leading blanks            :
:     '                  2 = drop trailing blanks           :
:     '                  4 = drop all blanks                :
:     '                  8 = single up on all blanks        :
:     ' Return with S$(S) selectively deblanked             :
:                                                           :
:     IF (S(S) AND 8)<>8 THEN ^+3^                          :
:     S1=INSTR(S$(S)," ")  : IF S1=0 THEN ^+2^              :
:     S$(S)=LEFT$(S$(S),S1)+MID$(S$(S),S1+2) : GOTO ^-1^    :
:     IF (S(S) AND 5)=0 THEN ^+2^                           :
:     WHILE LEFT$(S$(S),1)=" ":S$(S)=MID$(S$(S),2):WEND     :
```

```
:        IF S(S) AND 6 THEN WHILE RIGHT$(S$(S),1)=" " :    :
:          - S$(S)=LEFT$(S$(S),LEN(S$(S))-1) : WEND       :
:        IF (S(S) AND 4)=0 THEN RETURN                    :
:        S1=INSTR(S$(S)," ") : IF S1=0 THEN RETURN        :
:        S$(S)=LEFT$(S$(S),S1-1)+MID$(S$(S),S1+1) :GOTO ^-1^  :
+--------------------------------------------------------+
```

13.9 BUGLER

This is a little fun program from Chapter 4 that composes bugle
calls. It is useful for breaking apartment leases.

```
+--------------------------------------------------------+
:    ^BUGLER.PRE^   ' Program composes bugle calls       :
:       DEF FNR$=MID$("CEG",1+INT(3*RND),1)               :
:       WHILE 1                                           :
:          A$="" : B$=""                                  :
:          FOR I=1 TO 5 : A$=A$+FNR$  : NEXT I            :
:          FOR I=1 TO 7 : B$=B$+FNR$  : NEXT I            :
:          PLAY "XA$; P8 XA$; P8 XB$;"                    :
:          SOUND 32767, 60                                :
:          WEND                                           :
+--------------------------------------------------------+
```

13.10 CLICHE

Under the pretense of learning about parallel arrays, we
managed to have a little fun with this ancient idea in Chapter 5.

```
+--------------------------------------------------------+
: ^CLICHE.PRE^                                           :
:   ' Program to print fractured sayings       2-11-85   :
:   DIM H1$(100), H2$(100)       ' the parallel arrays   :
:   ON ERROR GOTO ^+2^        ' continue at end of data  :
:   WHILE 1:READ H1$(N),H2$(N):N=N+1:WEND  ' read data   :
:   WHILE 1                                              :
:      PIN=INT(N*RND)         ' random pin from 0 to N-1 :
:      PRINT:PRINT H1$(PIN); H2$(PIN)        ' display   :
:      SOUND 32767,30                        ' delay     :
:      WEND                                              :
:                                                        :
:   DATA "A good man ","is hard to find"                 :
:   DATA "A pretty girl ","is like a melody"             :
:   DATA "A rolling stone ","gathers no moss"            :
:   DATA "A stitch in time ","saves nine"                :
:   DATA "A thing of beauty ","is a joy forever"         :
:   DATA "An apple a day ","keeps the doctor away"       :
:   DATA "An idle mind ","is the devil's playground"     :
+--------------------------------------------------------+
```

```
:    DATA "Charity ","begins at home"                          :
:    DATA "Half a loaf ","is better than none"                 :
:    DATA "Happiness ","is just a guy named Joe"               :
:    DATA "History ","is bunk"                                 :
:    DATA "Ignorance ","is bliss"                              :
:    DATA "The love of money ","is the root of all evil"       :
:    DATA "The pen ","is mightier than the sword"              :
:    DATA "The rain in Spain ","falls mainly in the plain"     :
:    DATA "Virtue ","is its own reward"                        :
+-------------------------------------------------------------+
```

13.11 CULL

This routine removes alien bytes from a string. (*See* Chapter 4.)

```
+-------------------------------------------------------------+
:   ^CULL.LIB^    ' Sub to delete alien bytes      2-11-85    :
:      ' Enter with  S$(S) = data string to be culled         :
:      '             S$(S-1) = the authorized characters      :
:      ' Return with S$(S)   = the culled string              :
:      '             S$(S-1) = undisturbed                    :
:                                                             :
:    . GOSUB ^ALIEN^                                          :
:      WHILE S(S)        ' as long as have aliens, zap them   :
:        S$(S)=LEFT$(S$(S),S(S)-1)+MID$(S$(S),S(S)+1)         :
:        GOSUB ^ALIEN^                  ' any more aliens?    :
:      WEND                                                   :
:    RETURN                                                   :
+-------------------------------------------------------------+
```

13.12 DATIME

This routine returns the current date and time as a single ASCII digit string in decreasing order from century (CC) through second (ss). The string is 14 digits long but will retain its integer precision when used with the VAL function. Hence, the routine can be used to time two successive intervals to the nearest second by subtraction.

If less precision is required, the routine also returns two special strings with the date and the time separated.

```
+-------------------------------------------------------------+
:   ^DATIME.LIB^   ' Sub returns date-time as string  6-3-84  :
:      ' Enter without arguments                              :
:      ' Return S$(S)=time in form "CCYYMMDDhhmmss"           :
```

```
:       ’          S1$  =date part in system form "MM-DD-CCYY"  :
:       ’          S2$  =time part in system form "hh:mm:ss"   :
:     ’ Pushes one stack level                                 :
:                                                              :
:     S2$=TIME$ : S1$=DATE$ : S=S+1                            :
:     S$(S)=RIGHT$(S1$,4)+LEFT$(S1$,2)+MID$(S1$,4,2)           :
:      - +LEFT$(S2$,2)+MID$(S2$,4,2)+RIGHT$(S2$,2)             :
:     RETURN                                                   :
+--------------------------------------------------------------+
```

13.13 DSMSIMUL

This program simulates dynamic memory management with variable-size blocks. It treats the screen as the memory being managed, so you can watch as blocks are reserved and and released. (*See* Chapter 7 for details.)

```
+--------------------------------------------------------------+
: ^DSM SIMUL.PRE^        ’ DSM Simulator      2-11-85          :
:    DEFINT A-Z : CLS : DIM DSS(2000)                          :
:    DSS(0)=0 : DSS(1)=2000 : DSS(2000)=0                      :
:                                                              :
:    ’ set up for monochrome or color adapter                 :
:    GOSUB ^VIDEO.LIB^                                         :
:    VIDRAM! = S!          ’ start of video RAM               :
:                                                              :
:     ’ fill dynamic space with random busy blocks            :
:    DEF SEG=VIDRAM!                                           :
:    SO=1+INT(50*RND) : GOSUB ^RESERVE.LIB^                    :
:    IF SO THEN S$="x" : GOSUB ^SHOW^ : GOTO ^-1^             :
:                                                              :
:    WHILE 1  ’loop forever, releasing and reserving          :
:       ’ find a busy block                                    :
:       SO=1+INT(2000*RND) : IF DSS(SO)>=0 THEN ^+0^          :
:       ’ release it                                           :
:       DSS(SO)=-DSS(SO)  : S$=" " : GOSUB ^SHOW^            :
:       ’ reserve a block                                      :
:       SO=1+INT(50*RND) : GOSUB ^RESERVE.LIB^               :
:       IF SO THEN S$="x" : GOSUB ^SHOW^                      :
:    WEND                                                      :
:                                                              :
: ^SHOW^        ’ sub to display block SO on screen           :
:   DEF SEG = VIDRAM!                                          :
:   FOR I=SO+1 TO ABS(DSS(SO))-1:POKE 2*(I),ASC(S$)          :
:      NEXT I                                                  :
:   RETURN                                                     :
+--------------------------------------------------------------+
```

13.14 ERRMESS

This routine returns a readable error message for the more popular error codes. It is part of the error-management policies mentioned in Chapters 11 and 12.

```
+----------------------------------------------------------------+
:   ^ERRMESS.LIB^   ' Convert error code to message 1-29-85    :
:     ' NOTE: To preserve machine state, this routine          :
:     ' uses global variable names  ERRRx                      :
:     ' Enter  with ERRRN = BASIC error number (from ERR)      :
:     ' Return with ERRR$ = the error message or ""            :
:                                                              :
:     RESTORE ^+1^                                             :
:     DATA  6, "Overflow"                                      :
:     DATA  7, "Out Of Memory"                                 :
:     DATA  9, "Bad Subscript"                                 :
:     DATA 14, "Out Of String Space"                           :
:     DATA 15, "String Too Long"                               :
:     DATA 16, "Bad String Expression"                         :
:     DATA 24, "Device Timeout"                                :
:     DATA 27, "Printer Not Ready"                             :
:     DATA 52, "Bad File Name or Channel"                      :
:     DATA 53, "File Not Found"                                :
:     DATA 54, "Bad File Mode"                                 :
:     DATA 55, "File Is Already Open"                          :
:     DATA 61, "Disk Is Full"                                  :
:     DATA 64, "Bad Filename"                                  :
:     DATA 67, "Too Many Files"                                :
:     DATA 68, "No Such Device"                                :
:     DATA 70, "Write-Protected Disk"                          :
:     DATA 71, "Drive Not Ready"                               :
:     DATA 72, "Diskette Fault"                                :
:     DATA  0, ""                                              :
:     READ ERRR1,ERRR$                                         :
:     WHILE ERRR1>0 AND ERRR1<>ERRRN                           :
:       READ ERRR1,ERRR$ : WEND                                :
:     RETURN                                                   :
+----------------------------------------------------------------+
```

13.15 FILLER

This program processes words with the pipeline technique. (*See* Chapter 9.)

```
+----------------------------------------------------------------+
:   ^BOSS^                    ' Sub to supervise Filler program :
:     DEFINT A-Z                                                :
:     DIM QH(10), QT(10), QLINK(1000), QDATA$(1000)             :
```

```
:      QH(0)=1                 ' intialize dynamic space stack   :
:      FOR S0=1000 TO 1 STEP -1 : GOSUB ^RELEASE^ : NEXT S0      :
:      LINE INPUT  "Enter Source File Name  "; INFILE$          :
:      LINE INPUT  "Enter Target File Name  "; OUTFILE$         :
:      INPUT  "Enter text width  "; COLUMNS                     :
:      OPEN "I",1,INFILE$ : OPEN "O",2,OUTFILE$                 :
:      WHILE STOPWRITE=0       ' until WRITER detects text end   :
:         GOSUB ^READER^        ' read source lines from file    :
:         GOSUB ^WORDER^        ' break source lines into words   :
:         GOSUB ^LINER^           ' pack words into lines        :
:         GOSUB ^WRITER^           ' write lines to file         :
:         WEND                                                   :
:      CLOSE                                                     :
:      END                                                       :
:                                                                :
: ^READER^                    ' Sub to read lines from file     :
:    IF STOPREAD THEN RETURN              ' ignore calls?        :
:    IF QH(0)=0 THEN RETURN               ' out of space?        :
:    GOSUB ^RESERVE^                   ' get an available slot   :
:    IF EOF(1)         ' on eof, set flag and force marker       :
:       - THEN STOPREAD=1 : QDATA$(S0)=".EOTEXT."                :
:       - ELSE LINE INPUT #1, QDATA$(S0)     ' read a line       :
:    S2=1 : GOSUB ^APPEND^           ' append line to queue 1    :
:    RETURN                                                      :
:                                                                :
: ^WORDER^                   ' Sub to break lines into words     :
:    IF QH(1)=0 THEN RETURN               ' out of lines?        :
:    IF QH(0)=0 THEN RETURN               ' out of space?        :
:    IF W$<>"" THEN ^WORDER 2^          ' handle leftovers       :
:    W$=QDATA$(QH(1)):S1=1:GOSUB ^DROP^          'get a line     :
:    WHILE LEFT$(W$,1)=" ":W$=MID$(W$,2):WEND    ' unblank       :
:    IF W$="" THEN          ' if blank line, send null word      :
:       - S0=QH(0) : QH(0)=QLINK(S0) : QDATA$(S0)="" :           :
:       - S2=2 : GOSUB ^APPEND^ : RETURN                         :
: ^WORDER 2^      ' move a word off working line to queue 2      :
:    GOSUB ^RESERVE^                      ' get a free slot      :
:    S1=INSTR(W$+" "," ")                    ' first blank       :
:    QDATA$(S0)=LEFT$(W$,S1-1) 'peel a word off into slot        :
:    S2=2 : GOSUB ^APPEND^         ' append word to queue 2      :
:    W$=MID$(W$,S1+1)              ' shift past the word         :
:    WHILE LEFT$(W$,1)=" ":W$=MID$(W$,2):WEND    ' unblank       :
:    RETURN                                                      :
:                                                                :
: ^LINER^    ' Sub to fill words from q2 into lines in q3        :
:    IF QH(2)=0 THEN RETURN               ' out of words?        :
:    IF QH(0)=0 THEN RETURN               ' out of space?        :
:    S$=QDATA$(QH(2)):S1=2:GOSUB ^DROP^    ' get next word       :
:    IF S$<>"" AND S$<>".EOTEXT." THEN ^LINER 2^                 :
:    IF L$<>"" THEN GOSUB ^LINER 4^   ' force partial line       :
:    L$=S$ : GOSUB ^LINER 4^ : RETURN     ' force word out       :
: ^LINER 2^      ' if word fits add it to line else new line     :
:    IF LEN(L$) + LEN(S$) + 1 <= COLUMNS                         :
```

```
:          - THEN L$=L$ + S$ + " "            ' add word to line    :
:          - ELSE GOSUB ^LINER 4^ : L$=S$+" "           ' new line   :
:          RETURN                                                    :
: ^LINER 4^                          ' Sub to send L$ to queue 3     :
:          GOSUB ^RESERVE^ : QDATA$(S0)=L$    ' get, fill a slot     :
:          S2=3 : GOSUB ^APPEND^             ' output it to queue 3  :
:          RETURN                                                    :
:                                                                    :
: ^WRITER^                           ' Sub to write lines to file    :
:          IF QH(3)=0 THEN RETURN              ' out of lines?       :
:          S$=QDATA$(QH(3)):S1=3:GOSUB ^DROP^          ' next line   :
:          IF S$<>".EOTEXT." THEN PRINT #2, S$ ELSE STOPWRITE=1      :
:          RETURN                                                    :
:                                                                    :
: ^APPEND^   ' Sub to add data item S0 to end of queue S2           :
:          IF QH(S2)=0             ' if queue is empty, set it up    :
:          - THEN QH(S2)=S0 : QT(S2)=S0                              :
:          - ELSE QLINK(QT(S2))=S0 : QT(S2)=S0                       :
:          QLINK(S0)=0                  ' clear new tail pointer     :
:          RETURN                                                    :
:                                                                    :
: ^DROP^        ' Sub to release the first item of queue s1         :
:          S0=QH(S1) : QH(S1)=QLINK(S0) : GOSUB ^RELEASE^            :
:          RETURN                                                    :
:                                                                    :
: ^RELEASE^        ' Sub to release element S0 to free stack         :
:          QLINK(S0)=QH(0) : QH(0)=S0    'slot S0 is new top slot    :
:          RETURN                                                    :
:                                                                    :
: ^RESERVE^                     ' Sub to find an available slot S0    :
:          S0=QH(0) : QH(0)=QLINK(S0)           ' returns top slot   :
:          RETURN                                                    :
+--------------------------------------------------------------------+
```

13.16 HXLATE

This routine is one of a pair of routines that translate strings containing arbitrary binary codes into Hex ASCII for transmission as pure ASCII display codes. (*See* Chapter 4.). This one accepts a string containing any ASCII codes from 0 to 255 and translates it to Hex ASCII. Here it has been recast as a standard library subroutine. The reverse translation routine is AXLATE.LIB.

```
+--------------------------------------------------------------------+
: ^HXLATE.LIB^                                                       :
:       ' Sub to convert string to Hex ASCII      2-11-85            :
:     .' Enter with  S$(S) = ASCII string                            :
:       ' Return with S$(S) = Hex ASCII string                       :
```

```
:                                                               :
:      FOR S1 = 1 TO LEN(S$(S))                                 :
:          S$=HEX$(ASCII(LEFT$(S$(S),1)))   ' hex bytes         :
:          S$(S)=MID$(S$(S),2) + S$   ' append to rest          :
:          NEXT S1                                              :
:      RETURN                                                   :.
+-----------------------------------------   ----------------+
```

13.17 LJUST

```
+------------------------------------------ ------------------+
:   ^LJUST.LIB^   ' Sub to strip left blanks   1-31-85        :
:      ' Enter and return with S$(S)                          :
:                                                             :
:      WHILE LEFT$(S$(S),1)=" "                               :
:          S$(S)=MID$(S$(S),2):WEND                           :
:      RETURN                                                 :
+-------------------------------------------------------------+
```

13.18 LOWERC

This is simply a slightly modified clone of UPPERC.LIB to convert strings to lowercase. It could have been coded as a function option of UPPERC.LIB, but the call for conversion to lowercase is so rare that it is not worth wasting the space to include the lowercase function every time.

```
+--------------------------------------------------------------+
: ^LOWERC.LIB^   ' Sub to convert to lowercase      2-11-85 :
:   ' Enter  with S$(S) = any string                           :
:   ' Return with S$(S) = string with letters lowercased       :
:                                                              :
:   S1=LEN(S$(S))                                              :
:   WHILE S1                                                   :
:     S2=ASC(MID$(S$(S),S1,1))                                 :
:     IF S2>64 AND S2<91 THEN MID$(S$(S),S1,1)=CHR$(S2+32) :
:     S1=S1-1                                                  :
:     WEND                                                     :
:   RETURN                                                     :
+--------------------------------------------------------------+
```

13.19 MENU

This routine inputs a word from a specified word list. It is useful for developing a menu-driven program. It also contains an interesting use of the function flag for editing the input from the keyboard. In effect, the caller uses the function flag to look over the shoulder of the subroutine and tell it what to do at certain points.

```
+-----------------------------------------------------------------+
:  ^MENU2.LIB^   ' Handle menu-driven kb input    2-11-85    :
:     ' Enter with                                           :
:     '        S$(S) the menu,  e.g. "ADD,SUB,READ,...,FIND" :
:     '         S(S) the function flag for editing input     :
:     '             1 strip leading blanks off input         :
:     '             2 strip trailing blanks off input        :
:     '             4 strip all blanks from input            :
:     '             8 upper case the input                   :
:     '            16 retry until get good input             :
:     '            32 print menu as prompt                   :
:     ' Return S(S)=n, the nth word in menu was input        :
:     '    if S(S)=0 then S$(S) is the keyboard input        :
:     '    as entered (and edited) but not found in menu     :
:     '                                                      :
:  IF S(S) AND 32 THEN PRINT S$(S)                           :
:  S=S+1 : LINE INPUT S$(S)                                  :
:  S(S)=S(S-1) AND 7 : GOSUB ^BLANKS.LIB^                    :
:  IF S(S-1) AND 8 THEN GOSUB ^UPPERC.LIB^                   :
:  S=S+1 : S$(S)=S$(S-2) : GOSUB ^RANK.LIB^ : S=S-1          :
:  IF (S(S+1)=0) AND (S(S) AND 16) THEN   ^MENU2.LIB^        :
:  S$(S)=S$(S+1) : S(S)=S(S+1)                               :
:  RETURN                                                    :
+-----------------------------------------------------------------+
```

13.20 NOBLANKS

This routine deletes all blanks from a string.

```
+-----------------------------------------------------------------+
:  ^NOBLANKS.LIB^    ' Sub to delete all blanks  1-28-85    :
:     ' Enter  with S$(S) = any string                      :
:     ' Return with S$(S) = string without blanks           :
:                                                           :
:  S1=INSTR(S$(S)," ") : IF S1=0 THEN RETURN                :
:  S$(S)=LEFT$(S$(S),S1-1) + MID$(S$(S),S1+1)               :
:  GOTO ^-2^                                                :
+-----------------------------------------------------------------+
```

13.21 OCCURS

This routine counts the number of times a given string S$(S) occurs in another given string S$(S−1). It is useful for selecting *n*th occurrences of delimiters for various operations such as editing, deletion, or parsing.

```
+---------------------------------------------------------------+
:  ^OCCURS.LIB^  ' Count occurrences of one string   12-5-84  :
:    ' Enter  with S$(S) the occurring string                  :
:    '               S$(S-1) the containing string             :
:    ' Return with S(S) the number of occurrences              :
:    ' Pops 1 stack level                                      :
:                                                              :
:    S$=S$(S) : S=S-1 : S(S)=0 : S1=INSTR(S$(S),S$)            :
:    WHILE S1                                                  :
:        S(S)=S(S)+1 : S1=INSTR(S1+LEN(S$),S$(S),S$) : WEND    :
:    RETURN                                                    :
+---------------------------------------------------------------+
```

13.22 PEEL

As discussed in Chapter 4, the delimiter is one useful way of packing variable-length fields into a string. The following set of routines perform the reverse function: they PEEL one field from a given string. Several versions are provided to accommodate the various methods used. All of the routines push the field on the S$( ) stack and leave the remainder of the given string as the second stack item.

```
+---------------------------------------------------------------+
:  ^PEEL.LIB^  ' Peel a field to delimiter S(S)   12-10-84   :
:    ' Enter  with S$(S) a delimited string to be peeled       :
:    '               S(S) the ASCII code of the delimiter      :
:    ' Return with S$(S) a peeled field (or null)              :
:    '               S$(S-1) rest of the string (or null)      :
:    ' Pushes one stack item and preserves S(S)                :
:                                                              :
:    S1=INSTR(S$(S)+CHR$(S(S)),CHR$(S(S)))                     :
:    S$(S+1)=LEFT$(S$(S),S1-1)       ' the field               :
:    S$(S)=MID$(S$(S),S1+1)          ' the rest                :
:    S=S+1                           ' raise the stack         :
:    RETURN                                                    :
+---------------------------------------------------------------+
```

```
+---------------------------------------------------------------+
:  ^PEEL1.LIB^  ' Peel field to blank delimiter   12-10-84  :
:    ' Enter  with S$(S) a blank-delimited string              :
:    ' Return with S$(S) a peeled field (or null)              :
:    '               S$(S-1) rest of the string (or null)      :
:    ' Pushes one stack item and changes S(S)                  :
:                                                              :
:    S(S)=32 : GOSUB ^PEEL.LIB^                                :
:    RETURN                                                    :
+---------------------------------------------------------------+
```

```
+----------------------------------------------------------------------+
:  ^PEEL2.LIB^   ' Peel field to comma delimiter    12-10-84 :
:     ' Enter  with S$(S) a comma-delimited string           :
:     ' Return with S$(S) a peeled field (or null)           :
:     '             S$(S-1) rest of the string (or null)     :
:     ' Pushes one stack item and changes S(S)               :
:                                                            :
:     S(S)=44 : GOSUB ^PEEL.LIB^                             :
:     RETURN                                                 :
+----------------------------------------------------------------------+

+----------------------------------------------------------------------+
:  ^PEEL3.LIB^    ' Peel field to delimiter      12-10-84 :
:    ' Enter  with S$(S) a self-delimited string, in which :
:    '        the first byte is the delimiter for the string :
:    ' Return with S$(S) a peeled field (or null)           :
:    '            S$(S-1) rest of the string, once again    :
:    '                    prefixed with the delimiter       :
:    ' Pushes one stack item and changes S(S)               :
:                                                            :
:    S(S)=ASC(LEFT$(S$(S),1)) : S$(S)=MID$(S$(S),2)         :
:    GOSUB ^PEEL.LIB^                                        :
:    IF S$(S-1)<>"" THEN S$(S-1)=CHR$(S(S-1))+S$(S-1)       :
:    RETURN                                                  :
+----------------------------------------------------------------------+
```

13.23 PREBASIC

The BASIC preprocessor program is discussed, and the source
is listed in Chapter 2. Here its numbered version is given, so you
may enter it the very first time.

```
+----------------------------------------------------------------------+
:  110 DEFINT A-Z                                            :
:  120 DIM I$(1000)                                          :
:  130 DIM O$(1000)                                          :
:  140 DIM LAB$(1000)                                        :
:  150 DIM L(100),L$(100)                                    :
:  160 DIM S$(10),S(10)                                      :
:  170 QUOTE$=CHR$(34) : HAT$="^" : APOST$="'"               :
:  180 MAXL=0 : MAXO=0 : NEXTO=1 : S=1                        :
:  190 CLS : ON ERROR GOTO 1270                              :
:  200 PRINT "  Welcome To PREBASIC     Version 2-14-85"     :
:  210 PRINT                                                 :
:  220 INPUT "Input  File Name      "; IFILE$                :
:  230 OPEN "I",#1,IFILE$                                    :
:  240 INPUT "Output File Name      "; OFILE$                :
:  250 OPEN "O",#2,OFILE$                                    :
:  260 INPUT "Library Drive (as X:) "; LIBDRIVE$             :
:  270 S$(S)= "Leave Comments": GOSUB 1330                   :
:  280 OPT1$=S$(S)                                           :
```

```
: 290 S$(S)= "REM ---- Label ": GOSUB 1330         :
: 300 OPT2$=S$(S)                                  :
: 310 PRINT "Reading Input    ..." : GOSUB 370     :
: 320 PRINT "Re-labelling      ..." : GOSUB 810    :
: 330 PRINT "Writing Output  ..." : GOSUB 1110     :
: 340 PRINT MAXO; " Lines Written To File "; OFILE$:
: 350 PRINT "Normal End Of Program"                :
: 360 END                                          :
: 370 S=S+1                                        :
: 380 MAXI=0                                       :
: 390 WHILE NOT EOF(1)                             :
: 400 LINE INPUT #1, I$(MAXI+1):MAXI=MAXI+1:WEND   :
: 410 FOR TL=1 TO MAXI                             :
: 420 S$(S)=I$(TL)                                 :
: 430 WHILE 1                                      :
: 440 GOSUB 1420                                   :
: 450 IF LEFT$(S$(S),1)<>HAT$ THEN 640             :
: 460 S1=INSTR(2,S$(S)+HAT$,HAT$)                  :
: 470 LAB$=MID$(S$(S),2,S1-2)                      :
: 480 S$(S)=MID$(S$(S),S1+1)                       :
: 490 S=S+1:S$(S)=LAB$                             :
: 500 GOSUB 1450                                   :
: 510 GOSUB 1480 : LAB$=S$(S)                      :
: 520 GOSUB 1180 : IF S(S)=0 THEN 560              :
: 530 PRINT "Duplicate Label ";HAT$;S$(S);HAT$;    :
: 540 PRINT " Ignored."                            :
: 550 BEEP : GOTO 620                              :
: 560 MAXL=MAXL+1                                  :
: 570 L$(MAXL)=S$(S)                               :
: 580 L(MAXL)=NEXTO                                :
: 590 IF LAB$(NEXTO)<>"" THEN 610                  :
: 600 LAB$(NEXTO)=S$(S):GOTO 620                   :
: 610 LAB$(NEXTO)=LAB$(NEXTO)+", "+S$(S)           :
: 620 S=S-1                                        :
: 630 WEND                                         :
: 640 IF OPT1$="Y" THEN 680                        :
: 650 GOSUB 1420                                   :
: 660 IF LEFT$(S$(S),3)="REM" THEN 760             :
: 670 GOSUB 1220                                   :
: 680 GOSUB 1420                                   :
: 690 IF LEFT$(S$(S),1)<>"-" THEN 760              :
: 700 S$(S)=MID$(S$(S),2) : GOSUB 1420             :
: 710 S=S+1:S$(S)=O$(NEXTO-1):GOSUB 1220           :
: 720 GOSUB 1550 : O$(NEXTO-1)=S$(S) : S=S-1       :
: 730 O$(NEXTO-1)=S$(S+1)+" "+S$(S):GOTO 780       :
: 740 PRINT "Continued Line NOT Joined (too long): ";:
: 750 PRINT S$(S)                                  :
: 760 IF S$(S)="" THEN 780                         :
: 770 O$(NEXTO)=S$(S) : MAXO=NEXTO : NEXTO=NEXTO+1 :
: 780 NEXT TL                                      :
: 790 CLOSE #1 : S=S-1                             :
: 800 RETURN                                       :
```

```
:    810 CL=1                                                      :
:    820 WHILE CL<MAXO                                             :
:    830 HAT1=INSTR(O$(CL),HAT$)                                   :
:    840 HAT2=INSTR(HAT1+1,O$(CL),HAT$)                            :
:    850 IF HAT1=0 OR HAT2=0 THEN 1080                             :
:    860 S=S+1:S$(S)=MID$(O$(CL),HAT1+1,HAT2-HAT1-1)               :
:    870 GOSUB 1480:GOSUB 1450                                     :
:    880 LAB$=S$(S)                                                :
:    890 IF INSTR("+-",LEFT$(LAB$,1))=0 THEN 910                   :
:    900 S(S)=CL + VAL(LAB$):GOTO 1040                             :
:    910 GOSUB 1180                                                :
:    920 IF S(S) THEN 1040                                         :
:    930 S$(S)=LAB$                                                :
:    940 OPEN "I",1,LIBDRIVE$+S$(S)                                :
:    950 GOSUB 370                                                 :
:    960 GOSUB 1180:IF S(S) THEN 1040                              :
:    970 PRINT:PRINT "Missing Label ";HAT$;LAB$;HAT$;              :
:    980 PRINT "    Stubbed In New Line "; 100+10*CL               :
:    990 O$(NEXTO)="PRINT " + QUOTE$ + "Stub For Label "           :
:   1000 O$(NEXTO)=O$(NEXTO)+ LAB$ + QUOTE$ + " : STOP"            :
:   1010 MAXO=NEXTO : NEXTO=NEXTO+1                                :
:   1020 MAXL=MAXL+1:L$(MAXL)=LAB$:L(MAXL)=NEXTO                   :
:   1030 S(S)=MAXO                                                 :
:   1040 S1$=LEFT$(O$(CL),HAT1-1):S3$=MID$(O$(CL),HAT2+1)          :
:   1050 O$(CL) = S1$ + MID$(STR$(100+10*S(S)),2) + S3$            :
:   1060 S=S-1                                                     :
:   1070 GOTO 1090                                                 :
:   1080 CL=CL+1                                                   :
:   1090 WEND                                                      :
:   1100 RETURN                                                    :
:   1110 FOR WL=1 TO MAXO                                          :
:   1120 IF LAB$(WL)="" OR OPT2$="N" THEN 1150                     :
:   1130 PRINT #2, USING "#### &"; 95+10*WL;                       :
:   1140 PRINT #2, "REM        --- " + LAB$(WL) + " ---"           :
:   1150 PRINT #2, USING "#### &"; 100+10*WL, O$(WL)               :
:   1160 NEXT WL                                                   :
:   1170 RETURN                                                    :
:   1180 S1=MAXL                                                   :
:   1190 WHILE L$(S1)<>S$(S) AND S1>0 : S1=S1-1 : WEND             :
:   1200 S(S)=L(S1)                                                :
:   1210 RETURN                                                    :
:   1220 S1=INSTR(S$(S),APOST$) : IF S1=0 THEN RETURN              :
:   1230 IF INSTR(S1,S$(S),QUOTE$) THEN RETURN                     :
:   1240 IF INSTR(S1,S$(S),HAT$  ) THEN RETURN                     :
:   1250 S$(S)=LEFT$(S$(S),S1-1) : GOSUB 1550                      :
:   1260 RETURN                                                    :
:   1270 IF ERL=940 THEN RESUME 970                                :
:   1280 IF ERL=730 THEN RESUME 740                                :
:   1290 RESUME 1300                                               :
:   1300 BEEP : PRINT : PRINT "Error"; ERR;                        :
:   1310 PRINT "At Line"; ERL; "In PREBASIC Program"               :
```

```
: 1320 END                                                        :
: 1330 ' Return with S$(S)="Y" if kb replied positive             :
: 1340 '              S$(S)="N" if kb replied negative             :
: 1350 PRINT S$(S);                                                :
: 1360 PRINT "   (Y N) ? "; : LINE INPUT S$(S)                     :
: 1370 GOSUB 1480                                                  :
: 1380 IF S$(S)="YES" THEN S$(S)="Y"                               :
: 1390 IF S$(S)="NO"  THEN S$(S)="N"                               :
: 1400 IF S$(S)<>"Y" AND S$(S)<>"N" THEN 1360                      :
: 1410 RETURN                                                      :
: 1420 WHILE LEFT$(S$(S),1)=" "                                    :
: 1430 S$(S)=MID$(S$(S),2):WEND                                    :
: 1440 RETURN                                                      :
: 1450 S1=INSTR(S$(S)," ") : IF S1=0 THEN RETURN                   :
: 1460 S$(S)=LEFT$(S$(S),S1-1) + MID$(S$(S),S1+1)                  :
: 1470 GOTO 1450                                                   :
: 1480 S1=LEN(S$(S))                                               :
: 1490 WHILE S1                                                    :
: 1500 S2=ASC(MID$(S$(S),S1,1))                                    :
: 1510 IF S2>96 AND S2<123 THEN MID$(S$(S),S1,1)=CHR$(S2-32)       :
: 1520 S1=S1-1                                                     :
: 1530 WEND                                                        :
: 1540 RETURN                                                      :
: 1550 WHILE RIGHT$(S$(S),1)=" "                                   :
: 1560 S$(S)=LEFT$(S$(S),LEN(S$(S))-1):WEND                        :
: 1570 RETURN                                                      :
```

13.24 RANK

This routine finds the rank number of a given word in a comma list of words. For one use, see the routine MENU2.LIB.

```
: ^RANK.LIB^  ' Find rank of a word in a list   2-11-85   :
:       ' Enter with  S$(S) the list   e.g. "one,IT,ONE,ALL" :
:       '             S$(S-1) a word   e.g. "ONE"          :
:       ' Return with S(S) = the rank of the word, e.g. 3  :
:       '             S$(S) = the given word              :
:       ' Pops one stack level                            :
:                                                         :
:       S1=INSTR(","+S$(S)+",",","+S$(S-1)+",")           :
:       IF S1=0 THEN S=S-1 : S(S)=0 : RETURN              :
:       S=S+1 : S$(S)="," : S$(S-1)=LEFT$(S$(S-1),S1-1)   :
:       GOSUB ^OCCURS.LIB^ : S=S-1 : S(S)=S(S+1)+1        :
:       RETURN                                            :
```

13.25 RESERVE

This routine reserves a block of cells from a dynamic storage space array DSS(). The allocation algorithm is developed in Chapter 7.

```
: ^RESERVE.LIB^  ' Sub to reserve dynamic space  10-11-84  :
:    ' Reserves a variable-length block of cells in DSS().  :
:    ' Uses linked list of free and busy blocks.  Cell 1    :
:    ' is first block.  Link is negative if block is busy.  :
:    ' To initialize:                                       :
:    '     DIM DSS(max):DSS(O)=0:DSS(1)=max:DSS(max)=0       :
:                                                           :
:    ' Enter with   SO=n = number of cells requested        :
:    ' Return with SO=address of block of n+1 cells (or O)  :
:    '         cells SO+1 thru SO+n are now available        :
:    '         to release:   DSS(SO)=-DSS(SO)               :
:                                                           :
:    S1=1          ' S1, S2, and S3 are 3 successive blocks  :
: ^RESERVE.LIB 1^                                           :
:    ' find first free block S1                             :
:    IF S1=0 THEN SO=0 : RETURN     ' out of space           :
:    S2=DSS(S1):IF S2<=0 THEN S1=-S2:GOTO ^RESERVE.LIB 1^    :
:    S3=DSS(S2)      ' free/busy flag of block S2            :
:                    ' S1 is a free block and S2 follows it  :
:    ' while S2 is also free, merge S2 into S1               :
:    WHILE S3>0 : DSS(S1)=S3 : S2=S3 : S3=DSS(S2) : WEND     :
:                                                           :
:    ' if free block S1 is too small, try next block        :
:    IF S2-S1<=SO THEN S1=-S3 : GOTO ^RESERVE.LIB 1^         :
:                                                           :
:    ' carve new busy block SO out of free block S1         :
:    SO=S2-SO      ' compute address of new busy block       :
:    DSS(S1)=SO    ' link block S1 to SO and flag it free    :
:    DSS(SO)=-S2   ' link block SO to S2 and flag it busy    :
:    RETURN                                                 :
```

13.26 RJUST

This subroutine strips right blanks.

```
: ^RJUST.LIB^    ' Sub to strip right blanks  2-13-85       :
:    ' Enter and return with S$(S)                          :
:                                                           :
:    WHILE RIGHT$(S$(S),1)=" "                              :
:       S$(S)=LEFT$(S$(S),LEN(S$(S))-1):WEND                :
:    RETURN                                                 :
```

13.27 SKELETON

Here follows skeleton code for both a library routine and for a complete program. Such skeletons are useful as "starter code".

```
+------------------------------------------------------------+
:  ^SKELETON.LIB^    ' Sub to xxxxx      date                :
:     ' Enter with  S(S) = xxx                               :
:     '                                                      :
:     ' Return with S(S) = xxx                               :
:     '             S$(S) = xxx                              :
:     ' Note:  xxx                                           :
:                                                            :
:     code                                                   :
:     code                                                   :
:     RETURN                                                 :
+------------------------------------------------------------+


+------------------------------------------------------------+
:  ^SKELETON.PRO^   ' Standard program framework   2-11-85   :
:     ' Use this as starter code for a new program           :
:     ' Order is important to compiler                       :
:                                                            :
:     ' Identify program and version                         :
:     PROGRAM$ = "program name"                              :
:     VERSION$ = "version date"                              :
:     AUTHOR$  = "programmer"                                :
:                                                            :
:     ' Set default variable names                           :
:     DEFINT A-Z                                             :
:     ' Dimension arrays                                     :
:     DIM S(10),S#(10),S$(10)                                :
:     ' Define functions                                     :
:     DEF FNMIN(A,B) = -(A<=B)*A -(B<A)*B                    :
:     ' Set up error trapping                                :
:     ON ERROR GOTO ^GLOBAL ERROR HANDLER^                   :
:     ' Clear screen and soft key line                       :
:     KEY OFF : CLS                                          :
:     ' Switch to text mode                                  :
:     SCREEN 0,0,0 : WIDTH 80                                :
:     ' Hide the cursor                                      :
:     LOCATE ,,0                                             :
:     ' Find the start of the video RAM                      :
:     GOSUB ^VIDEO.LIB^ : VIDEO! = S!                        :
:                                                            :
:     '          I N I T I A L I Z E                         :
:                                                            :
:     ' Welcome the user and identify the programmer         :
:     LOCATE 8,1                                             :
:     PRINT "Welcome To "; PROGRAM$                          :
:     PRINT "  version  "; VERSION$                          :
:     PRINT                                                  :
```

```
:       PRINT "    by     "; AUTHOR$                    :
:                                                       :
:       ,   ... initialization code                    :
:                                                       :
:       ,        M A I N    D R I V E R                 :
:       ,   ... main program code                       :
:                                                       :
:       END                                             :
:                                                       :
:       ,        S U B R O U T I N E S                  :
:       ,                                               :
:       ,   ... subroutine code                         :
:                                                       :
: ^GLOBAL ERROR HANDLER^                                :
:       ERRRCODE=ERR : ERRLINE=ERL                      :
:       ' Handle expected errors                        :
:       IF ERRRCODE<>27 THEN ^+3^                       :
:       LINE INPUT "Hit RETURN When Printer Ready";ERRR$ :
:       RESUME                                          :
:      .IF ERRRCODE<>71 THEN ^+3^                       :
:       LINE INPUT "Hit RETURN WHEN Drive Is Ready";ERRR$ :
:       RESUME                                          :
:                                                       :
:       ' Unexpected error                              :
:       RESUME ^+1^                                     :
:       PRINT "Error"; ERRRCODE;"At Line"; ERRRLINE     :
:       GOSUB ^ERRMESS.LIB^ : PRINT ERRRMESS$           :
:       PRINT "In Program ";PROGRAM$                    :
:       STOP    ' to let user look at variablesND       :
:       END                                             :
+--------------------------------------------------------+
```

13.28 SORT

This is the sort routine developed in Chapter 6 and recast to work as a library subroutine. It expects the unsorted data in the S$() stack and returns a sorted chain whose links are stored in S().

```
+--------------------------------------------------------+
: ^SORT.LIB^    ' Sub to sort into a chain    2-12-85    :
:       ' Enter with  S$(S-1..S-n) = n items to be sorted :
:       ,         and  S$(S) = count of items to be sorted :
:       ' Return with S(S)  = head pointer to sorted chain :
:       ,         and  S(S-1..S-n) = links in sorted order :
:       ,         and  S$() unchanged                    :
:       ' Note: sort is ascending and stable             :
:                                                        :
:       S1=VAL(S$(S))-1 ' counts unsorted nodes          :
:       IF S1<2 THEN S(S)=0 : RETURN      ' empty chain  :
```

```
:      S2=1              ' counts sorted nodes            :
:      S3=S-2            ' starts unsorted data           :
:      S(S)=S-1          ' points to first node           :
:      S(S-1)=0          ' first node is end of sorted chain :
:      FOR S8=1 TO S1                                     :
:          IF S$(S3) < S$(S(S))                           :
:              - THEN S(S3)=S(S) : S(S)=S3     ' push     :
:              - ELSE S4=S(S):S5=S2:GOSUB ^SORT LIB 2^    :
:          S2=S2+1 : S3=S3-1                              :
:          NEXT S8                                        :
:      RETURN                                             :
:                                                         :
: ^SORT LIB 2^  ' Sub to insert key node (stably)         :
:      ' Enter with a chain of S5 nodes starting at node S4 :
:      '     and a key node S3 to be inserted AFTER node S4 :
:      ' Return with node inserted                        :
:                                                         :
:      WHILE S5>1       ' find center node S6 of chain S4 :
:          S6=S4 : FOR S7=1 TO S5\2:S6=S(S6):NEXT S7      :
:          IF S$(S6)<=S$(S3)     ' binary split the chain :
:              - THEN S4=S6 : S5=S5-S5\2     ' right half :
:              - ELSE S5=S5\2                 ' left half :
:          WEND                                           :
:      S(S3)=S(S4):S(S4)=S3  ' insert node S3 behind S4   :
:      RETURN                                             :
+---------------------------------------------------------+
```

13.29 STRING

This routine is an example of using strings to store special data values. (*See* Chapter 4.)

```
+---------------------------------------------------------+
: ^STRING.LIB^  ' Sub to get string constant  11-20-84    :
:      ' Enter  with S(S) = the desired number            :
:      ' Return with S$(S) = the desired string constant  :
:                                                         :
:      ON S(S) GOSUB ^+1^,^+2^,^+3^,^+4^,^+5^,^+6^,        :
:          -  ^+7^,^+8^ : RETURN                           :
:      '  1   Capital Letters in ASCII (65 - 90)          :
:      S$(S)="ABCDEFGHIJKLMNOPQRSTUVWXYZ" : RETURN        :
:      '  2   Lowercase Letters in ASCII (97 - 122)       :
:      S$(S)="abcdefghijklmnopqrstuvwxyz" : RETURN        :
:      '  3   Base 10 Digits in ASCII (48 - 57)           :
:      S$(S)="0123456789" : RETURN                        :
:      '  4   Base 10 Digits in Binary (0 - 9)            :
:      FOR S1=0 TO 9:S$(S)=S$(S)+CHR$(S1):               :
:          - NEXT S1:RETURN                                :
:      '  5   Hexadecimal Digits in ASCII                 :
:      S$(S)="01234567890ABCDEF" : RETURN                 :
```

```
:   ' 6    String byte index codes  (1 - 255)
:   FOR S1=1 TO 255:S$(S)=S$(S)+CHR$(S1):
:       - NEXT S1:RETURN
:   ' 7    PI to 50 places
:   S$(S)="3.1415926535897932384626433832795O
:       - 288419716939937510"  : RETURN
:   ' 8    Date-Time as digits  "CCYYMMDDhhmmss"
:   S$=DATE$+TIME$:S$=MID$(S$,7,4)+LEFT$(S$,2)
:       - +MID$(S$,4,2)+MID$(S$,11,2)+MID$(S$,14,2)
:       - +MID$(S$,17,2,2):S$(S)=S$:RETURN
```

13.30 TELLER

This program comes from Chapter 8. It simulates a customer line in a four-teller bank.

```
:   ^TELLER^   CLS : PRINT "Teller Program"
:       ' Task master give control to tasks in turn
:       GOSUB ^ARRIVE^:GOSUB ^DISPLAY^:GOSUB ^NEXT^
:       GOTO ^-1^
:
:   ^ARRIVE^   ' task to greet customers at the door
:       WHILE LEN(WQ$)<30 AND RND>.3
:           WQ$ = WQ$+CHR$(65+INT(26*RND))+SPACE$(1+2*RND)
:           WEND
:       RETURN
:
:   ^DISPLAY^   ' task to update the screen
:       LOCATE 4,1   : PRINT 1; W1$
:       LOCATE 8,1   : PRINT 2; W2$
:       LOCATE 11,11 : PRINT STRING$(30,"-")
:       LOCATE 12,10 : PRINT WQ$; SPACE$(30);
:       LOCATE 13,11 : PRINT STRING$(30,"-")
:       LOCATE 16,1  : PRINT 3; W3$
:       LOCATE 20,1  : PRINT 4; W4$
:       RETURN
:
:   ^NEXT^   ' task to move a customer to a teller
:       IF LEN(WQ$) = O THEN RETURN   ' is queue empty?
:       FOR I=1 TO 1000*RND : NEXT    ' simulate delay
:       NC$=LEFT$(WQ$,1) : WQ$=MID$(WQ$,2)
:       IF NC$=" " THEN ^-1^   ' ignore spaces in queue
:       ON 1+INT(4*RND) GOTO  ^+1^, ^+2^, ^+3^, ^+4^
:       W1$=NC$ : RETURN   ' move next customer to teller 1
:       W2$=NC$ : RETURN
:       W3$=NC$ : RETURN
:       W4$=NC$ : RETURN
```

13.31 UNPACK

This routine unpacks a comma list into individual items and leaves them on the stack. The routine is unusual in that it leaves the unpacked items above the current stack pointer. This arrangement lets other library subroutines use it to unpack parameters passed to them and then use them in processing.

```
: ^UNPACK.LIB^    ' Sub to unpack a comma-list      9-10-84   :
:    ' Enter  with S$(S)=item list with comma delimiters     :
:    '                    e.g.  "string,to,be,unpacked"      :
:    ' Return with S$(S)=as given                            :
:    '             S(S) =count n of unpacked items, e.g. 4   :
:    '             S$(S+1) thru S$(S+n) the unpacked items   :
:    '             e.g.  S$(S+1) = "string"                  :
:    '                   S$(S+2) = "to"                       :
:    '                   S$(S+3) = "be"                       :
:    '                   S$(S+4) = "unpacked"                 :
:    ' Note:  parameters are returned ABOVE stack pointer    :
:                                                            :
:    S0=0 : S$=S$(S)                                         :
:    WHILE S$<>""                                            :
:      S0=S0+1 : S1=INSTR(S$+",",",")                        :
:      S$(S+S0)=LEFT$(S$,S1-1) : S$=MID$(S$,S1+1)            :
:      WEND                                                  :
:    S(S)=S0                                                 :
:    RETURN                                                  :
```

13.32 UPPERC

This routine converts a string to uppercase.

```
: ^UPPERC.LIB^   ' Sub to convert to capitals      2-10-85  :
:    ' Enter  with S$(S)=string to be processed             :
:    ' Return with S$(S)=string with letters capitalized    :
:                                                           :
:    S1=LEN(S$(S))                                          :
:    WHILE S1                                               :
:      S2=ASC(MID$(S$(S),S1,1))                             :
:      IF S2>96 AND S2<123 THEN MID$(S$(S),S1,1)=CHR$(S2-32):
:      S1=S1-1                                              :
:      WEND                                                 :
:    RETURN                                                 :
```

13.33 VFILE

This routine sets up and manipulates a v-file, that is, a random access file in which variable-length blocks can be dynamically reserved and released. The routine is fully discussed in Chapter 7.

```
+-------------------------------------------------------------------+
: ^VFILE.LIB^     ' Sub for random file DSM       10-12-84       :
:     ' Provides 4 functions for sharing random file space.   :
:     ' Uses linked list of free and busy blocks.            :
:     ' Every block starts with 2-byte link field. Link is   :
:     ' minus if block is busy; plus if free; 0 if last.      :
:     ' Record 1 is first block.  VLR is last block.         :
:     ' Handles errors by returning error code in S(S).       :
:     ' Fields VB$ as buffer for user's convenience.          :
:     ' Uses hardwired parameters:                            :
:     '      VB$          file buffer                         :
:     '      VF$          file name                           :
:     '      VL$          link to next record                 :
:     '      VCH          channel                             :
:     '      VRL          record length                       :
:     '      VLR          last record number                  :
:     ' Enter  with S(S) = function code                      :
:     '                and parameters as shown for function   :
:     ' Return with S(S) = 0=normal;  >0=error code           :
:     ' Function:                                             :
:     '      1 = Create and open new file                     :
:     '             uses   VF$, VB$, VL$, VCH, VRL, VLR        :
:     '      2 = Open an existing file                        :
:     '             uses   VF$, VB$, VL$, VCH, VRL             :
:     '      3 = Reserve a block of S0 records                :
:     '             uses   VL$, VCH                            :
:     '             returns S0=record address or 0            :
:     '      4 = Release block S0                             :
:     '             uses   VL$, VCH                            :
:     ON ERROR GOTO ^+4^                                       :
:     ON S(S) GOSUB ^VFILE.LIB 1^,^VFILE.LIB 1^,              :
:              - ^VFILE.LIB 3^,^VFILE.LIB 4^                   :
:     S(S)=0                                                   :
:     ON ERROR GOTO ^GLOBAL ERROR HANDLER^ : RETURN            :
:     S(S)=ERR : RESUME ^-1^       ' local error handler      :
: ^VFILE.LIB 1^     ' create or open                          :
:     OPEN "R",VCH,VF$,VRL                                     :
:     FIELD #VCH, VRL AS VB$ : FIELD #VCH, 2 AS VL$            :
:     IF S(S)=2 THEN RETURN    ' open only                     :
:     LSET VL$=MKI$(VLR) : PUT #VCH,1                          :
:     LSET VL$=MKI$(0)   : PUT #VCH,VLR                        :
:     RETURN                                                   :
: ^VFILE.LIB 3^     ' reserve a block of S0 records           :
:     S1=1             ' start looking at this block          :
```

```
:  ^VFILE.LIB 3b^                                             :
:     IF S1=0 THEN S0=0 : RETURN      ' out of space          :
:     GET #VCH,S1 : S2=CVI(VL$)                               :
:     IF S2<=0 THEN S1=-S2 : GOTO ^VFILE.LIB 3b^             :
:     GET #VCH,S2 : S3=CVI(VL$)                               :
:     WHILE S3>0       ' merge free blocks                    :
:         GET #VCH,S1 : LSET VL$=MKI$(S3) : PUT #VCH,S1       :
:         S2=S3 : GET #VCH,S2 : S3=CVI(VL$)                   :
:         WEND                                                :
:     IF S2-S1<=S0 THEN S1=-S3 : GOTO ^VFILE.LIB 3b^         :
:     S0=S2-S0         ' allocate; S0 is new busy block       :
:     GET #VCH,S1 : LSET VL$=MKI$(S0)   : PUT #VCH,S1         :
:     GET #VCH,S0 : LSET VL$=MKI$(-S2) : PUT #VCH,S0          :
:     RETURN                                                  :
:  ^VFILE.LIB 4^      ' release block S0                      :
:     GET #VCH,S0                                             :
:     LSET VL$=MKI$(ABS(CVI(VL$)))                            :
:     PUT #VCH,S0                                             :
:     RETURN                                                  :
+-----------------------------------------------------------+
```

13.34 VIDEO

The IBM PC screen is memory-mapped, meaning that every screen position corresponds to a location in memory. The start of the video memory, as it is called, is different for monochrome than for color graphics adapters. This routine returns the video memory start address for the machine.

```
+-----------------------------------------------------------+
:  ^VIDEO.LIB^    ' Sub to find start of video ram  2-11-85 :
:     ' Returns S!  =  45056 if mono   47104 if color card  :
:     DEF SEG=0                                             :
:     S! = 47104! + ((PEEK(&H410) AND 48)=48)*2048          :
:     RETURN                                                :
+-----------------------------------------------------------+
```

13.35 YESNO

A recurring problem in programming is the need to ask the keyboard user a question that can be answered "yes" or "no." Since the user may answer in a variety of ways, with a mix of upper- and lowercase, this problem can become irritating to have to solve at every turn. The following two routines come in handy. YESNO allows a number of responses, such as YES for Y and NO for N. YESNO2 requires either Y or N.

```
+---------------------------------------------------------------+
:   ^YESNO.LIB^   ' Prompt and input Y or N    5-26-84          :
:      ' Enter  with S$(S) = the prompt string                  :
:      ' Return with S$(S)="Y" if kb replied positive           :
:      '              S$(S)="N" if kb replied negative           :
:      PRINT S$(S);                                             :
:      PRINT "  (Y N) ? "; : LINE INPUT S$(S)                   :
:      GOSUB ^UPPERC.LIB^                                       :
:      IF S$(S)="YES" THEN S$(S)="Y"                            :
:      IF S$(S)="NO"  THEN S$(S)="N"                            :
:      IF S$(S)<>"Y" AND S$(S)<>"N" THEN ^-4^                   :
:      RETURN                                                   :
+---------------------------------------------------------------+

+---------------------------------------------------------------+
:   ^YESNO2.LIB^ ' Sub to prompt for Y or N answer   2-10-85 :
:      ' Enter  with S$(S) = the prompt message                 :
:      ' Return with S$(S) = "Y" if user replied positive       :
:      '               = "N" if user replied negative           :
:                                                               :
:      PRINT S$(S);                                             :
:      PRINT "  (Y N) ? "; : LINE INPUT S$(S)                   :
:      GOSUB ^UPPERC.LIB^                                       :
:      IF S$(S)<>"Y" AND S$(S)<>"N" THEN BEEP:GOTO ^-2^         :
:      RETURN                                                   :
+---------------------------------------------------------------+
```

Index

!	floating point 5
"	string constant 8
#	channel 20, 160
#	floating point 5
$	string 5
%	integer 5
'	comment 3, 5, 37
*	operator 7
+	operator 7, 8
−	continuation line 38
−	operator 7
/	operator 7
:	statement separator 3, 11, 38
⟨	operator 7
⟨=	operator 7
⟨⟩	operator 7
=	operator 7
⟩	operator 7
⟩=	operator 7
\	operator 7
∧	label 25, 32
∧	operator 7

array—*Continued*
  dimensioning 9
  duplicate 118
  file 121-23
  introduction 105-7
  name 9
  operator 9
  parallel 111-13, 117-18, 124, 198, 273
  pointer 115-21
  queue 180-84
  random 123-24
  review 9
  stack 214-15
  string 9, 66, 75-76, 108-9, 211
  subarray 118
  virtual 123
artificial intelligence 90, 101, 108, 128, 132, 170, 208
ASC 72
ASCII 76-80, 95, 96, 268, 278
assembly line, *see* pipeline

A

aging 188
aligning data 187
AND 7
animating 19
argument, *see* parameter
arithmetic 97, 98, 268
array
  advanced 107-8
  auxiliary 198
  basket 109-112, 213
  buffer string 88

B

backspacing 218
BASIC 1-4, 6, 21, 26, 61, 107, 253, 270
  and DOS 21-22
  environment 21
  extending 49
  translating to PREBASIC 47
basket, *see* array
BASPRE 47, 50
batching data 189
Beethoven's Ninth 100
binary 142

O

ON ERROR GOTO   17, 241
ON-GOTO   3
OPEN   86
operator   7
operator precedence   9
OPTION BASE   9, 106
OR   7
ordering   187

P

parameter   3, 236, 247, 250–54
parameter passing   3, 16, 97, 111, 220,
  251–54
parsing   97
personalized software   228–29, 242–43,
  246, 269
PERT   207
pin   113–15, 129, 154, 198
pipeline   172, 193, 205, 207, 276
  example   196–205
  introduction   193–96
  using   205–8
pointer   61, 66, 101, 108, 115-22, 125,
  130, 179, 184, 219
Polish notation   222
pop   49, 209
POS   19
PREBASIC   25–29, 22, 29–31, 47–50,
  207
  BASIC to   270–72
  comment   37, 235
  continued line   37–38
  documenting   38–39
  installing   46
  label   32–35
  library   35–36, 233, 252
  line number   32
  macro   49
  program   39–46
  translating BASIC to   47
  with line numbers   282–85
preprocessor   27
PRINT   18, 19

priority   215
procedure block   11
program library   4, 30, 35
program
  2-COLUMN PAGER   205
  4BANGER   222, 266
  ALIEN   81, 269
  APPEND SEQUENTIAL FILE   186
  ASTRADD   268
  AXLATE   268
  BANGER   227, 269
  BASPRE   270
  BLANKS   255, 272
  BUGLER   100, 273
  CARD DECK   68, 69
  CARD SHUFFLE   123
  CHAIN SORT   145
  CHAIN SORT TEST   146
  CLICHE   124, 273
  COPY SEQUENTIAL FILE   14, 16,
    186
  CULL   82, 274
  DATIME   274
  DSM SIMULATOR   162, 275
  ERRMESS   261, 276
  EXTRACT SEQUENTIAL FILE   186
  FILLER   196–205, 276
  FNMAX   7
  HORSE RACE   19
  HXLATE   96, 278
  KEYBOARD INPUT   18
  LJUST   279
  LOWERC   279
  machine language   103
  MENU   279
  NOBLANKS   280
  OCCURS   259, 280
  PEEL   281
  PREBASIC   39–46, 282
  PRINT SCREEEN   102
  QUEUE IN ARRAY   181
  RANDOM FILE   20, 122
  RANK   285
  RESERVE   158, 286
  RJUST   286
  SEQUENTIAL FILE ACCESS   185
  SKELETON   21, 249, 287
  SORT   288
  STRING   99, 289
  TELLER   191, 290
  TRACK RANDOM RECORDS   177
  TRUCK RENTAL   133
  UNPACK   291
  UPPERC   291

T